Horses in Midstream

Horses in Midstream

U.S. Midterm Elections
and Their Consequences,
1894–1998

ANDREW E. BUSCH

University of Pittsburgh Press

Published by the University of Pittsburgh Press, Pittsburgh, Pa. 15261
Copyright © 1999, University of Pittsburgh Press
All rights reserved
Manufactured in the United States of America
Printed on acid-free paper
10 9 8 7 6 5 4 3 2 1

A CIP catalog record for this book is available from the Library of Congress and the
British Library.

To Katherine Noelle

CONTENTS

ACKNOWLEDGMENTS

I would like to thank Gary C. Jacobson and numerous anonymous reviewers for their valuable suggestions, as well as Sara Green for her research assistance. I would also like to express my appreciation to Niels Aaboe, Hope Kurtz, and the rest of the hard-working staff at the University of Pittsburgh Press.

Introduction

American politics is nearly unique among North Atlantic industrial democracies in that the United States regularly holds national legislative elections midway through the term of its executive officer.[1] In those "midterm" elections, mandated by the United States Constitution, all 435 seats in the House of Representatives and one-third of U.S. Senate seats are up for election. In addition, most American states now elect their governors and other statewide officers in midterm election years.

Despite the potentially profound impact of midterm elections, they have traditionally been the poor stepchild of American electoral studies in most respects. The two questions that have drawn the most attention of political scientists—Why does the president's party almost always lose seats in Congress in midterm years? and What explains the variation in those losses from year to year?—have produced a substantial amount of literature but no consensus. The question of what difference midterm elections make to American politics has been little discussed, possibly due to the presumption that the most important consequences flow from presidential rather than midterm elections. For most of the twentieth century, the federal government has been at the center of American politics, and the president has been at the center of the federal government; even when they have not been, they have seemed so.

The dramatic midterm elections of 1994, which swept the Republican Party into control of both houses of Congress for the first time in forty years, and of 1998, which saw a reversal of the normal midterm pattern in the House for the first time since 1934, have refocused attention on the phenomenon of midterm elections. This refocusing has led to a rediscovery of the importance of selected midterm elections in American political history, yet no thorough examination of this subject has been undertaken. Given the potential importance of midterm elections, the substantial scholarly silence on the question of their role in American politics is surprising and unfortunate.

This book will examine midterm elections from 1894 to 1998. Because our chief goal is to study the consequences of midterm elections, and the consequences of 1998 are not yet fully apparent, the main focus will be on midterms from 1894 to 1994, a 100-year span bracketed by two of the most dramatic midterm elections in American history. This period was chosen for a variety of reasons. The data, both quantitative and qualitative, are much more reliable within that era than before. Furthermore, 1894 was a crucial juncture in American politics, government, and society. In a sense, the realignment of 1894–1896 can be seen as the beginning of modern industrial America. The 1890s can also be seen, in many respects, as a major turning point in the creation of the modern Congress, at least in terms of careerism and what Nelson Polsby called "institutionalization."[2]

The "Why and How Much" Debate

Scholars of congressional elections have been largely occupied with the following two questions: Why does the president's party almost always lose congressional seats in midterm elections? And what factors lead to the substantial variations in losses suffered by presidents across the years? While these questions are theoretically distinct, they have become intertwined in numerous academic theories. There are four theories that attempt to explain the regularity and extent of presidential party losses in midterm elections: the "coattails" theory, the "surge-and-decline" theory, the "national conditions," or "referendum," theory, and the "presidential-penalty" theory.

Coattails

Perhaps the first theory propounded about midterm election patterns, the coattails theory holds that midterm losses are the consequence of presidential coattails being withdrawn. In marginal districts, members of the presidential victor's party are swept into office by the top of the ticket. Two years later, the same marginal representatives, bereft of strength at the top of the ticket and left to their own resources, are swept back out.[3] Some scholars have referred to this as the "regression to the mean" theory, since it postulates a return to a more normal state of affairs after the abnormal gains of a presidential year.[4] A potentially complementary theory stresses the importance of "exposure," though the exposure thesis can stand alone and explains congressional results in both midterm and presidential years. The more seats a congressional party holds above its "normal" number, measured by past performance, the more exposed it is—and the more difficulty it will have in the next election.[5]

Surge and Decline

An elaboration on the coattails theory, the surge-and-decline theory was first presented by Angus Campbell in 1960. Surge and decline emphasizes the impact of turnout: according to the original manifestation of the argument, peripheral voters (mostly unaffiliated) are mobilized to vote for the winning presidential candidate and incidentally benefit that party's candidates for Congress. Two years later, these voters drop out of the electorate, hurting the presidential party's congressional candidates.[6] This theory found support in the significantly lower voter turnout rates in midterm elections. However, while it claimed to explain why the president regularly lost seats in Congress, it had more difficulty explaining variations in those losses.[7]

The surge-and-decline theory has since been modified by several scholars. Richard Born and James E. Campbell have both argued that surge and decline was essentially true but that the real effect comes from a presidential-year surge not of independent voters but of weak partisans. Campbell also acknowledged that surge and decline went too far in denying the importance of national political and economic factors, and he sought to incorporate those factors into a revised model.[8]

National Conditions (or Referendum)

The chief alternative theory revolves around the argument that the original surge-and-decline theory failed to account for conditions at the time of the midterm elections; it was totally dependent on turnout variations of two years before. This theory—or, more accurately, cluster of theories—claimed that national conditions were central to understanding midterm election results. This national-conditions model asserts that the midterm election results represent a national referendum of sorts and are the product of election-year factors, representing the electorate's appraisal of the state of the economy, overall presidential performance, and/or party competence. Several variations of the referendum model have appeared.

The economic stimulant to voting behavior was discussed by Anthony Downs in *An Economic Theory of Democracy*.[9] Economic factors were also cited by Gerald H. Kramer, who argued that short-term national economic conditions—particularly trends in real personal income—were crucial to midterm election outcomes.[10] Howard S. Bloom and H. Douglas Price concluded shortly thereafter that bad economic conditions hurt the president's party in midterm elections but that prosperity was not a significant factor.[11] Some scholars have also argued that voter evaluations of economic performance seem to be long term in nature and are not subject to easy manipulation.[12]

Additionally, numerous students of congressional elections have deemed presidential popularity to be a significant factor in midterm elections. Studies of selected midterm elections have purported to show an effect by presidential popularity—not among partisans but among independents—starting with congressional races and proceeding all the way down the ballot.[13] Combining these two insights, Edward Tufte constructed a model of congressional elections dependent on a combination of economic conditions and presidential popularity.[14] To a large degree, Tufte's analysis has served as the touchstone for subsequent attempts to build a referendum model, though it is not clear whether presidential popularity, party evaluations, and voter perceptions of the economy should be considered equal independent variables or whether some depend directly on others.[15] The idea that midterm congressional elections turn on national issues also received support from a study of 1982 campaign literature, which showed that House and Senate candidates focused primarily on issues such as unemployment, inflation, and government spending rather than on local issues or constituency service.[16]

Like the surge-and-decline model, however, the national conditions (or referendum) model contained weaknesses that future scholars sought to correct with elaborations and modifications. Long before the referendum model had a name, Donald E. Stokes and Warren E. Miller questioned whether voters had sufficient information about congressional candidates to be able to render a referendum-style judgment.[17] Numerous scholars have likewise disputed the salience of presidential popularity and economic conditions in the congressional vote, either in the aggregate or on the individual level.[18] Others have argued that the referendum model focused too exclusively on presidential popularity at the expense of broader party evaluations, which they introduced into the model.[19]

Samuel Kernell and Gary C. Jacobson have attempted to bridge the "congressional elections are local" versus "congressional elections are national" gap by introducing an attenuated form of the referendum model. In this model of congressional elections, national conditions are decisive, but only through the indirect mechanism of influencing the calculations of potential congressional candidates ("strategic politicians"). National conditions are assumed by political actors to be important, so those conditions affect decisions by members of Congress to retire, by prospective members to run, and by contributors on all sides to give. It is the relative strength and resources of candidates at the local level which ultimately determine election outcomes.[20]

Presidential Penalty

Finally, some scholars have argued that midterm election patterns are best understood by attributing to voters a simple desire to, in essence, punish the president's party for holding the White House.[21] Kernell argued that presidential popularity or unpopularity was not uniformly important. Rather, midterm elections are characterized by "negative voting"; the president's unpopularity hurts his party more than his popularity helps it.[22] This notion received some support from Priscilla Southwell's study of the 1974, 1978, and 1982 midterm elections, which indicated that voter turnout was stimulated in 1982 by disapproval of Ronald Reagan's economic policies.[23] Robert Erikson and Gerald C. Wright point out that "the congressional vote for the president's party drops 4 percent to 5 percent in the midterm, and this seems to occur regardless of how the economy is doing or how the public feels about the president."[24] This punishment may be meted out in the form of negative voting or for the deliberate purpose of obtaining greater balance in government. The desire for balance in government is cited also by Morris Fiorina in his study of divided government.[25] This notion, too, has come under attack as presuming too much knowledge and issue-orientation on the part of the electorate.[26]

This debate continues to engage students of electoral behavior and is not limited to an analysis of midterm elections at the congressional level. Various scholars have also claimed to have found evidence for both the surge-and-decline theory and the referendum theory at the state and local level, and even internationally, in analogous elections.[27]

What Difference Does It Make?

In contrast to the attention lavished on the "why and how much?" debate, very little literature has grappled with the question of what difference midterm elections generally, and the anti-administration tendency of those elections specifically, make to American politics. Occasionally, a scholar will address this question in passing, but the question is important enough to merit more focused attention. Two recent pieces of scholarship, however, point in the direction of a framework for studying that question.

First, David R. Mayhew has argued that selected midterm elections have served an important creative function in American politics.[28] In Mayhew's view, these "innovative midterm elections" fundamentally changed the complexion of American politics by producing a long-term change in party or ideological control of Congress and the institution and substantial implementation of a new national policy agenda. According to Mayhew, the four innovative midterms were in 1810, when the western "war hawks" came to dominate Congress; 1866, when Radical Republicans attained a decisive advantage; 1910, which marked the beginning of the progressive dominance that characterized that whole decade; and 1938, which inaugurated the long reign of the "conservative coalition" in Congress.

Second, Alberto Alesina and Howard Rosenthal have developed a theory of "institutional balancing," which combines electoral cycles (including the midterm pattern) with macroeconomic cycles. Using a rational-choice framework, Alesina and Rosenthal concluded that "the midterm effect is part of the balancing effort of the electorate." That electorate faces two parties polarized between two goals of economic policy, both of which voters want represented: employment stimulation (Democrats) and inflation control (Republicans). Since the party of the president is known at the time of the midterm, it is easy for voters to know how to balance him and his economic priorities—simply by voting for the opposition.[29] One does not need to endorse Alesina and Rosenthal's undiluted rational-choice approach and relatively constrained focus on macroeconomics in order to appreciate the broader idea of the midterm election as a balancing force. Indeed, the question of voter agency may be less important than the argument that midterm elections impose a balancing effect regardless of voter agency.

The thesis of this book is twofold, drawing from, paralleling, and expanding upon the arguments raised by Mayhew, Alesina, and Rosenthal. First, midterm elections play a role that is both more important and more systematic than is generally acknowledged. They do matter, often a great deal. Second, the way they matter most is to serve as an integral part of the system of checks and balances established by the Founders, though the Founders would hardly have anticipated many of the ways that balancing takes place. Midterm elections do this in a multitude of ways, both negative and creative.

The assumption underlying this thesis is that midterm elections have for too long been viewed solely as dependent variables in American politics. Studied primarily in terms of their electoral outcomes and frequently explained by theories that hold those outcomes to be a product of previous elections (i.e., coattails, surge-and-decline, exposure), midterm elections have traditionally been seen as the end of a process or a cycle rather than as the beginning. And indeed, study of midterm elections cannot and should not be divorced from the context in which those elections take place, especially the events that precede them.

How the midterm election can serve as an important independent variable—or at least as an intervening and interdependent variable—must also be considered, however. For example, just as congressional scholars have devoted a great deal of attention to the question of how midterm elections are affected by the previous presidential election, it is time to devote attention to the equally sensible question of how midterm elections are related to the next presidential election. More broadly, it is time to examine more thoroughly how midterm elections, themselves, may contribute to future events as an integral part of a dynamic process.

Thus, the goal of this book will be to explore and delineate more fully the role of midterm elections in American politics, particularly their effect as a largely extraconstitutional complement to the system of checks and balances. In exactly what ways do midterm elections serve as an institutional check in American government, and how do they interact with existing checks? In what specific ways do midterm elections operate in a purely negative fashion to block the president, and in what ways do they operate in a broader, positive fashion to introduce innovation into the system? How have midterm elections contributed to realignments, to presidential politics, to the development of new issues and agendas? And can midterm elections be classified according to these criteria?

Midterm Elections and Checks and Balances in the American System

Since 1938, a consequence of each midterm congressional election has been elimination, practically speaking, of prospects for some policy departures wanted by the White House.
—RICHARD NEUSTADT

The counter-tendency inherent in the midterm election provides yet another check on the president.
—BARBARA HINCKLEY

Students of American politics are familiar with the multitude of mechanisms that serve to prevent excessive concentration of power and to require adequate deliberation rather than hasty action. Separation of powers between the executive, legislative, and judicial branches is foremost among those mechanisms. "The accumulation of all powers, legislative, executive, and judiciary, in the same hands," as Madison remarked in *Federalist* 47, "may justly be pronounced the very definition of tyranny."[1] That separation at the federal level was taken one step further by the principle of bicameralism, dividing the legislative branch (which the Founders assumed would predominate in a republic) into two parts. Since perfect separation of the branches was not practical and could not, in any case, prevent legislative usurpation, the legislative and executive branches were allowed to share in the exercise of some of the powers of the other (what we call checks and balances, in the narrow sense): the executive's veto gave him a share of the legislative power, while congressional war declaration and Senate powers over appointment and treaties gave the legislative branch a share of powers previously thought to be purely executive in nature.

Aside from the structure of the federal government, several other structural or theoretical mechanisms served to discourage an imbalance of political forces. The principle of constitutionalism—that statutory law and other political action have to be measured against the higher standard of a written constitution—represented a check in itself, as did the specific content of the United States Constitution, including the Bill of Rights and numerous rights written into the original Constitution. The division of power between federal and state governments served as a check. The large republic, as Madison argued in his celebrated essay in *Federalist* 10, comprehended a larger number of competing interests (or factions), making it less likely that a single interest could attain a stable majority and oppress the minority. And the republican principle of periodic elections guaranteed that the people would retain control over the officers of government.

These devices—separation of powers, bicameralism, checks and balances, a written constitution, federalism, the extended sphere of the republic, and frequent and regular elections—are justly regarded as standing at the heart of the American system. Yet the midterm election—a particular species of election with a very particular pattern attending it—must be considered another great check, a device which has evolved into a means of controlling the executive, reducing his party, and even introducing fundamental shifts in American politics. Its task has been not merely to check in a simple and negative sense, to prevent action by the president or his partisan allies, though it can most assuredly do that. Its task is also frequently to balance in a much broader sense: to end the dominance of one party and to clear the way for dominance by the other, and to serve as a positive tool for innovation and the long-term rejuvenation of the opposition party.

In the most basic sense, midterm elections are but a subset of the check offered by the process of regular elections. But where elections in general are instituted with the broad purpose of providing for consent of the governed and to give the people the means to remove officers from power, the midterm election pattern virtually guarantees that the president's party will be hurt at regular intervals. The extent of that damage may vary considerably, but the fact of it rarely does. In that sense, midterm elections are that subset of elections that predictably reduce the president's strength. However, they interact with numerous other checks in a much broader and more complex fashion, as will be seen.

This midterm check has hardly ever been recognized as such, though a few scholars, such as Richard Neustadt and Barbara Hinckley, have—often in passing—remarked upon this structural consequence of midterm elections. Yet there are numerous indications that midterm elections serve as an important check in American politics. It is striking, for example, that all of the academic theories attempting to explain the midterm pattern include some version of the notion that midterm elections serve as a potential opportunity for the electorate to check the executive. This is demonstrated most obviously in the presidential penalty theory, but is also clearly present in the referendum model. The strategic politicians thesis includes this notion carried out indirectly, and both the coattails and the surge-and-decline ideas hold that the president's party loses seats because of a withdrawal from the electorate of previously supportive voters. Thus, while scholars disagree about the question of voter agency, the virtually unanimous conclusion is that presidential party losses somehow have to do with the president and can be interpreted as either a direct or an indirect blow against him. As we will see, the notion of midterm elections producing a check on the president is also widely accepted by politicians, themselves, who do ascribe agency to voters.

Furthermore, there is a clear general trend of post-midterm congresses being less productive and more contentious—that is, more prone to gridlock—than pre-midterm congresses. David Mayhew's study of divided government, which concluded that production of important legislation was as likely in divided as in unified government, also concluded that post-midterm congresses were consistently less productive than pre-midterm congresses in both divided and unified governments. According to Mayhew, in only one instance from 1946 through 1990 was the second half of a presidential term more productive than the first, and on average major legislative acts fell by almost one-fourth after midterm elections.[2] A review of all public bills enacted from 1892 to 1996, not attempting to separate important from less-important bills, shows a similar though more modest pattern. In three-fifths of cases, legislative productivity dropped; overall, while there were wide variations, post-midterm productivity fell by more than 5 percent on average. Under particular circumstances that will be discussed later, productivity dropped much further and much more regularly (table 1.1).

Students of the presidential veto have also concluded, upon examining veto patterns, that midterm congresses are more contentious than congresses elected in presidential years. Jong R. Lee determined that midterm congresses are more likely to overturn vetoes, even when the research is controlled for other factors. Furthermore, when the opposition controls Congress—a phenomenon made more likely by midterm elections—both vetoes and overrides are more likely.[3] Altogether, Lee argued that "congresses elected at midterm are much more rebellious than might be expected simply from the loss of presidential partisans."[4] Gary W. Copeland confirmed that opposition control has been a significant factor in the likelihood of both vetoes and veto overrides. From 1860 through the Carter

Table 1.1 Legislative Pr͟ ͟ctivity Before and After Midterm Elections

	Increases	Declines	Avg. Before	Avg. After	Change
"Important bills" (1947–1990)	1	9	13.8	10.1	-26.8%
All public bills(1893–1996)	11	15	688.7	651.9	-5.3%

Source: Data from David R. Mayhew, *Divided We Govern* (New Haven: Yale University Press, 1991), 118; George B. Galloway, *History of the House of Representatives* 2d. ed. (New York: Thomas Y. Crowell Company, 1976), 375–76; Robert Moon and Carol Hardy Vincent, *Workload and Activity Report: United States Senate, 1946–1992* (Washington, D.C.: Congressional Research Service, 1993), 15; Norman J. Ornstein, Thomas E. Mann, and Michael J. Malbin, *Vital Statistics on Congress 1995–1996* (Washington, D.C.: Congressional Quarterly Press, 1996).

Table 1.2 Vetoes and Veto Overrides, 1892–1996

	Vetoes	Vetoes as % of Public Bills	Veto Override Attempts	Veto Override Success (% of Attempts)
Pre-midterm Congresses	892	5.0%	70	18 (25.7%)
Post-midterm Congresses	973	5.7%	128	54 (42.2%)

Source: Data from *Presidential Vetoes, 1789–1988* (Washington, D.C.: GPO, 1989); *Presidential Vetoes, 1989–1994* (Washington, D.C.: GPO, 1994).

presidency, Copeland counted 16 percent more vetoes after midterm elections than before, although he argued that the difference was largely explained by other factors.[5]

From 1892 to 1996, there were more vetoes and considerably more veto overrides in post-midterm congresses than in pre-midterm congresses. While the aggregate number of vetoes was influenced by a few presidencies in which post-midterm vetoes vastly outnumbered pre-midterm vetoes, post-midterm veto override efforts grew consistently across administrations.[6] Veto override attempts doubled in post-midterm congresses, as did the proportion of those attempts that succeeded (table 1.2).

Presidential support scores for the Eisenhower administration through the first Clinton administration also demonstrate that presidents clearly experience greater difficulty in promoting their own agendas after midterm elections (table 1.3). Of the eleven cases from 1953 through 1996, presidential support scores as calculated by *Congressional Quarterly* declined after midterm elections in all but one case: John F. Kennedy, whose support score increased after 1962, also happened to be the one president in this period whose party had largely escaped the midterm curse. The average decline in the other ten cases was 11.1 percentage points (a decline of about one-eighth). Because presidential support scores in Congress have a tendency to decline throughout a president's term, one might ask whether the post-midterm drop is merely part of a secular trend throughout the presidency. The answer is no. The average yearly decline from the first to the last year of a presidency during this period was only 2.7 percent, and in only one of the ten cases was post-midterm decline smaller than the average decline over the course of the presidency (Gerald Ford's administration).[7]

Several other scholars have modified the *Congressional Quarterly* scoring system but have obtained similar results. Gary King and Lyn Ragsdale calculate that post-midterm support scores in the House declined in all seven cases from 1957 through 1984. And in all seven cases, that decline was greater than the average annual decline suffered by each president; overall, the average post-midterm decline was nearly four times greater

Table 1.3 Presidential Support Scores Before and After Midterm Elections

	Increases	Declines	Avg. Before	Avg. After	Change %
CQ score*	1	10	72.5	66.1	-8.8
Ragsdale/ King score**	0	7	63.2	58.5	-7.4
Bond/Fleisher score***	2 (H)	6	69.1	63.9	-7.5
	2 (S)	6	69.2	62.6	-9.5

* Congress combined, 1953–1996. Data from *Congressional Quarterly Weekly Report*, December 19, 1992, 3896; Carroll J. Doherty, "Clinton's Big Comeback Shown in Vote Score," *Congressional Quarterly Weekly Report*, December 21, 1996, 3427. Yearly scores were averaged to produce a single pre-midterm or post-midterm score.
** House only, 1957–1984. Data from Gary King and Lyn Ragsdale, *The Elusive Executive* (Washington, D.C.: Congressional Quarterly Press, 1988), 73–74. Yearly scores were averaged to produce a single pre-midterm or post-midterm score.
*** House and Senate separately, 1953–1984. Data from Jon R. Bond and Richard Fleisher, *The President in the Legislative Arena* (Chicago: University of Chicago Press, 1990), 78. Scores were originally formulated as pre-midterm and post-midterm (by numbered Congress).

than the average annual decline (4.6 percent versus 1.2 percent).[8] Jon R. Bond and Richard Fleisher, counting only important conflictual votes from 1953 through 1984, concluded that, in both the House and the Senate, presidential support scores fell following midterm elections in six of eight cases.[9]

Presidential support scores are not flawless instruments; they do not always distinguish important from trivial issues (although Bond and Fleisher sought to do so), and they cannot distinguish between presidents whose high support scores reflect influence over a pliant Congress and those whose scores reflect accommodation to a hostile Congress.[10] Nevertheless, together with other indicators, post-midterm support scores tell a consistent story: the president suffers from midterm elections.

While almost impossible to quantify, it is likely that presidents are often forced off of their agendas in more subtle ways as well. Post-midterm congresses undoubtedly alter the content of legislation and the priority given to one piece of legislation over another, generally in ways unsympathetic to the president. Alberto Alesina and Howard Rosenthal, for example, hold that, even if midterm elections do not cause stalemate, they do alter the nature of policy by balancing the wishes of the executive with those of a strengthened opposition.[11] A Democratic Congress unchanged by the election of 1994 may well have passed a welfare reform measure in 1995 or 1996, yet very few would argue that it would have been the same welfare reform measure that was actually enacted.

If presidents consistently face a more difficult time after midterm elections—if they are more easily stymied—this phenomenon is, nevertheless, only part of the story, for there is also a more creative role played by midterm elections. The midterm election is capable of serving as the leading edge of positive change, in both the electoral and the policy realms.

This role is strongly suggested by circumstantial evidence and will be more thoroughly examined throughout this book. In the sixteen midterm elections preceding a presidential loss by the opposition party, the opposition gained only an average of thirty House seats and one Senate seat. On the other hand, in the ten midterm elections preceding a presidential win by the opposition, the opposition gained an average of forty-four House seats and six Senate seats. And if one looks only at an important subset of opposition presidential wins—midterm elections immediately preceding the partisan realignments of 1896 and 1932—the opposition party took over the House both times and gained an average of eighty-three House and seven Senate seats. These correlations are far from perfect and may be weakening; there are examples of large congressional losses not leading to presidential defeat by the president's party. The 1994 elections come immediately to mind as an important counter example. Nevertheless, a rough correlation does exist and invites a closer examination.

How Do Midterm Elections Impose an Added Check?

If there is both substantial evidence and tantalizing suggestion that midterm elections contribute to both stymieing presidents and replacing them, the all-important question is "how?" It is one thing to show correlation, quite another to provide a compelling reason to believe that the correlation reflects some degree of causation.

There are at least seven often overlapping yet distinct ways in which midterm elections contribute to the American system of checks and balances. In short, midterm elections change the composition of Congress, undermine the president's plebiscitary claim to an electoral mandate, provide the opposition with intangible momentum, provide an opportunity for the opposition to thrust forward new issues and also to develop new leadership, exacerbate splits in the president's party, and ensure a balancing force in state government.

Midterm Elections Change the Composition of Congress

The first, most obvious, and most fundamental mechanism by which midterm elections serve as an institutional check is the utter consistency, in a broad sense, of the tendency of midterm results to shift the composition of Congress in ways detrimental to the president. Indeed, one of the most important and best known patterns of American politics has been the anti-administration pattern attending midterm elections, the exception of 1998 notwithstanding (table 1.4). There are three ways in which congressional composition changes: a loss of seats by the president's party, a disproportionate loss of seats by the president's allies within his own party (or disproportionate gain by his strongest enemies within the opposition party), and loss of control of one or both houses of Congress, in either partisan or ideological terms.

PARTISAN SEAT LOSSES

The barometer most frequently used to measure party fortunes in midterm elections is the number of seats lost by the president's party in the House of Representatives.[12] In the twenty-six midterm elections from 1894 through 1994, the president's party lost House seats in every midterm election except that of 1934, when Franklin Roosevelt's Democrats picked up nine House seats. (This feat, of course, was repeated by Democrats in 1998.)

Table 1.4   President's Party Seat Shift in Midterm Elections, 1894–1998

Year	House	Senate
1894	-116*	-5*
1898	-21	+7
1902	-16†	+2
1906	-28	+3
1910	-57*	-10
1914	-59	+5
1918	-19*	-6*
1922	-75	-8
1926	-10	-6
1930	-49*	-8
1934	+9	+10
1938	-71	-6
1942	-55	-9
1946	-55*	-12*
1950	-29	-6
1954	-18*	-1*
1958	-48	-13
1962	-4	+3
1966	-47	-4
1970	-12	+2
1974	-48	-5
1978	-15	-3
1982	-26	+1
1986	-5	-8*
1990	-8	-1
1994	-52*	-8*
1998	+5	0

Source: Data from Norman J. Ornstein, Thomas E. Mann, and Michael J. Malbin, *Vital Statistics on Congress 1995–96* (Washington, D.C.: Congressional Quarterly Press, 1996).
*Loss of party control
†Because of an increase in the size of the House, Theodore Roosevelt's Republicans gained 9 seats at the same time Democrats were gaining 25, representing a net loss of 16 for the president's party.

The worst presidential performance was a loss of 116 seats in 1894, and the smallest loss was four seats in 1962. Losses varied considerably between those extremes, but the average House loss was thirty-six seats. In contrast, in only three of the twenty-six presidential elections from 1896 through

1996 did the party of the winning presidential candidate lose House seats (1960, 1988, and 1992). The president's party consistently loses seats because it consistently suffers a fall-off of approximately 5 percent in its national vote share in midterm elections. Indeed, from 1894 though 1994, the two-party vote share of the president's party in congressional elections fell in every election except that of 1926. (Because of variations in vote distribution across districts, the Republicans still lost seats in 1926 despite a rising vote share, and Democrats still gained seats in 1934 despite a falling vote share.)

In the Senate, the potential for change is muted by the fact that only about one-third of Senate seats, as opposed to all House seats, are subject to contest in any midterm election.[13] Furthermore, because of the staggered terms, there can be wide variations from year to year in the number of presidential party seats up for election. Nevertheless, the general pattern seen in the House applies to the Senate, as well, though not with the same constancy. As in the House, the president's party begins midterm Senate elections at a disadvantage, having lost seats in eighteen of the twenty-six midterm elections from 1894 through 1994. On average, when data are controlled for factors like the economy, the president's party loses one seat for every three seats it must defend over the opposition party.[14] Gains were recorded in the other eight elections, indicating that, while midterm tides may rock the Senate, it is buffered to a degree that the House is not. The average net Senate seat loss was about three, and results ranged from a net loss of thirteen in 1958 to a net gain of ten seats for the president's party in 1934. Two-thirds of midterm elections saw seat shifts within the range of plus or minus seven. Although little difference can be seen in the House between first midterms and subsequent midterms for presidents or parties, second midterms are generally particularly devastating for the president's party in the Senate (table 1.5).[15]

In an age that is generally acknowledged to be characterized by a decline of parties, how important can a partisan shift in Congress truly be? Party remains a crucial cue for congressional floor voting, as it remains one of the greatest cues in the electorate; indeed, within Congress, party unity scores are generally higher today than they were a generation ago.[16] Party is still key to the organization of Congress: the majority controls the crucial positions of committee chairmanships as well as (especially in the House) the terms by which bills and amendments can be offered and debated.

Furthermore, despite complaints by George Wallace and others that "there's not a dime's worth of difference" between the major parties, the Republicans and Democrats are, indeed, different. Within the context of

Table 1.5 Average Congressional Seat Change in Midterm Elections, 1894–1994

	House	*Senate*
Midterms in which president's party lost seats (out of 26)	25	18
Average presidential party seat change	-36	-3.2
President's first midterm seat losses (n = 19)	-35.8	-2.2
President's subsequent midterm seat losses (n − 7)	-36.1	6.4
Party's first midterm seat losses (n = 11)	-35.4	+2.7
Party's subsequent midterm seat losses (n=15)	-36.3	-5.9

liberalism broadly understood, which has always defined the mainstream of American politics, they offer significantly different policy prescriptions and priorities. Regardless of the absolute liberalism or conservatism of the district and the candidates, the Republican candidate in any given district is almost always relatively more conservative than the Democrat.[17] And as Philip Klinkner has shown, the major parties also have quite distinct internal cultures with sometimes profound implications, though these distinctions are often submerged from easy public view.[18] It was not until the Republican takeover of the House, for example, that political scientists began to understand that numerous features of the House since the 1950s had been Democratic, rather than simply congressional, institutions.

FACTIONAL SEAT SHIFTS

While partisan seat shifts are the clearest indication of waning presidential strength, no discussion of the compositional change of Congress in midterm elections would be complete without consideration of shifts within each party. Alesina and Rosenthal rate the change in overall composition of Congress—not just the numerical partisan balance or partisan control—

as a crucial outcome of midterm elections.[19] David Mayhew likewise argues that compositional change has been more important than mere numerical shifts in partisan balance for producing "innovative midterms." For example, one of his innovative midterms (1866) saw a shift of only six seats in the House but much greater change in the internal composition of the majority Republicans in favor of a policy of radical reconstruction.[20] In David Brady's view, while partisan seat change is the single most important factor, the very fact of massive membership turnover is, itself, at the heart of the realignment process, providing a force of energy which can break through the clogged legislative arteries and take policy in a dramatically new direction.[21] This view might easily be extrapolated to consider the importance of compositional turnover in conditions that fall well short of realignment.

Thus, midterm elections can hurt the president not merely through the mechanism of party but through the specific nature of the American party system—that is to say, the philosophically heterogeneous quality of our major parties. Party is central to the check inherent in midterm elections not just because the president's party loses seats and prestige but because midterm elections have historically held such a powerful potential to alter the internal composition of each party, usually in ways that hurt the president. His personal and philosophical allies often suffer disproportionately, another piece of inferential evidence bolstering the presidential penalty theory of the midterm pattern; his intrapartisan rivals are bolstered within party councils; his strongest partisan enemies are likewise frequently bolstered. Indeed, presidents face double jeopardy, in that the composition of their party can be changed both in the general election and in intraparty nomination contests. There are several indications of this compositional effect (table 1.6).

First, it is possible to compute general election seat shifts by region and compare those to the president's intraparty base as well as to the base of his intraparty opposition. These aggregate data are, of course, only a rough and imprecise way of getting at the question—the danger of the ecological fallacy looms large here—but they can at least provide some evidence worth pondering. When we look at the president's regional party base and the regional base of his intraparty opposition, midterm elections conformed to the expectation expressed above—that the composition of the president's party shifts against him—in two-thirds of cases (17 of 26). The president's base and intraparty opposition were calculated by reference to his share of national convention delegates or, in a few recent cases, primary results by region.[22] This approach to defining a president's

Table 1.6   Factional Composition Changes in the House, 1894-1994

Year	Pres. Intraparty Base	Pres. Intraparty Opposition	Intraparty Regional Shift	Intraparty Ideological Shift	Opp. Party Ideological Shift
1894	N,M	B,W,S	-57	*	
1898	B,M,S,W	N	25		*
1902	M,N	S,W,B	12		
1906	M,N	S,W,B	-20		
1910	S,W,B	M,N	35	*	*
1914	M,N,S	B,W	-60		
1918	M,N,S	B,W	1	*	
1922	S,B,M,N	W	-70	*	*
1926	S,B,M,N	W	-10	*	
1930	N,W,S,B	M	-9	*	*
1934	M,W,N,B	S	11		
1938	M,W,N,B	S	-72	*	
1942	M,W,N,B	S	-49	*	
1946	B,M,W,N	S	-54	*	
1950	B,M,W,N	S	-25	*	
1954	N,B	M,W,S	-4		
1958	N,B	M,W,S	6	*	*
1962	N,M,W	S,B	10		
1966	N,M,W	S,B	-26	*	
1970	B,S,M	N,W	-9		
1974	N,M,B	W,S	-17	*	
1978	S,B	W,N,M	7	*	*
1982	W,S	N,M,B	23	*	*
1986	W,S	N,M,B	-3		
1990	N,W,M	B,S	-8		
1994	S,M	B,N,W	-14	*	*

Pres. intraparty base= Regional base of the president (in order of support). See Appendix A.
Pres. opposition base= Regional base of the president's intra-party opposition. See Appendix A.
Intraparty regional shift= Shift of regional balance within president's party (seat change in president's base minus seat change in intraparty opposition base).
Intraparty ideological shift= Ideological shift against the president within his own party, emphasized by contemporary or historical analysis.
Opp. party ideological shift= Ideological shift in favor of the president's strongest foes within the opposition party as emphasized by contemporary or historical accounts.
B= Border states (KY, MD, MO)
M= Midwest states (IL, IN, IA, KS, MI, MN, NE, ND, OH, SD, WI)
N= Northeast states (CT, DE, ME, MA, NH, NJ, NY, PA, RI, VT, WV)
S= Southern states (AL, AR, FL, GA, LA, MS, NC, OK, SC, TN, TX, VA)
W= Western states (AK, AZ, CA, CO, HI, ID, MT, NV, NM, OR, UT, WA, WY)
Source: Data from Guide to U.S. Elections, 2nd ed. (Washington, D.C.: Congressional Quarterly, 1985); America Votes (Washington, D.C.: Congressional Quarterly), 1986, 1990, 1994.

intraparty regional base is not without flaws, chief of which is that regional success in the nominating stage does not translate automatically into success in Congress, but it is more valid than a measurement of general election results and much less cumbersome than an attempt to disaggregate regional support on legislative votes over the last century. The intraparty regional compositional shift seen in table 1.6 is derived by comparing seats gained or lost from base regions with seats gained or lost in opposition regions. For example, in 1894 Democrats lost eighty-three seats in Grover Cleveland's base areas of the Northeast and Midwest, while losing only twenty-six seats in the opposition South, border states, and West, so the balance within his own party was fifty-seven seats worse for the president.

In several cases, the regional data obscure important nuances. In fourteen clearly identifiable cases, the president's party shifted against him ideologically as a result of primary and/or general election results,[23] and in at least ten cases the opposition party became more ideologically hostile. Such ideological shifts are necessarily assessed on a more impressionistic basis than are the regional bases of support or opposition, but they can also help capture important information. Altogether, twenty-three of twenty-six cases saw at least one type of compositional shift, and two of the remaining cases came in the anomalous years (1934 and 1962) when the president's party escaped the midterm pattern altogether (see chapter six).

Another possible indirect measure of the overall composition of Congress can be found in the relative level of support for the so-called "conservative coalition" of Republicans and Southern Democrats. From 1957 through 1992, conservative coalition support shifted against the president after midterm elections twice as often as it shifted in his favor. In both the House and the Senate, conservative coalition scores grew worse six times and better only three times after midterm elections ("worse" meaning lower for a Republican president, higher for a Democratic president). Furthermore, when charting shifts in conservative coalition scores against midterm election partisan seat changes, a rough correlation is evident. In all three of the House cases in which the president's position improved after the midterm, his party had suffered much lower than average losses; in two of the three Senate cases, his party had actually gained seats.[24]

Bond and Fleisher have also constructed several indices of factional composition from 1953 to 1984, reaching results that are more ambiguous but which still generally confirm the potential of midterm elections to alter party composition on both sides. Bond and Fleisher divide each party into a base (conservative Republicans, liberal Democrats) and a cross-pressured faction (liberal Republicans, conservative Democrats). According to their calculations, the president's ideological base in the Senate shrank as a proportion of his party, and his opponents' ideological base grew (these two are not necessarily concomitant), after five of eight midterm elections. In the House, the opposition base also grew proportionally five of eight times, although the president's base as a proportion of his own party shrank only three of eight times.[25] Perhaps more to the point, when taking into account both the number of members in the president's party base and their statistical level of support for the president, the president's post-midterm "effective party base" fell in the House seven of eight times, by an average of over 14 percent.[26]

There is no question that the measurement of factional composition is more difficult than the measurement of partisan seat swings and that it brings less consistent results. Most measurements posit intraparty compositional change as a probability, in contrast to the near certainty of partisan change. Accordingly, it must be considered a secondary feature of midterm elections in general, though in particular cases it may be vital. Nevertheless, some form of the factional effect does seem more likely than not, given the available evidence, and must be thought of not in isolation but in combination with the partisan effect.

The change in both partisan and factional strength are crucial because, all other things being equal, presidents are more successful with more rather than fewer copartisans in Congress and more rather than fewer ideological allies across parties. As James P. Pfiffner remarks, "The greater the margin of party members in each house presidents have, the better their chances are when they begin to seek a majority of votes on any particular measure."[27] More broadly, Bond and Fleisher argue that "members of Congress do provide levels of support for the president that are broadly consistent with their partisan and ideological predispositions. Facing a Congress composed of a more favorably predisposed cast of actors does increase the chances of presidential success."[28] When thinking about the seat losses suffered by the president's allies in any given midterm election, it is important to remember that one must multiply by two the seats lost to fully grasp the magnitude of the loss: when the president's party, for example, loses twenty-five seats, the gap between it and the opposition shifts not by twenty-five votes but by fifty.

LOSS OF CONGRESSIONAL CHAMBERS

The degree to which seat losses translate into loss of control of one or both houses of Congress depends, of course, on both the extent of seat losses and the margin of control prior to the midterm elections. Nevertheless, a clear pattern is observable here as well. Matthew Soberg Shugart points out that, from 1868 through 1992, only about two of five presidential elections have produced an opposition Congress, while almost half of midterm elections have done so.[29] Interestingly, Shugart's findings also indicate that other countries utilizing a presidential system and midterm elections—most in Latin America—experience a similar pattern but to a lesser extent. Among the twelve countries studied, divided government was more commonly the product of nonconcurrent (midterm) elections than of concurrent elections by a ratio of almost two to one. Nevertheless, U.S. midterms are one-third more likely to produce an opposition Congress than is the international average.[30]

In the United States, no party since 1894 has lost preexistent partisan control of Congress at the same time it was winning the presidency. Presidential elections have coincided with a shift in party control in favor of the president's party in the House only twice (1948 and 1952) and in the Senate five times (1912, 1932, 1948, 1952, and 1980). In contrast, since 1894 midterm elections have been the occasion for a shift in party control— always moving to control by the president's opposition— seven times in the House (1894, 1910, 1918, 1930, 1946, 1954, and 1994) and six times in the Senate (1894, 1918, 1946, 1954, 1986, and 1994).

Accordingly, without midterm elections, divided government would be much less likely; before the decline of party in the electorate and of presidential coattails in the last half of the twentieth century, it would have been almost nonexistent. As a consequence of midterm shifts in party control of Congress, midterm elections have frequently served as a vehicle for the creation (or strengthening) of divided government. On eight occasions since 1894, midterm elections have produced divided government where it did not exist at all or (as in 1986) added a second legislative chamber to opposition control. On five other occasions, all since 1958, midterm elections have maintained divided government that already existed by adding to the House (and usually Senate) margins of the already-existing opposition majority (1958, 1970, 1974, 1982, 1990). Thus, since the Eisenhower administration, midterm elections have more often had the effect of deepening divided government than of creating it.

Taking the earlier manifestation of these tendencies into account, Pearl Olive Ponsford produced in the 1930s a polemic against the political consequences of midterm elections, arguing that they were an unmitigated evil leading to divided government and political paralysis. In Ponsford's view, midterm elections should be eliminated.[31] This argument was taken up decades later by Lloyd Cutler and others, who proposed concurrent four-year terms for president, House, and Senate in order to make divided government less likely.[32]

Much recent scholarship has made a credible argument that divided government is not, by itself, responsible for governmental gridlock. Rather, this argument goes, divided government is primarily a symptom, a consequence and manifestation of the social division and ambivalence about the role of government which is truly responsible for gridlock. Indeed, some presidents have achieved much despite an opposition Congress, while others have failed even when blessed with a Congress controlled by their own party; divided government (and, by extension, any strengthening of the president's congressional opposition) is not an insuperable obstacle to legislative achievement. There are far too many factors affecting legislative outcomes for any one factor, including divided government, to be unduly elevated. As evidence for this proposition, advocates point to studies that show little average difference in production of major legislation between periods of unified government and periods of divided government.[33]

However, other studies have reached the opposite conclusion—that the conventional wisdom about the tendency of divided government to produce legislative gridlock is correct.[34] Furthermore, presidential support scores in Congress are consistently about 20 percent lower in divided government than in unified government.[35] Even when gridlock does not result, presidents are checked in more subtle ways; they are probably forced into unpleasant compromises more often when the opposition controls Congress. The most that can be said with certainty is that "divided government is but one factor in determining policy success or failure."[36]

Such an analysis is, in any case, ultimately inadequate for understanding the potential effects of midterm elections for several reasons. First and foremost, it is important to distinguish here between divided government, per se, and the central effect of midterm elections, which may, but does not have to, lead to divided government—the decline in strength primarily of the president's party and secondarily of his intraparty allies. Because the ideological composition of Congress is a crucial factor, it is also possible that a hidden form of divided government may result—a form that leaves the external shell of unified government intact but places the president's ideological opponents in practical control of Congress. There were, for example, two winners in 1938—Republicans and conservative Democrats— and it was this combination that bedeviled Franklin Roosevelt for the rest of his presidency. The results of the 1966 midterm elections convinced even Democratic congressional leaders that Lyndon Johnson had gone too far, too fast. In neither case did the opposition party take formal control of

Congress; in both cases the president was stymied, nonetheless. Conversely, as in 1981 through 1982, a president may face divided government formally but still hold an ideological majority. Only the midterm elections of 1982, which deprived the Republican–Boll Weevil bloc of working control of the House, restored the reality (as opposed to simply the appearance) of divided government.

Thus, the partisan dynamic underlying midterm elections is both central to their importance and nuanced beyond a simple calculation of partisan seat shifts or control of legislative chambers. Altogether, partisan seat losses, factional seat losses, and the partisan and/or ideological divided government that may result from those seat losses combine to form a powerful check. In a very real sense, the anti-administration pattern of midterm elections reinforces the principles of separation of powers and bicameralism. In recognition of this fact, V. O. Key remarked that "the mutually independent election of President and Congress" is "essential" to separation of powers.[37] Students of political parties—as well as practitioners like Thomas Jefferson and Woodrow Wilson—have long seen parties as a bridge across separation of powers. The opposite is also true: midterm elections reducing the president's strength in Congress, partisan and otherwise, widen the separation between the branches.

Likewise, on two occasions since 1894, midterm elections have been the occasion for unified party control of Congress to be disrupted. On both occasions, the House shifted party control while the Senate remained under the control of the president's party until the next election. This phenomenon was more frequent before 1894, when it happened seven times (although sometimes unified congressional control was reestablished by the president's party in the next election). Only thrice has the reverse happened—a midterm election that unified both houses of Congress under the same party—and only once since 1894.[38] Scholars who question the importance of divided government acknowledge the potentially stifling consequences of a split legislative branch, particularly on budget issues.[39] Even when there is no partisan division between the houses brought about by midterm elections, the House often changes more quickly than the Senate when there are large-scale philosophical or partisan shifts underway. Congruence of party can consequently mask a widening of differences below the surface.

Midterm Elections Undermine the President's Plebiscitary Authority

Public explanation, argument, and rhetoric—as well as public prestige and popular support—have become central to the modern presidency in a variety of ways.[40] Richard Neustadt's groundbreaking work on presidential power argued that a president's power was defined largely by his persuasiveness and that one of the most important factors determining persuasiveness was his public standing. In Neustadt's view, a president's prestige "may not decide the outcome in a given case but can affect the likelihoods in every case and therefore is strategically important to his power."[41] As Mary Stuckey argues, the president has become the nation's "interpreter-in-chief."[42] To Samuel Kernell, "going public" has become a central strategy of the modern presidency.[43]

Since at least the administration of Woodrow Wilson, this rhetorical drive has taken the form of presidents claiming a popular mandate in their elections, to the extent that their authority is legitimized by this mandate primarily and by the Constitution only secondarily.[44] Indeed, in Neustadt's view, the president's "power"— his ability to get things done through persuasion—has outstripped his "powers," or his constitutionally granted authority.[45] Thus, presidential interpretations of presidential election outcomes—at least to the extent that they have been accepted by the broader public—have fundamentally transformed the very nature of presidential power, energizing the presidency as a popular office.

Even though political scientists are generally skeptical about interpreting election results as a conscious popular mandate for particular policies,[46] incoming presidents can always claim to have obtained such a mandate because they have always, by definition, just won a presidential election. However, presidents are almost always at a disadvantage in midterm elections and must explain not personal victories but party defeats. If the interpretation of popular mandate associated with presidential elections has been an important factor in presidential power, then presidents have a strong stake—and a difficult task—in shaping a midterm interpretation. A pattern of interpretation of midterm election results offered by presidents, as well as by members of both parties in Congress, can be seen in the thirteen postwar midterm elections from 1946 through 1994.

When providing midterm election explanations, presidents are almost always on the defensive, struggling to maintain the appearance of their popular mandate.[47] The president's primary imperative is to minimize the loss of his own prestige, to shore up the appearance that he still governs by popular mandate. Consequently, as one might expect, presidents generally attempt to avoid personal responsibility as far as possible. Indeed, in only one case out of thirteen did a president explicitly accept responsibility (Clinton in 1994). In seven of thirteen cases, the administration explicitly denied that the midterm results contained a referendum on the president.

In two of those cases, presidents in their second terms pointed to their reelection landslides two years earlier as evidence of the improbability of a general repudiation of their administrations (Eisenhower in 1958 and Reagan in 1986). Twice presidents seemed to blame the voters. The first time was in 1958, when Dwight Eisenhower as much as accused the voters of confusion, saying he was unsure that voters "did this thing deliberately."[48] Bill Clinton in 1994 simultaneously accepted what he called "my share" of the responsibility, while claiming that voters had simply misunderstood how beneficial his program was.[49]

By far the most common explanation was the inevitability of history. In two-thirds of the cases (eight of thirteen), the president argued that the midterm results were largely meaningless because the president's party always loses seats; sometimes, especially when losses were relatively low, this interpretation shaded into a claim of some sort of moral victory. In two of these cases, as well as in a separate case, the president was able to argue explicitly that the results constituted a form of victory—not just a moral victory in comparison to past congressional losses but a victory based on actual gains in governorships or in the Senate. These arguments were as close as presidents could come to a mandate argument but were strictly defensive. Presidents sought to preserve the remnants of a mandate from two years before but could not conjure the image of a fresh mandate.

Other explanations offered by presidents or their administrations, in order of frequency, were national conditions, local conditions, and campaign weaknesses. Twice, presidents acknowledged some form of an ideological or policy mandate for the opposition in the elections: in 1974, when Gerald Ford said the elections constituted a mandate for the Democrats to deal with inflation, and in 1994, when Bill Clinton acknowledged that voters wanted smaller, more effective, and less intrusive government.[50] Only once, again in 1994, did the president say that voters deliberately chose divided government or did the administration blame the president's own party in Congress, although the latter explanation was offered by the chairman of the Democratic National Committee, not by the president himself.[51] In any event, presidents tried to reduce midterm losses to mechanistic factors whenever plausible but were often forced to acknowledge, either implicitly or explicitly, popular dissatisfaction.

While the president was forced on the defensive, his congressional opposition attempted to seize the initiative and delegitimize the president's earlier mandate, replacing it with a popular mandate of their own to change course.[52] In more than half of the cases (seven of thirteen), opposition members of Congress claimed an ideological or policy-specific mandate.

In six cases, the vote was interpreted as a more generic anti-administration signal, and in an additional three cases a generic party mandate was claimed. In four elections, opposition members of Congress pointed to voters' concerns about the economy, and in two cases administration scandal was cited. In six cases the more modest interpretation was advanced that the election results signaled a desire by voters for moderation or more balance in government, although such an argument itself implied a repudiation of the president's current direction. Only very rarely did a member of the victorious party hold that the election results carried no clear message.[53] The more extravagant election explanations were the dominant explanations when party control of Congress changed, and party takeover was more consistently connected to claims of an opposition mandate than were large seat gains without party takeover. In this sense divided government does seem to be important, not because of its effect on legislative production but because of the way it undermines presidential mandate claims.

Finally, the president's party in Congress offered a pattern of midterm explanation that was frequently closer to that of the president's opposition than to the president's. Institution was often more important than party in channeling midterm election explanations. It is possible to systematically compare the three by combining and reformulating categories of explanation (table 1.7).

Only on the most obviously partisan dimensions does the president's party remain wedded to the president. The president and his party in Congress largely have stood together against the opposition party on questions of an ideological and partisan mandate as well as on the question of campaign shortcomings. They both uniformly have rejected the notion of a partisan mandate, which the opposition party claimed about one-quarter of the time. They both also have been highly reluctant to acknowledge an ideological mandate, while the opposition party has used this explanation more than half the time. And both the president and his congressional party have occasionally blamed their losses on poor technical execution of the campaign, an explanation entirely avoided, for obvious reasons, by the victors.

However, on at least seven other dimensions, the pattern of explanation by the president's party in Congress is closer to that of the congressional opposition than to that of their own president. Both congressional parties have shied away from the historical precedent and local conditions explanations often used by presidents; unlike presidents, both congressional parties have also entirely avoided self blame or blaming the voters. Both the president's party and the opposition have frequently attributed mid-

Table 1.7 Midterm Election Explanations: President, Opposition Party in Congress, and President's Party in Congress, 1946–1994

Explanation	President Used	Average Seat Loss	Opposition Party in Congress Used	Average Seat Gain	Presidents Party in Congress Used	Average Seat Loss
History/victory	9	18/2	0	—	2	7/5
No repudiation of pres.	7	28/5	2	15/-1	3	31/2
Local conditions	4	27/2	0	—	1	29/6
Campaign shortcomings	3	35/10	0	—	2	7/5
Scandal	1	48/5	2	39/6	2	39/6
National conditions	4	44/5	4	22/3	4	30/3
Desire for change	1	52/8	0	—	4	34/4
President responsible*	1	52/8	6	32/4	7	39/5
Opposition party mandate	0	—	3	24/2	0	—
Ideological/policy mandate	2	50/7	7	30/7	0	—
Desire for balance/centrism	1	52/8	6	31/5	4	41/6
Failures of Congress	1	52/8	0	—	0	—
Dumb voters	2	50/11	0	—	0	—
No explanation offered	0	—	1	4/-3	3	22/6

*In the case of the president's party in Congress, six of the instances blamed presidential unpopularity in some form; the seventh blamed insufficiently vigorous campaigning by a popular president.

term election results to a referendum on the president. In more than half of the cases (seven of thirteen), a member of the president's party in Congress publicly placed at least some of the responsibility on the president. In six cases, the unpopularity of the president was blamed. Sometimes this responsibility was narrowly focused, as in arguments that Harry Truman's Brannan farm plan hurt some Democrats in 1950; at other times, as in 1994, the drag from the White House was said to be more general.[54] Members of the president's party publicly held him responsible in one manner or another in three of the four elections featuring a change in party control (1946, 1954, and 1994).

Indeed, the president's party was more likely to make such arguments than was the opposition party (much more likely, if the more generic explanations of people desiring change were euphemisms for an anti-administration vote). The anti-administration explanation leaves the president's party in Congress unscathed; the opposition, on the other hand, prefers a broader party, ideological, or policy interpretation and, thus, has an interest in not allowing the results to be personalized to the same extent. And members of the president's congressional party and the opposition are both much more likely than the president to attribute party shifts to a desire by the electorate for greater balance or centrism.

Altogether, rhetoric claiming a popular mandate has been the source of much of the growth of the power of the presidency in the twentieth century. As a result, midterm elections—which almost always hurt the president's party to some extent—do not merely pose a tangible threat by reducing the president's congressional strength. They also threaten the appearance of the president's popular grounding and, hence, strike at the heart of the modern plebiscitary presidency. The plebiscitary moral authority of the president is almost necessarily damaged in the process of midterm explanation: his voice grows weaker and more isolated, while that of the opposition grows stronger.

The president seeks to limit the damage, resorting whenever possible to the argument that "history did it," an implicit claim of moral victory which leaves his mandate intact. This line of explanation, however, is always defensive and frequently implausible. The president can try to play the mandate game after midterm elections, but he is not playing on his field. Instead, he finds himself in a no-win situation: either he must accept responsibility for his party's defeat or he must admit that his fate is in the hands of impersonal forces beyond his control. In this way, midterm elections might be said to enhance the check of constitutionalism itself. To the extent that the presidency's embrace of plebiscitary power contradicts the essential spirit of constitutionalism—that we are to be governed by written law, not by charismatic personality—midterm elections blunt that tendency. Presidents often unwittingly contribute to the antiplebiscitary effect of midterm elections by seeking to make the elections a test of their own popularity, a referendum that is stacked against them from the beginning.

Furthermore, the president's position vis-à-vis Congress can be doubly damaged in the struggle over midterm interpretations. More often than not, the opposition party is energized by its own claim of a popular mandate which supersedes that of the president, a claim that is especially powerful when it makes large gains or takes control of one or both chambers. And his own party often splits: party bonds frequently prove insufficient to produce a common interpretation between the president and his co-partisans in Congress.

Midterm Elections Provide Intangible Political Momentum to the President's Opponents

Midterm interpretations by the president and his opponents are not offered in a vacuum; outside commentators add their voices, and the public makes a judgment. As a result, connected with the question of midterm explanation is the issue of momentum. Far more difficult to measure than seat changes in Congress, intangible political momentum can nevertheless be a crucial component for a party's future success. Momentum can be thought of simply as the common perception of who is "up" and who is "down." Because the president's party almost always loses seats in Congress, his opponents are virtually guaranteed of gaining at least some political momentum, a shot in the arm that rejuvenates their spirits and reestablishes their viability as an alternative political force. By definition, that opportunity for momentum comes at a propitious moment, immediately following a presidential loss.

Just a few examples may help to illustrate how potentially important midterm elections can be to reviving the flagging fortunes of the out party. After nearly a decade of disaster, Republicans gained seventy-one House seats in 1938, reestablishing themselves as a competitive force. After the debacle of 1964, which had led commentators to ask whether Republicans would survive as a party, the GOP gained forty-eight House seats and won headlines proclaiming REPUBLICANS STRONGER THAN WAS EXPECTED IN OFF-YEAR VOTE,[55] THE REPUBLICAN TIDE,[56] GOP'66: BACK ON THE MAP,[57] and THE REPUBLICAN RESURGENCE.[58] Following the fiasco of 1974 and Jimmy Carter's 1976 presidential win, Republicans gained a modest fifteen House and three Senate seats in 1978 but were able to declare (and seemed to believe) that the tide had turned again in their favor. And Democrats, shell-shocked by the election of 1980 and the legislative triumphs of Ronald Reagan during 1981 through 1982, were stiffened in their resolve by the midterm election of 1982, in which they gained twenty-six House seats and regained working control of that chamber.

Media interpretations consistently support the opposition party's claims of disabling the president's mandate, if not of constructing its own. In only seven cases of twenty-six from 1894 through 1994 did the post-election analysis of the *New York Times* fail to declare a fairly clear defeat for the president and his party and a triumph for his opposition, and in two of those cases (1934 and 1962) the president's party had actually broken the pattern of midterm losses (Appendix E). It should be pointed out that the *Times,* like all publications, is sometimes influenced by its own agenda and is never clairvoyant or unchallenged; the quality of its instant analysis does not always hold up well under historical scrutiny. Nevertheless, the analyses produced by this leading news publication do serve to provide a rough barometer of contemporary media interpretation of who gained, who lost, and why.

While seemingly ephemeral, momentum can lead to a variety of more tangible political consequences. Wavering potential presidential candidates may choose to jump into the fray or to refrain from jumping. At lower levels, potential challengers and candidates for open seats make strategic calculations about whether it will be a good year or a bad year for their party. While a variety of factors are weighed in those calculations, results of the most recent midterm election almost certainly play a part. As Gary C. Jacobson says, "political career strategies are shaped by what happened in the previous election as well as by current national conditions. Politicians, like generals, are inclined to prepare for the last war."[59] For instance, Republicans were not able to take full advantage of Ronald Reagan's 1984 landslide because potential candidates were discouraged by the party's poor showing in 1982; similarly, Republicans may well have held on to congressional control in 1996 because many Democrats believed that Republicans would continue their successes of 1994 and chose to avoid potential challenges or to retire as incumbents.

Perceptions of momentum can also make fundraising easier and can motivate the grassroots volunteer base. Jacobson, for example, discusses potential contributors as strategic actors whose decisions are heavily influenced by "expectations about the likelihood of electoral success."[60] Money is more likely to flow to candidates for open seats than to challeng-

Table 1.8 Post-Presidential vs. Post-Midterm Campaign Spending, 1978–1994

	Total House	Open House Seats
Out-party change after presidential election	+28%	+36%
In-party change after presidential election	+21%	+22%
Ratio, out- vs. in-party spending changes after presidential election	4-3	3-2
Out-party change after midterm election	+22%	+13%
In-party change after midterm election	+10%	-4%
Ratio, out- vs. in-party spending changes after midterm election	2-1	4-1

Source: Data from Norman J. Ornstein, Thomas E. Mann, and Michael J. Malbin, *Vital Statistics on Congress 1995–96*, 81–82.

ers and to challengers running against incumbents who won their most recent election narrowly rather than by a wide margin. Midterm elections tend to reduce the margins of in-party incumbents across the board, thus making a larger number appear vulnerable and attracting stronger challengers and more opposition money than would otherwise be the case.

While good records of political fundraising and spending became available only after the 1974 Federal Election Campaign Act amendments, a rough pattern is visible in House election spending. (Senate races are too few in number and too idiosyncratic to make a useful indicator.) In all House elections from 1978 through 1994, the out-party's mean spending increased faster than that of the in-party following midterm elections by an average ratio of two to one. (Following presidential elections, the out-party also outpaced the in-party but in only three out of four cases and by a ratio of four to three.) In the all-important House open-seat contests, the average in-party spending actually fell by 4 percent, while out-party spending increased by an average of 13 percent after midterm elections. Altogether, the out-party's spending consistently outpaced the in-party's by significantly wider margins following midterm elections (table 1.8).

It is also worthwhile to consider another set of midterm elections, less regular and more idiosyncratic than others, which also play an important part in the milieu of electoral politics between presidential elections. These are the special elections that are called to fill vacancies that arise between regular congressional elections. Seldom is there a large enough number of special elections or a large enough net partisan turnover in those elections to make much difference in the composition of Congress, although Democratic victories in special elections gave them control of the House after the crucial midterm election of 1930. From 1944 to 1994, there were twenty-five two-year periods between regular congressional elections. Those periods averaged 8.0 special elections in the House and 2.4 in the Senate (table 1.9). The average net seat change is one-half a seat in the Senate and nearly one seat in the House, with no net shift greater than three seats in the Senate or four in the House in any two-year period. Nevertheless, there are at least two crucial facts about them which merit attention.

First, despite their seemingly idiosyncratic nature, "special elections are manifestations of usual partisan forces operating in a slightly different

Table 1.9 Special Elections for House and Senate (1944–1994)

	House	Senate
Special elections per interelection period (avg.)	8.0	2.4
Average loss by the president's party (seats)	.8	.5
'nter-election periods with presidential losses	12	11
Periods with presidential gains	4	2
Periods with no net party change	9	12

Source: Data from Norman J. Ornstein, Thomas E. Mann, and Michael J. Malbin, *Vital Statistics on Congress 1995–96* (Washington, D.C.: C.Q. Press, 1996), 53–54. See Appendix F.

context."[61] This means that, like all other midterm elections, special elections show a consistent bias against the administration party. In House special elections from 1944 through 1994, the president's party made a net seat gain in only four of the twenty-five two-year periods; in Senate special elections, that figure was two of twenty-five. Altogether, losing periods for the in-party outdid winning periods by a ratio of three to one in the House and a ratio greater than five to one in the Senate. (There was no net partisan shift in over one-third of House cases and nearly half of Senate cases.)

Christopher J. Anderson, Andrew M. Appleton, and Daniel S. Ward calculate that the president's party consistently loses votes in special House elections. Overall, opposition parties lost only 12 percent of their seats that were contested in special congressional elections, while the president's party lost 47 percent of its special election seats from 1960 through 1991. Furthermore, Anderson, Appleton, and Ward hold that both the rate of seat turnover and the anti-administration bias of special congressional elections have increased since Lee Sigelman calculated in 1981 that 80 percent of seats did not change parties and that, when they did, the out-party gained by a three-to-one margin.[62] Sigelman also discovered that the president's party did consistently better in special elections held in presidential election years than in those held during midterm years.[63] In the view of Anderson, Appleton, and Ward, "these results suggest that the 'presidential penalty' found by Erikson (1988) in U.S. midterm elections may be at work in special elections as well."[64] Evidence was also found of a consistent surge-and-decline effect, not only in American special elections but, interestingly, in British and Canadian by-elections.[65]

Second, it is obvious that many of these special elections serve as bellwethers for media interpretation of national trends. Indeed, as Anderson, Appleton, and Ward argue, "While textbooks on Congress all but ignore such contests, the media and political elites seem to take such elections quite seriously as barometers of public attitudes toward the president and political parties."[66] This tendency may lead to over-interpretation of special election results but is not irrational: "It is the absence of an incumbent in special elections that makes them particularly appropriate for performing the barometer function. By removing the personal vote, special elections may afford an opportunity for voters to send signals about broader political concerns, and in so doing, provide information about future political behavior."[67] In fact, Anderson, Appleton, and Ward argue that presidential approval (though, perhaps surprisingly, not the economy as an independent variable) has a moderate impact on the special election vote and that "the performance of the president's party in the barometer election is also a powerful predictor of change between the two general elections."[68] Accordingly, special elections often change the political climate dramatically, even as they leave the aggregate partisan balance essentially undisturbed. To cite a few important examples:

- When Republican Heather Wilson won a surprise victory in New Mexico's First Congressional District in May 1998, many Republicans took it as a sign that congressional failure to act on President Clinton's agenda would bring no adverse electoral consequences. Some also interpreted Wilson's win as a sign that Democratic hopes of regaining the House in 1998 were futile.[69] While these interpretations were overdrawn, they clearly influenced the course of events in 1998.

- The narrow January 1996 Senate victory by Democrat Ron Wyden in Oregon was widely interpreted as a signal of voter disenchantment with the congressional Republican "revolution." Subsequent Democratic fundraising and candidate recruitment improved markedly. Democrats succeeded in Oregon after having lost a special House election in California in October 1995, which they had hoped to bill as a bellwether.

- A June 1993 special Senate election in Texas provided an important boost for Republicans fighting Bill Clinton's budget proposals when Kay Bailey Hutchison won a lopsided victory over Bob Krueger to fill Lloyd Bentsen's seat. In the view of one major news magazine, "Hutchison may have beaten Krueger, but the real loser was President Clinton."[70] Only a month before, a hard-fought Democratic special election victory in Wisconsin was said to have given congressional Democrats a "badly-needed [but apparently short-lived] shot in the arm."[71]

- In November 1991, Democrat Harris Wofford completed a stunning forty-point comeback to defeat Republican Dick Thornburgh in a special Senate election in Pennsylvania. President Bush, who had been widely considered unbeatable in his impending quest for reelection, was suddenly declared vulnerable by a host of pundits.

- President Bush suffered another "major embarrassment" when Democrat Jill Long of Indiana won a special House election in 1989 in a district thought to be a Republican stronghold.[72]

- When Congressman Phil Gramm of Texas switched parties from Democrat to Republican, resigned his seat, and won a special election in 1983 against the normal anti-administration pattern, Ronald Reagan's strength in the South was confirmed and evidence was clear that party switchers could win. Since that time, a dozen House Democrats and two Senate Democrats have switched parties.

- During Jimmy Carter's presidency, Republicans made a net gain of five House seats in special elections, more than in any other pair of consecutive interelection periods, foreshadowing the gains of 1980.
- Most observers interpreted the April 16, 1974, victory of Democrat Richard VanderVeen in Michigan's 5th Congressional District—Gerald Ford's former district—as a referendum against the Nixon administration.[73]
- John Tower became the first Republican to win statewide office in Texas since Reconstruction when he won a special election to fill Lyndon Johnson's U.S. Senate seat in May 1961. The Tower special election spurred and accelerated the process of partisan realignment in Texas, as over 150 influential Democrats left the Democratic Party and backed Tower. One said that he hoped Tower's campaign would be a "spark that will cause conservative Democrats all over Texas to join the Republican Party."[74]
- In spring 1918, Republican William Lenroot won a special Senate election in Wisconsin despite (or perhaps because of) being called unpatriotic by President Woodrow Wilson. Lenroot's victory damaged Wilson's prestige and presaged the Republican takeover of Congress that fall.
- Democrat John J. Mitchell's narrow special election win in 1910 in Massachusetts House District 4—traditionally a Republican district—was assumed by many to bode well for Democrats later in the year. Indeed it did, although Mitchell himself lost reelection in November.[75]

In each of these cases (and many others), the national media and the parties drew lessons with national implications, turning largely local events into battles of prestige between the president and his opponents. Sometimes the president gained. More often than not, he lost without even being on the ballot. The odds are against him. The relative paucity and irregularity of special elections should not be confused with irrelevance. To the contrary, the fact that there are so few special elections elevates the importance of each one by focusing the eyes of the attentive public.[76]

The momentum that out-parties gain as a result of midterm elections— whether regular or special—does not inevitably carry them into the White House in two years. The Republicans of 1938 and the Democrats of 1982 did not see the White House for fourteen and ten years, respectively. But they lived to fight another day, their resolve stiffened, and in the process they made life much more difficult for the President. In almost every case since 1956, the overall decline in presidential support scores after midterm elections has been accounted for primarily by a larger opposition contingent and a greater willingness of the out-party to vote against the president.[77] Even if some midterms like 1938 or 1966 do represent merely a predictable return to equilibrium—and it is far from clear that they should be seen exclusively in that light—the perception of victory is crucial.

Parties exist not only to win presidential elections but also to organize Congress and to provide the nation with a strong, viable, and competitive alternative for policy and for offices at all levels. The anti-administration pattern of midterm elections virtually guarantees that the out-party will obtain momentum that will restore a measure of its vitality. No matter how low a party may fall, the midterm pattern means that there is a built-in mechanism for the revival of both its membership and its spirit. While numerous factors have contributed to the maintenance of America's two-party system, the nearly automatic revitalization offered by midterm elections has surely been one of those factors.

Midterm Elections Provide an Opportunity for Development of New Issues by the Opposition

A study of the 1950 midterm elections done by William A. Glaser noted two crucial political consequences of those elections and their aftermath: the effect on the leadership of both parties and the effect on both new and old issues. For example, "Korea, communism, and corruption" was tested successfully as a Republican campaign theme in 1950; it carried Dwight Eisenhower into the White House two years later.[78]

Such an analysis can easily be extended to other midterm elections. The midterm campaign, itself, is a perfect opportunity to place new issues before the public. More importantly, the post-midterm congressional opposition, especially in (but not limited to) cases in which that opposition takes or solidifies control of Congress, can embarrass and stymie the president, develop and promote an alternative agenda, and define differences with the in-party. Possessing bolstered numbers, a claim to public mandate, and a sense of momentum, the strengthened opposition may seek to develop issues by passing an extensive legislative program, inviting presidential vetoes, or even simply preventing the president from acting. To cite just two crucial examples, the congresses elected in 1894 and 1930 succeeded in both stymieing the president and developing the issues of currency and social welfare which stood at the heart of the realignments of 1896 and 1932.[79] Even in instances much less dramatic than realignment, midterm elections frequently lead to a change in policy direction of some magnitude.

Midterm Elections Provide an Opportunity for the Development of Leadership by the Opposition

There are two senses in which this phenomenon occurs: midterm elections can produce a new crop of future leaders for the out-party, and by bolstering the out-party in Congress, they provide an opportunity for out-party congressional leaders to attain greater importance. First, Glaser and his colleagues made the argument that the 1950 midterm elections provided the out-party with an important opportunity to develop new leadership. The effect of midterm elections in introducing new leadership can be seen by reviewing major-party presidential nominees since 1894. In twenty cases of twenty-eight, presidential nominees started their national political careers or obtained the elected position from which they launched their presidential bids in midterm election years (or, in Lyndon Johnson's case, an odd-year special House vacancy election). A twenty-first, Franklin D. Roosevelt, was first elected governor of New York in 1928, a presidential election year, but faced a crucial reelection campaign in the midterm year of 1930 (table 1.10). While both parties have obtained new leaders from midterm elections, the anti-administration pattern of midterm elections means that the out-party is more likely to benefit. And indeed, by more than a two-to-one margin, these figures were propelled in midterm elections as members of the president's opposition.

Second, midterm elections may contribute to the development of opposition leadership within Congress. In the aftermath of a presidential election, all eyes are on the president, himself. After midterm elections—given increased membership and a new sense of vitality—the opposition party may be able to showcase its congressional leadership as a vigorous and competent alternative to the leadership offered by the president's party. Such figures as Champ Clark, Henry Cabot Lodge, and Lyndon Johnson were elevated to majority party leadership as a result of midterm elections. Superior leadership may be important in taking advantage of the strategic and tactical opportunities of the moment, and it may produce a favorable popular impression that could carry over into the next presidential election. Needless to say, this does not always happen; circumstances are not always right, and sometimes the out-party leadership either makes mistakes or simply is not up to the task. But to contemplate the importance this factor may hold, imagine the possible consequences in November 1996 if Newt Gingrich had not misstepped so severely in late 1995 and early 1996. The midterm election of 1994 gave Republicans an enormous opportunity, although they ended up not taking advantage of it.

Table I.10 Major Party Presidential Nominees Whose Presidential Bids or
Political Careers Were Launched by Midterm Elections

Nominee (Party-Year)	Midterm	Office
Bryan (D-1896, 1900, 1908)	1890	House*
T. Roosevelt (R-1904)	1898	Governor
Wilson (D-1912, 1916)	1910	Governor*
Hughes (R-1916)	1906	Governor*
Harding (R-1920)	1914	Senate*
Coolidge (R-1924)	1918	Governor*
Davis (D-1924)	1910	House*
Smith (D-1928)	1918	Governor
F. Roosevelt (D-1932, 1936, 1940, 1944)	1930	Governor (reelect)*
Dewey (R-1944, 1948)	1942	Governor*
Truman (D-1948)	1934	Senate
Nixon (R-1960, 1968, 1972)	1946/1950	House*/Senate*
Kennedy (D-1960)	1946	House
Johnson (D-1964)	1937	House
McGovern (D-1972)	1962	Senate
Carter (D-1976, 1980)	1970	Governor*
Reagan (R-1980, 1984)	1966	Governor*
Mondale (D-1984)	1966	Senate
Bush (R-1988, 1992)	1966	House*
Dukakis (D, 1988)	1974, 1982	Governor*
Clinton (D-1992, 1996)	1978, 1982	Governor**

Note: Johnson was elected in a special House vacancy election; Mondale was appointed to the Senate in 1965 before having to run for election in 1966. T. Roosevelt also ran as a third-party nominee in 1912. Strom Thurmond and George Wallace, who both ran as third-party candidates, also won their governorships in midterm years (1946 and 1962, respectively).
* President's opposition
**President's opposition in 1982

Midterm Elections Often Exacerbate Splits in the President's Party

According to David Mayhew's analysis, large partisan seat shifts are, in them-selves, not crucial to "innovative midterms," the handful of midterm elec-tions which have had profound significance for American politics. Like-wise, changes in public opinion and unresolved high-stakes policy struggles may be important but are hard to quantify and are almost certainly not a sufficient cause. In Mayhew's view, majority-party factionalism emerges as the one irreducible factor contributing to innovative midterms; not only must high-stakes conflict polarize the parties but it must polarize factions within the tottering majority party.

There are at least three ways in which midterm elections contribute to splits within the president's party. First, the pressures of the upcoming midterm election may exacerbate intraparty splits by forcing philosophical or policy issues to the forefront or by leading to abandonment of the president's position by his congressional copartisans. There were a variety of reasons that Bill Clinton's health care reform proposal died in 1994, and not the least of them was that Democrats lost their nerve. With midterm elections pending and popular opinion turning against the plan, Democrats were unwilling to stake their political futures on the president's proposal.

Second, the process of interpreting midterm election results, which was discussed above as undermining the president's plebiscitary authority, also frequently has the effect of splitting the president's party. The president's party in Congress—on the losing end almost invariably in the House and usually in the Senate—generally does not find useful either of the obvious explanations—that the election was no mandate against the president or that it was a mandate against the president and his party. Thus, while the president seldom blamed his party in Congress, his party in Congress showed much less reluctance to blame him. Furthermore, the willingness of members of the president's party to openly blame him for their plight indicates the degree to which midterm elections have the capacity of damaging intraparty relations, disrupting the president's coalition, and harming his standing as party leader and legislative leader.

A brief review of the president's party outside of Congress indicates that midterm elections have served as opportunities for competing elements of the party—such as interest groups, party auxiliaries, state and local party leaders, and varying party factions—to make an argument for reformulating the party position. Failure by the president and party as a whole was a common explanation offered by these outside forces. More often than not, these interpretations stressed deviation by the president/party from the essential ideals of the party. Sometimes these interpretations conflicted with each other, and sometimes they conflicted with the predominant interpretations offered by members of the same party in Congress. For example, 1946 saw claims that the Democratic disaster flowed from Truman being insufficiently "progressive."[80] In the aftermath of the 1958 elections, one set of Republican state party leaders argued that the election results proved that the party was too conservative, while another set argued that the election results were traceable to Eisenhower's moderate "me-tooism."[81] In 1970, despite historically low losses, Republican liberals in the Ripon Society claimed that an opportunity for gains had been squandered by the Nixon administration's strategy of "positive polarization."[82] In 1990, Republicans outside of Congress openly blamed George Bush's tax increase for midterm failure.[83] And in 1994, Jesse Jackson held the election results to be the consequence of Bill Clinton's failure to inspire his liberal base, an interpretation generally at odds with the predominant interpretation among congressional Democrats.[84] Thus, outside of Congress, intraparty criticisms were usually part of a broader debate over the future direction of the party, indicating that midterm elections might have the sort of catalytic impact on party change that is often assumed to be reserved for presidential elections.

Finally, midterm elections can exacerbate party splits precisely because of the way in which party composition is frequently shifted. As noted above, the faction of the president's party which is most closely aligned with the president often suffers disproportionate losses, leaving the president's own party less well disposed toward him than it had been previously. The post-1894 Democrats were shorn of their pro-Cleveland and pro-gold wing; the post-1910 Republicans had a decidedly more progressive tinge; the post-1966 Democrats had lost many of their most ardent pro–Great Society members; the post-1982 House Republicans had lost many of the so-called "Reagan robots." Conversely, the newly bolstered presidential opposition tends to be more cohesive than the president's party, especially in post-midterm congresses that precede a change in White House control.

The possibility that midterm losses weaken a president in his own party also finds some support in the fact that major intraparty challenges to presidential incumbents have historically been associated with above-average midterm losses. Such challenges have occurred in six of the twenty-six presidential elections considered here, and losses in the midterm elections preceding those six elections have averaged thirty-eight in the House (slightly above the 1894–1994 average) and nearly six in the Senate (nearly double the 1894–1994 average).[85] This phenomenon may be receding somewhat, as it does not account for the challenges of 1980 and 1992 (following lower-than-average presidential losses) or the lack of a challenge in 1996 (following greater-than-average losses). Prior to 1980, the average midterm loss suffered by presidents facing an intraparty challenge was fifty-two in the House and eight in the Senate. However, the effect of midterm elections is not always dependent on the size of seat shifts. A loss of seats, even if not enough to lose partisan control of Congress, can cause a president to lose working control of one or both chambers and to lose control of the agenda; it can embolden his enemies, paralyze his friends, and push him in a direction that undercuts his own electoral base. For example, Edward Kennedy's challenge against President Jimmy Carter in 1980 was provoked by Carter's rightward shift, a shift driven in no small part by the character of the 1978 midterm campaign.

The Pattern of Midterm Elections at the State Level Has a Long-Term Balancing Effect in American Politics

Just as the president's party traditionally suffers at the national level, it also usually loses ground at the state level. This pattern has only grown in importance. In 1900, most states either elected their governors only in presidential election years or had two-year gubernatorial terms, requiring gubernatorial elections in both presidential and midterm years. Today, almost all states use four-year terms for governor, and most hold their state elections in midterm years, often in a deliberate effort to remove gubernatorial politics from direct entanglement with presidential campaigns. This means that the out-party has a built-in tendency to make disproportionate gains at the state level at the very time it has lost possession of the White House. The specific consequences of this balancing tendency are discussed in detail in chapter two but can be summarized as follows. The out-party momentum and development of new leadership which midterms foster at the national level also characterize midterms at the state level. To give just a few examples, Woodrow Wilson, Earl Warren, Thomas Dewey, Edmund Muskie, George Romney, Ronald Reagan, Michael Dukakis, and Bill Clinton all emerged in midterm elections. In particular, the leadership effect is crucial for long-term party viability, as the out-party is guaranteed a strong crop of new office holders in state legislatures, the "farm team" of American politics. Governors have long been associated with grassroots party building; state governments can develop alternate policy agendas; and those state governments are, within limits, responsible for congressional redistricting. Just as the anti-administration pattern of midterm elections exaggerates the effect of separation of powers and bicameralism, it also reinforces the check inherent in the principle of federalism by making it much more difficult for the president's party to forge a national policy that transcends the federal-state divide.

Categories of Midterms

The seven factors contributing to the midterm check are each usually present to some degree, but their relative weight varies from election to election. Some midterms see huge compositional changes in Congress, others quite modest changes. Some see great shifts in momentum and great difficulty for the president's interpretative efforts; others see much smaller momentum effects, with the president merely forced to blame history while claiming a moral victory for smaller-than-average losses. Some see obvious issues thrown to the forefront; others are more muddled. And the opportunities provided to the out-party by midterm elections are not always exploited by skillful leadership.

Consequently, while midterm elections in general provide an additional check on the president and his party, the precise manner in which that check is applied and the impact that it has on future events can vary considerably. The check provided by midterm elections is relatively nuanced and capable of exerting itself in complex and long-lasting ways. Thus, it makes sense to try to construct categories into which historical midterms can be placed. The evidence points to at least four basic categories:

- Normal midterms: Most midterm elections from 1894 through 1994 can be considered "normal" midterms, elections in which the president's party loses seats, and he is at least modestly harmed. However, they do not foretell great long-term partisan shifts, and typically the president's party goes ahead to win the next presidential election. At a minimum, these midterms represent the most basic form of negative check, although some may also have an important impact on policy formation.

- Preparatory midterms: Not only may midterm elections serve as a negative check stymieing the president, but they can also serve as a positive balance, a creative force in American politics. Not least, midterm elections have proven able to propel significant changes in party control of the White House, not only preceding but contributing to realignments and other long-term shifts in presidential power. These "preparatory" elections are only one factor of many leading to shifts at the presidential level, but they have often been crucial and just as often overlooked in subsequent analysis.

- Calibrating midterms: A simple negative check on the president and a total reversal of partisan power are not the only possible outcomes. Midterm elections can serve the purpose of moderating presidential initiatives in periods of great change without reversing them. These midterm elections give the electorate the opportunity to soften the edges of change without jettisoning either the program of change or the agent of change.

- Creative exceptions: On rare occasions—to be exact, three in the period from 1894–1998—presidential parties escaped the midterm curse. In doing so, they gained all of the advantages for themselves which midterms usually confer on their opponents. Twice, these exceptions have been crucial elements of periods of great policy innovation, and they prove by indirection the importance of the midterm pattern to slowing presidential action in most instances.

These four categories are descriptive in nature rather than analytically predictive. That is to say, they look backwards to observe the characteristics of midterm elections historically. They are not categories established in the abstract prior to any knowledge of specific cases, and no claim is advanced that it is possible to place most future midterms into the categorization scheme until they, too, have become an established part of history (though 1998 is not difficult to place as an exception). Such a scheme carries with it the obvious limitation that categorization can usually be assigned only in retrospect; even then, the placement of midterms into the categories depends ultimately on judgments that might not be universally shared. As will be seen, it is even possible to argue that certain midterms might fit simultaneously in more than one category. Yet it is difficult to imagine how the classification of midterm elections can avoid these dilemmas, especially if one accepts the proposition that elections in general and midterm elections in particular are highly contingent events, presenting opportunities but no guarantees to the victors.

This proposition—that midterm elections can produce effects and that they can produce a wide-ranging variety of effects depending on circumstances and human decision—is indeed fundamental to the classification scheme and the central argument of the book. The categorization scheme is largely constructed around the question of subsequent control of the presidency, not least due to the combination of simplicity and obvious importance. Either midterms did or did not precede presidential change (a simple question) and either they did or did not seem to contribute to that change (a more difficult question, but not impossible to perceive). And if they did on both counts, no one can dispute the importance of such a consequence.

As this chapter examined the national-level factors producing the midterm check, chapter two will examine more closely the seventh factor discussed above: the role of midterm elections at the state level in maintaining long-term party equilibrium. This chapter and the next establish a framework for answering the question of how midterm elections provide both a negative check and a creative balance. The remainder of this book will place midterms into the four categories and, in doing so, will more thoroughly explore the nature of those categories and the range of effects of midterm elections on American politics.

TWO

State Midterm Elections

While attention is generally focused on the results of midterm elections in Congress, there is another venue of midterm elections—the states—which also exhibits a consistent anti-administration pattern carrying significant and occasionally profound consequences. In a variety of ways, state midterm elections complement the national factors working to impose a check on the president and his party.

The pattern attending congressional midterm elections is clearly operative at the state level, as well. In both gubernatorial and state legislative elections, the president's party consistently suffers losses in midterm years. In an early study of this subject, V. O. Key concluded that oscillations in state legislative strength from 1938 through 1950 were closely tied to national trends, and subsequent research has confirmed that notion.[1] As Key remarked, "Evidently, in the public mind—at least in the framework of these great cycles of sentiment—no sharp differentiation between state and national affairs prevails."[2]

Furthermore, this check has grown in importance, for two reasons. First, at the beginning of the twentieth century, the vast majority of states held their gubernatorial elections in presidential election years. Since 1940, the number of states holding gubernatorial elections in presidential election years has fallen from thirty to eleven, and the number of states with four-year (rather than two-year) gubernatorial terms has doubled from twenty-three to forty-eight (only New Hampshire and Vermont retain two-year terms). Hence, today, most states elect their governors only in midterm election years, along with some four to ten other statewide officials such as lieutenant governor, attorney general, and treasurer.[3] Every state elects at least one of its legislative houses every two years, meaning that at least half of those elections are in midterm years. No state holds its lower house elections only in presidential years; just four states—Kansas, Minnesota, New Mexico, and South Carolina—hold their state senate elections only in presidential years (see table 2.1). The shift in gubernatorial election scheduling has been driven largely by the desire of states to delink the election of state officers from the presidential race.[4] Second, as Key pointed out, the decline of one-party states since 1950 has removed a possible buffer against midterm fluctuations.[5]

Consequently, midterm elections at the state level pose a greater threat to the president's party than ever before. James E. Campbell noted in a 1986 essay that the president's party lost at least 1 percent of state legislative seats in three of every four midterm elections from 1944 to 1984 (308 of 402 state legislatures). In those years, the mean seat loss was 7.3 percent, and Campbell detected a surge-and-decline pattern, with midterm losses oscillating symmetrically with the previous presidential vote. In Campbell's view, "There is a pulse to state legislative elections, a regular pattern of gains and losses very much like that observed in congressional elections. Moreover, the pulse is regulated by presidential election politics."[6]

John E. Chubb concurred, pointing out that, from 1950 to 1988, the president's party had lost no fewer than eight and as many as twenty-four state legislative chambers, averaging a loss of thirteen. Only once in the previous fifty years had the president's party increased its share in either the upper or lower legislative chambers. Chubb calculated that presidential coattails were much more important than gubernatorial or Senate coat-

Table 2.1 State Offices Up for Election, 1996–1999

	1996	1997	1998	1999
Governors	11	2	36	3
State senate*				
Chambers	43	1	42	3
Seats	1,194	40	1,121	131
State house				
Chambers	43	2	45	4
Seats	4,787	180	5,033	407

Source: Data from *The Book of the States 1996–97*, vol. 31 (Lexington, Ky.: Council of State Governments, 1996).
*For the purposes of this table, the unicameral legislature of Nebraska is classified as a state senate, meaning that there are 50 state senates and 49 state houses nationwide.

tails and that withdrawal of those presidential coattails in midterm years cost the president's party over 4 percent of lower-house seats. Declining turnout cost nearly an additional 1 percent, and national economic conditions contributed to further losses.[7]

James E. Piereson, Dennis M. Simon, Charles W. Ostrom Jr., and Robin F. Marra concluded that the referendum model was operative even down to the state legislative level. Peireson's study of the 1970 elections indicated that evaluations of Richard Nixon had a substantial impact on the vote choice of independent voters at all electoral levels, and Simon, Ostrom, and Marra argued that midterm elections, even as far down as the state legislative level, depend on an "underlying evaluation of the real world that allows us to view elections as coherent national events."[8] Peireson also concluded in a study of state elections from 1910 through 1970 that national tides had a consistently greater impact than the factor of incumbency, although less than party strength.[9] Other studies have confirmed that party and partisan tides are a crucial factor—if not *the* crucial factor—in state legislative races.[10]

In gubernatorial elections, until Republican successes in 1986, the president's party had gone more than sixty years without increasing its share of governors in the midterm elections, losing an average of 6.2 governorships from 1950 to 1984. Early analyses by V. O. Key and Austin Ranney indicating a coattail effect in gubernatorial elections have been corroborated by subsequent research.[11] By Chubb's calculation, national conditions reduce the gubernatorial vote for the president's party by almost 2 percent per race.[12] Dennis M. Simon divided midterm election years from 1950 through 1986 into "good," "mediocre," and "bad" presidential years, depending on both the absolute level of presidential approval and changes in that approval over the previous two years.[13] In good years, the president's party won 50 percent of gubernatorial races, in mediocre years 41 percent, and in bad years less than 26 percent. In open races, the president's party won 51 percent in good years and only 18 percent in bad years. In sum, "evaluations of the president operate as an influence on the voting preferences of citizens in gubernatorial elections . . . the electoral fortunes of gubernatorial candidates are tied to the public standing of the president."[14]

John F. Bibby argued after the 1982 midterm elections that "midterm gubernatorial elections are highly susceptible to national trends. Indeed, change in partisan control of governorships is likely to be greater than is the extent of switched party control of seats in Congress."[15] In fact, according to Bibby, both gubernatorial and state legislative elections "are more dramatically affected by national trends during midterm elections than they are in presidential election years."[16] Or, as Chubb put it, "off-year election scheduling has largely freed governors from direct presidential coattails, but it has subjected them to midterm presidential punishment."[17] V. O. Key even argued that these national tides have intraparty factional effects in state politics, just as they do at the congressional level.[18]

Thus, state midterm elections operate on the same pattern as congressional midterm elections and, as far as the evidence indicates, for the same reasons. There are several possible effects of this phenomenon.

One potential effect that has been hypothesized is that states that elect opposition governors in midterm elections may be more likely to vote against the president's party in the next presidential election. However, in the words of Bibby, "Analysis of recent presidential elections [1968–1980] . . . reveals that there is virtually no relationship between control of a state's governorship and the outcome of the presidential voting in the state . . . Thus, whatever the substantial benefits of holding a governorship are, they do not extend to winning electoral votes for the party's presidential candidate."[19] Presidential elections since 1980 have similarly shown lack of a consistent pattern. On the other hand, there are at least five other broad sets of consequences which tend in the direction of providing an important balancing component in American politics.

Partisan Momentum

First, in the same way as congressional midterm results, opposition gains at the state level intangibly invigorate the national party, providing some measure of general momentum. As has already been discussed, this phenomenon was clearly present in 1966 and other years. Both overall gains in governorships and victories in specific bellwether states can contribute to the momentum. A few states (Virginia, New Jersey, Kentucky, Mississippi, and Louisiana) hold their state elections in odd-numbered years. Because there are so few of these cases, media attention tends to be focused more closely on them than on gubernatorial elections in regular midterm years, when so many statehouses are at stake and attention must be shared with congressional elections. In recent years, victories by Democratic gubernatorial candidates in New Jersey and Virginia in 1981 were declared by the media to be a caution signal for the "Reagan revolution"; Democratic wins in those states in 1989 were taken to represent a pro-choice backlash in the wake of the *Webster v. Reproductive Health Services* case. Republican victories in the 1993 gubernatorial elections in the same states were interpreted as a sign of trouble for the Clinton administration, while in 1995 Democratic successes in the Kentucky governorship and smaller-than-anticipated Republican gains in Virginia legislative elections were widely taken as a sign that the Republican tide of 1994 had stalled.

Governorships and Party Building

Second, more tangibly, it has long been held by students of American politics that governors play a particularly important role in party development. In short, "The governor is at the apex of the power structure of the state."[20] The governor is almost invariably considered the leader of his party in his state, serves as its chief spokesman, and has enormous influence (if not outright control) over the selection of his state's party chairman.[21] The governor's office can also serve as the central nervous system for his party, coordinating party-building efforts throughout the state and serving as a crucial support system for the state party.[22] Governors have also tended to have substantial influence in national party councils; Dwight D. Eisenhower, for example, probably owed his 1952 nomination to the influence of the crop of Republican governors elected in the 1950 midterm elections. This function of party leadership has perhaps been diminished by the reduction of gubernatorial patronage and, indeed, the whole decline of parties generally; there is evidence that governors often do not take their party leadership role as seriously as some outside observers would assume.[23] There is little question, however, that the parties, themselves, view possession of governorships as an important organizational advantage. As Bibby remarked, "Governors can provide state parties with the resources and leadership to build effective organizations."[24] And to the extent that national parties build their "inner core of professionals" by controlling state governments, as V. O. Key hypothesized, the midterm pattern at the state level is again clearly to the long-term disadvantage of the president's party.[25]

New Leadership

Third, state midterm elections have an important role in thrusting forward new leaders and potential candidates for higher office in the opposition party. Eighteen of forty-five presidential nominees from 1868 through 1996 last held the office of governor, and several other presidential nominees were governors at some earlier point in their careers. Of the thirty-four major-party presidential nominees to run from 1896 through 1996, fifteen have been governors at some point, fourteen held the governorship as their last office before their presidential bid,[26] eleven were elected or reelected in midterm years, and nine of those won their most crucial midterm races as members of the president's opposition (see table 2.2). The brief mid-century dominance of U.S. Senators over governors as presidential nominees, largely a function of the salience of foreign policy during the Cold War, can be said in retrospect to have come to an end in 1976. Governors have also fared quite well as vice-presidential nominees, and the vice-presidency is, of course, a major pathway to the presidency.[27] Not as easily quantified—but easily as important—are the potential presidential contenders whose careers were cut short by midterm defeat or whose stature was damaged by narrower-than-expected victory.

Recent cases particularly bear out this point. Since 1950, five governors or ex-governors have been nominated for president by a major party. Adlai Stevenson was elected governor of Illinois in 1948; Jimmy Carter won the governorship of Georgia in the 1970 midterm elections; Ronald Reagan first won the governorship of California in the 1966 midterm elections; Michael Dukakis first won the governorship of Massachusetts in the 1974 midterm elections and was returned in the 1982 midterm elections after a

Table 2.2 Governors and Former Governors as Major Party Presidential Nominees, 1896–1996

Governors Nominated	Elected or Reelected in Midterm Year	Won Midterm as President's Opposition
McKinley	T. Roosevelt	Wilson
T. Roosevelt	Wilson	Coolidge
Wilson	Hughes	Smith
Hughes	Coolidge	F. Roosevelt
Cox	Smith	Dewey
Coolidge	F. Roosevelt	Carter
Smith	Dewey	Reagan
F. Roosevelt	Carter	Dukakis
Landon	Reagan	Clinton
Dewey	Dukakis	
Stevenson	Clinton	
Carter		
Reagan		
Dukakis		
Clinton		

Note: Two other governors, Strom Thurmond and George Wallace, who ran third-party presidential campaigns, became governors in the midterm years of 1946 and 1962.

1978 defeat; and Bill Clinton was first elected governor of Arkansas in the 1978 midterm elections and was returned in the 1982 midterm elections after a 1980 defeat (Arkansas adopted a four-year gubernatorial term in 1990). In only the first case, that of Stevenson, was the governor not elected in a midterm election. In the midterm cases, of the six initial elections or revivals after defeat, the men in question were carried in by an anti-administration tide five times. (Clinton in 1978 was the sole exception.)

Of course, the president's opposition does not possess a monopoly on thrusting forward new presidential timber. Sometimes strong prospects of the president's own party will win despite the national trend, establishing or defending a career that puts them on the road to a presidential nomination. Since the president is not on the ballot, these copartisan victors can reap the benefits of greater public attention. In that sense, midterm elections can serve broadly as a jumping-off point for candidates of both parties. Nevertheless, the trend is clearly in favor of the president's opposition, and potential presidential candidates from that side are both theoretically and empirically more likely to benefit.

Below the presidential level, the party effects of midterm elections are potentially just as profound. Some scholars have even referred to state government as "a halfway house for men with political ambitions."[28] As Gary C. Jacobson has discussed at length, the best candidates for higher office tend to be officeholders from a lower or (better yet) equivalent office: "Other things being equal, the strongest congressional candidates are those for whom politics is a career."[29] Governors make particularly good candidates for U.S. Senate; state legislators and other statewide officeholders (such as lieutenant governors, secretaries of state, and state treasurers) make particularly good candidates for governor; and state legislators make particularly good candidates for U.S. House of Representatives. Elected officeholders seeking higher office already start with some geographical base (in the case of governors running for the Senate, a geographical base identical to that of a Senator). They also start with a base of activist supporters and financial contributors, crucial experience in the art of running and winning political campaigns, and name recognition that surpasses that of virtually all other potential candidates (barring famous entertainers and athletes).

Consequently, it is extremely important for parties to do well in lower-level elections. As Bibby remarked, "Party growth over the long term requires more than presidential victories . . . Legislatures are the recruiting ground for future congressmen, senators, and governors. Without a strong contingent of state legislators, a party's talent pool is severely restricted."[30]

Larry Sabato has calculated that nearly two-fifths of governors elected between 1900 and 1949 were state legislators or held some statewide office
(not including attorney general) immediately before becoming governor;
from 1950 through 1980, that number increased to nearly one-half. In the
words of Sabato, "The state legislature has come to dominate more and
more careers of future governors."[31] Furthermore, one of every eight governors from 1950 through 1980 went on to become a U.S. Senator; altogether, roughly one of every four Senators has been a governor.[32] (It should
also be noted that U.S. Senators occasionally run for governor, and when
they do, they usually win).

The holding of most gubernatorial and other statewide office elections in midterm years, and the holding of at least half of state legislative
elections at the same time, means that there is a built-in balancing mechanism from the bottom up. The president's opposition will bring into lower
office a crop of new office holders who will, in time, be in a position to run
strong campaigns for higher offices. This check on the president's party
may not be fully felt until long after the president, himself, leaves office; it
is a guarantee of two-party equilibrium over time.

Redistricting

Fourth, state government is responsible for a function which, at least at the
margins, can have substantial impact on later congressional contests: the
decennial redistricting process, which establishes new boundaries for U.S.
House districts. Debate has flourished in the field of electoral studies over
the question of exactly how much influence the redistricting process has
on partisan outcomes. Studies of the post-1960 and post-1970 redistricting concluded that redistricting had little net effect on the partisan distribution of seats nationally. Referring to the 1960 process, Robert Erikson
concluded that "partisan control of the districting scheme is not as important a determinant of partisan control of the state's congressional districts
as might be thought."[33] Despite having believed in 1978 that their gains at
the state level gave them "gerrymander insurance," Republicans throughout the 1980s complained that their seemingly permanent House minority status was due largely to Democratic gerrymandering at the state level.[34]
Many scholars acknowledged that Democrats had gained some benefit from
favorable districting; for example, Alan Abramowitz calculated that Democrats in the 1982 elections improved their swing ratio much more in the
seventeen states where Democrats had completely controlled the redistricting process after 1980. Democratic gains were much more limited where

Republicans had retained at least some leverage over the process.[35] Most studies, however, tended to downplay the significance of redistricting, pointing out that gerrymandering was easier to attempt than to successfully impose, that the effects of gerrymandering tend to be short lived, and that most states were not susceptible to an all-out gerrymander because of either split party control of state government or the involvement of judges in the process.[36] By some estimates, only eleven states were subject to obviously partisan gerrymanders after 1980.[37]

Nevertheless, redistricting has clearly made a difference in the 1990s. A study of post-1990 redistricting, for example, found that unfavorably redistricted incumbents attracted more experienced challengers.[38] As the post-1990 redistricting progressed, it became increasingly evident that Republicans were winning the redistricting wars. The benefit to Republicans of this turn of events became clear in 1994, when Republican congressional candidates did not have to swim against the tide of a Democratic presidential victory. It is not unlikely that Republicans owed their narrow House majority after 1994 (and, even more so, their narrower majority after 1996) to gains made in newly favorable districts of the 1990s. By one cautious estimate, post-1990 redistricting cost Democrats nine House seats nationwide in 1992 and another thirteen in 1994, enough to account for Republican control.[39] Other studies have shown the Republicans picking up six seats in the South alone in 1992 and 1994 due to redistricting attempts to create "majority minority districts."[40]

The struggle to more precisely define the effects of redistricting will doubtless continue, but two irreducible facts remain. First, House districts are ultimately the environments in which House candidates must run. They set parameters within which candidates, to be successful, must operate. The way district lines are drawn may offer a range of effects from profound to marginal but can never be irrelevant. Second, because state governments are given the task of redistricting and three-fourths of governors are elected for four-year terms in midterm years, there is a strong likelihood that the president's opposition will have a greater say in the redistricting process than would be the case if state elections more closely coincided with presidential elections. This greater say can be quite important, even if it often is not: studies have shown that when one party controls state government, it frequently attempts to gerrymander.[41] In half of cases— like 1960, 1980, and 2000—when presidential elections are held in census years, the incoming president's party will likely gain in state legislatures, mitigating the redistricting damage somewhat. Abramowitz, for instance, argues that "Republican efforts in 1980 state election campaigns may have helped to reduce Republican congressional losses in 1982."[42] In the other half of cases—those in which midterm years fall on the decennial census year—the anti-administration effect will usually be magnified by gains made by the opposition in state legislatures.

The 1990 redistricting was an exception: midterm presidential party losses were smaller than usual, and redistricting ultimately worked to benefit George Bush's party. Republican net losses of two governors in 1990 did not prevent the Republicans from doing well in the post-1990 redistricting largely because Republicans broke even in state legislative races[43] and won governors' races in several key states like California, Ohio, Michigan, and Illinois; partly because racial gerrymandering based on the Voting Rights Act Amendments of 1982 negated some of the effects of partisan gerrymandering; and partly because judges stepped in to draw the boundaries in several states. All other things being equal, it is still probably true that Republicans did not do as well as they would have without the midterm effect at the state level; they held California in 1990, for example, but still lost control of Texas and Florida—otherwise winnable states.[44] And if Republican redistricting successes after 1990 were largely made possible by a better-than-average midterm performance by the president's party, it is not too difficult to deduce the potential impact of midterm elections on redistricting in years when the results are more typical.

Policy Development

Finally and most broadly, midterm elections can provide a partisan reinforcement to the institutional check inherent in the federal system itself. The constitutional status of the states has been an ongoing point of contention since the Founding, and numerous questions remain in a state of flux, from the meaning and applicability of the Tenth Amendment to the breadth of the congressional Commerce Clause. Nevertheless, practically speaking, state governments remain essential to governance in America. Numerous crucial functions are primarily carried out at the state and local levels, education and law enforcement chief among them. Other functions, like many forms of workplace and environmental regulation, medical assistance for the poor, and construction and maintenance of highways, are shared. Many programs that are primarily federal, such as the food stamp program, are nevertheless administered by states. States play a central role in both of the processes established for amending the U.S. Constitution: in one case, two-thirds of states call for a constitutional amending convention to initiate the process, and in both cases three-fourths of states must agree to ratification of the amendment. Even elections for federal office and an important component of national defense—the national guard—are overseen by state governments. Alexander Hamilton argued in the *Federalist Papers* that "the people of each State would be apt to feel a stronger bias towards their local governments than towards the government of the Union";[45] after a period in the mid–twentieth century when this prediction was open to serious question, it seems today to be accurate once again. By 1980, substantial majorities or pluralities of poll respondents believed that state governments were more trustworthy, more caring, more accountable, more efficient, fairer, and less corrupt than the federal government.[46] Indeed, in Hamilton's view, the states could do more damage to the federal government than the federal government could do to the states. Consequently, the authors of the *Federalist* argued that states had the capacity to serve as focal points of popular resistance to federal usurpations.[47]

While this resistance no longer takes the form of the theory of "nullification" or "interposition" found in the writings of Thomas Jefferson and John C. Calhoun—and while, indeed, the entire balance of federal-state relations has shifted markedly in favor of the federal government since at least the 1930s—state midterm elections that go against the president's party can lead to a systematic policy shift, at the state level, away from the president's priorities. Most importantly, governors—of whom, again, three-fourths are elected in midterm years—play a central role in state policy development. And studies of state politics indicate that "most state legislatures surpass the United States Congress in partisan unity and cohesion,"[48] meaning that partisan shifts in legislative composition can have even greater effects at the state level than at the federal level.

By way of a negative check, states that fall under opposition control can resist federal policy implementation and enforcement, derailing or delaying federal initiatives by administrative foot dragging and legislative counter thrusts. The latter, while often falling prey to reversal by federal courts, can take years to overcome. This negative check is most evident in policy arenas that directly impact federalism itself. For example, Ronald Reagan's "new federalism" initiative of 1982—a proposed swap of federal and state programs in pursuit of a more rational sorting out of duties—died a quiet death largely because state and local officials did not embrace it. As observers have noted, the federal and state governments are often engaged in a policy dialogue that is not nearly as one-sided as the recent constitutional theory of unlimited federal supremacy would assume.[49] That dialogue almost surely grows more tendentious as the president's opponents grow stronger at the state level. And because the states in the 1990s are institutionally stronger players than at any time since before the Great Depression, they are better positioned in that dialogue.

Positively, states are "laboratories of democracy," as Supreme Court Justice Louis Brandeis observed, arenas in which a variety of alternative and innovative solutions can be simultaneously pursued. A variety of authors have demonstrated the ways in which states have served this role throughout American history, from public education and civil service reform to the income tax, conservation, regulation, and social insurance programs of the progressive era to environmental, law enforcement, welfare, economic development, and even civil rights innovations in more recent times.[50] As Terry Sanford argued, "The states test whether the opinions by which we live our lives and run our governments are myths or facts. This is federalism at its best—always probing, always testing, always seeking a better way."[51] Midterm governors from the opposition party—like Franklin Roosevelt (reelected in 1930), Pat Brown (elected in 1958), George Romney (elected in 1962), and Ronald Reagan (elected in 1966)—advanced serious programs that gained national attention. And it is no accident that most of the powerful political movements of American history originated at the state and local level.[52]

This capacity of the states to initiate innovation is important in itself. It is also important because this structural strength makes it possible for states to balance the president and his party, not just by obstructing administration policies but also by offering and pursuing solutions that move in a fundamentally different direction than the one preferred by the president. For example, while the welfare reform bill of 1996 was ultimately a product of compromise between President Clinton and congressional Republicans, the force moving the welfare reform debate steadily to the right was action at the state level in places like Wisconsin and Michigan (where governors Tommy Thompson and John Engler were elected and reelected in midterm years). Long before Bill Clinton signed the bill, his administration had been moved a considerable distance by the initiatives of reformist governors, whose bloc grew much larger in the 1994 midterm elections.[53] By the end of 1994, twelve states had requested federal waivers for major welfare changes; by the end of 1995, another seventeen had enacted substantial reforms. Further analysis showed that states where party control of the legislature had shifted in 1994 were significantly more likely to initiate reforms.[54] On another policy front, states and localities around the country proceeded with serious experiments with school voucher plans despite the president's pronounced hostility to such plans at the federal level.

James E. Campbell has speculated that "presidential coattails in state legislative elections may help bridge the federalism gap between national and state governments."[55] If this is true, then it is also true that the presidential penalty in state midterm elections widens the federalism gap. And the overwhelming preponderance of gubernatorial elections held in midterm years virtually guarantees that the latter effect will be more powerful than the former. Indeed, as the office of governor has become systematically more powerful since the 1950s, this potential effect has undoubtedly been strengthened further.[56]

There are numerous recent examples of the ongoing importance of states in the federal-state dialogue. Ann O'M. Bowman and Richard C. Kearney cite a variety of issues from antitrust to natural resources to environmental standards to state and municipal bonds, saying, "A final product of state resurgence has been an increased scope and intensity of conflict with the national government over intrusive federal laws and grant requirements that supersede state policy."[57] State and local law enforcement officials succeeded in 1997 in persuading the Supreme Court to overturn those portions of the Brady gun control act which forced them to serve a federal administrative purpose; many other state and local governments reacted to the Clinton administration's gun control initiatives in the 1990s by passing laws and ordinances making it easier for law-abiding citizens to carry concealed firearms for self defense. In recent years states have, at least for a time, ignored federal law and regulation concerning Medicaid funding for abortion, environmental land use, and a variety of other issues. Indeed, the movement in the federal courts and Congress away from support for unrestricted abortion on demand has been prompted in no small part by the simple unwillingness of many state governments to accept that policy framework. Larry Sabato observes that

> the states can provide an important check on national power, on the condition they themselves are vigorous enough to meet the challenge. For most of this century they have not been sufficiently vigorous, but the transformation of the states—the result of a stronger governorship, a reapportioned legislature, widespread constitutional revision, large-scale reorganization, and the spread of two-party competition, among other factors—has energized the states and enabled them to compete for authority and responsibility with the national government.[58]

What has been taken from the states through the breakdown of the theory of enumerated powers has thus at least partially been restored through the reality of the counter-administration partisan tendency of state midterm elections. At the very least, the president and his party cannot be guaranteed of a favorable reception in statehouses; the difficulties for the president in constructing a cross-federal coalition in favor of any particular national initiative are multiplied. It is indeed likely that state governments will, at least on some issues, actively set themselves up against the preferences of the administration. As long as the states remain responsible for large swaths of public policy, ambition at the state level will continue to counteract federal ambition. This would be the case to some extent regardless of the timing of elections or the partisan makeup of state governments, but it is all the more true given those factors.

Thus, in a variety of ways, there are sizable national consequences to the fact that most state elections are held in midterm years and that they exhibit the same anti-administration bias as congressional midterm elections. Midterm elections regularly provide the president's opposition with some measure of intangible momentum at the state level; thrust forward new political figures who, over time, develop into viable candidates for higher offices (including the presidency); burden the president's party with an almost automatic disadvantage during the crucial process of redistricting (though that disadvantage can be offset, as in 1990, by other factors); and strengthen the means available to the president's opposition to resist federal policies and to design alternative policies. Unlike midterm congressional elections, which register clear national results and can affect the president and national politics in a very short period of time, elections at the state level are decentralized, and their impact becomes clear only over time. In many ways—certainly in terms of policy development, grassroots candidate development, and redistricting—the effects take years to mature, but it is in precisely those ways that long-term party balance is built into midterm elections at the state level.

Summary and Conclusion

Midterm congressional elections have frequently exerted profound influence on American government and politics. They almost always shift the balance of power away from the president and his party, sometimes so dramatically as to inaugurate a new era in American politics. Upon examination, it is also clear that midterm elections at the state level can have significant anti–presidential party effects both in the short and long terms. Gubernatorial and state legislative elections in midterm years follow the same pattern as congressional midterm elections, a problem for the president's party which has been amplified by the growing number of states holding their gubernatorial elections at midterm.

Altogether, state midterm elections operate in a manner that confirms the general thesis that midterm elections serve as an institutional check on the president and his party. In the case of state elections, that check takes a wide-ranging form that in many respects does not bear full fruit until long after the president leaves office. In that sense, the check does not merely stymie the president but also provides a nearly automatic balancing mechanism for two-party competition. Successes at lower levels lead to later successes at higher levels in a variety of ways, from party building to congressional redistricting to the development of new candidates to the bolstering of an alternative public policy menu. Individual elements of this check may have only modest importance (redistricting, for example), but taken in combination they comprise a potentially formidable force.

THREE

Midterm Elections as the Vanguard of Change

I. REALIGNMENT AND THE ELECTIONS OF 1894 AND 1930

Both the 1896 and the 1932 realignments can be said to
have begun in the congressional elections prior to the
presidential realigning election.
— DAVID BRADY

While midterm elections in general make life more difficult for presidents, a negative checking power is not their sole characteristic. To the contrary, midterm elections are often closely connected to long-lasting electoral and policy changes. While they are never the only factor at work, these preparatory midterms help to lay the groundwork for a change in party control in the White House.

This chapter will examine the ways in which midterm elections contributed to the two generally acknowledged realignments between 1894 and 1998, the 1896 and New Deal realignments.[1] Despite the difficulties involved in classifying realignments (there is more than one scheme of classification) and even in assigning particular eras to those classifications (for example, no consensus exists about whether 1968 or, perhaps, 1980 was the beginning of a realignment), some broad agreement exists. Partisan realignment, as defined by scholars, is the most profound and most durable of electoral change, setting the parameters of politics for decades. It is also a larger-scale version of the lesser political changes that sweep the nation more frequently, an exaggerated model that can help provide insight into, and a framework for studying, those lesser changes. Realignments are, in sum, an extreme subset of political change in general. Midterm elections immediately preceding realignments are, therefore, only a subset of those midterm elections that prepare the ground for subsequent political change. Pre-realignment midterms can cast light on these preparatory midterms as a class, showing how midterms can serve as a mechanism for positively promoting change and reversing long-term patterns of party dominance.

Critical Election and Realignment Theory

V. O. Key initiated the discussion on realignment and critical elections with his article "A Theory of Critical Elections" in 1955. Key examined the shift of New England voters toward the Democratic Party in 1928, and defined "critical elections" as those in which "depth and intensity of electoral involvement are high, in which more or less profound readjustments occur in the relations of power within the community, and in which new and durable electoral groupings are formed."[2] Early scholarship on realignment tended to focus on defining it, as well as defining other elections in relation to it. Subsequent academic discourse has examined the questions of what factors of national politics contribute to (or at least coincide with) realignments, how realignment fits into broader political cycles, how realignment takes place at the level of the individual voter (i.e., conversion of existing voters or mobilization of new voters), and even whether realignment in the classical sense is possible in the modern "post-partisan" milieu of American politics.[3] Nevertheless, little systematic inquiry has been undertaken to study the possible role of midterm elections in the realignment process, though some scholarship sheds important indirect light on that question.

One important debate has concerned the question of whether realignment is primarily mass-driven or elite-driven. Paul Lechner argues that change at the elite level lags behind change at the mass level, while Stuart Elaine MacDonald and George Rabinowitz argue that at least some realignments are led by changes in agenda at the elite level.[4] MacDonald and Rabinowitz draw a distinction between two alternative realignment processes, "structural realignment" and "performance realignment." In structural realignment, the structure of conflict is shifted at the elite level first, where the agenda changes and the masses follow: "When structural change occurs . . . that change will be visible in the behavior of elites well before it becomes embedded in the mass party system."[5] In performance realignment, by contrast, realignment is due to a perception on the part of a decisive body of voters that the dominant party has failed in a matter of fundamental concern to the nation. In the view of MacDonald and Rabinowitz, the structural realignment model best fits most cases.

The MacDonald and Rabinowitz hypothesis points in the direction of a broader concept that has been taken up by a variety of scholars, not all of whom put precedence on structural change at the elite level. That concept is central to the role of midterm elections in the realignment process (and by inference in the process of change in general), revolving around the contingency of realignment—its nonmechanistic dependence on factors that are largely within the realm of political control. Jerome Clubb, William Flanigan, and Nancy Zingale emphasize the importance of performance and leadership by the newly advantaged party. In this view, realigning elections—or, more precisely, elections that in retrospect turned out to have served as the beginning of a realignment—provided an opportunity for the advantaged party by producing unified party control of government and an apparent mandate to act. These opportunities for policy innovation led to realignment only if successfully grasped: "To the extent that these policies were perceived as successfully managing and reducing crisis, the incumbent party's majority was sustained and strengthened in succeeding elections."[6]

Thus, while the conditions for realignment might exist, the extent and direction of any particular realignment is not inevitable. By this interpretation, the election of 1932 provided an opportunity for realignment; it was not the realignment itself. The New Deal realignment was made possible by the Great Depression, yet it was only solidified by the subsequent performance of Franklin Roosevelt and the Democratic Party. Clubb, Flanigan, and Zingale also discuss a handful of "realignments which might have been": the Democratic victory of 1852, blown apart by failure to achieve acceptable sectional compromise; the Democratic victory of 1892, undone by depression and Grover Cleveland's obstinacy; and 1964, when the massive Democratic victory was turned into a string of presidential defeats by Vietnam (and, one might add, popular reaction against cultural permissiveness and some aspects of the Great Society).

This emphasis on the nature of critical elections as opportunities rather than preordained events can also be seen in the work of other realignment scholars. Charles Sellers, for example, pointed out the chaotic and unstructured nature of the early stages of realignment. James Sundquist argued that realignment is a lengthy process that extends well before and after the "critical election" and that "leadership does matter, and the behavior of statesmen will have an impact at least on the power and scale and timing of the realignment."[7] J. Richard Piper, after delineating various levels of realignment, postulated that "major party realignments can easily be frustrated . . . by patterns on one level that inhibit changes developing in others."[8] And James Burnham, along with Clubb, Flanigan, and Zingale, made the case that realignment depends on a combination of crisis, issues, policy response, and political leaders, around which form a realignment symbol or set of symbols.[9]

Much has been written about the part that Congress plays in periods of realignment. This work has tended to focus on changes in the congressional parties' demographic and regional bases of support, the effects of vote-to-seat ratios on congressional realignments, the policy impact of the large membership turnover (both in the House as a whole and in committees) inherent in realignments, and changes in partisanship and party cohesion in Congress during realigning periods.[10] Theories of realignment emphasizing contingency and looking to performance and leadership leave open a significant space, however, for Congress to help drive realignment in ways that have so far been largely unexamined. MacDonald and Rabinowitz, for example, emphasize the importance of change at the elite level and specify Congress as the institution most likely to lead that change (not only during realignment), but they say little about how that might take place.[11]

This chapter will examine the midterm elections of 1894 and 1930—as well as the 54th Congress and the 72nd Congress, which gained power in those elections—in terms of the mechanisms for midterm influence specified in chapter one: compositional change in Congress and the states, damage inflicted on the president's plebiscitary prestige, political momentum for the president's opposition, issue development, development and/or showcasing of new leadership, and exacerbation of splits in the president's party. Three of those factors bear particularly heavily on the performance model of realignment: party cohesion, leadership, and issue development.

The Election of 1894, the 54th Congress, and Realignment in the 1890s

Composition

After two years of unified Democratic control of the Presidency and both houses of Congress, the Republicans dominated the midterm elections of 1894. They seized control of both houses of Congress, making the largest single gain in House seats in American history (116) and gaining five seats in the Senate. This victory was "indissolubly linked with the panic of 1893," which had occurred weeks after the inauguration of Grover Cleveland to his second term.[12] This panic had produced massive unemployment, financial collapse, and substantial labor unrest to add to the already notable agrarian unrest in the South and West. Since the plebiscitary presidency was not yet a standard feature of American politics, the anti-plebiscitary effect of midterms was muted, but Republicans clearly gained momentum heading into 1896. The *New York Times* offered that Democrats, having "dwarfed, bungled, and betrayed" their own program, had been "punished" and "rebuked in the only way open to the voters, by the accession of the rival party."[13]

The elections of 1894 also turned the Democrats from a national congressional party to a regional one by sweeping out of office northern Democrats and Democrats most closely associated with the Cleveland administration. House Democrats lost only 9 percent of their southern seats, but an astonishing 90 percent of midwestern and 87 percent of northeastern Democrats fell. In twenty-four states, Democrats failed to elect a single member of the House, and in six other states they elected only one. In all of New England, only one Democratic Congressman survived. Of eighty-nine House members in the Midwest, eighty-six were Republicans. Overall, 36 percent of House seats changed party control in 1894.[14] According to David Brady, "the realignment of the 1890s was first felt in the House in the 1894 election."[15] Similarly, Paul Kleppner pointed to 1894 as the crucial year of realigning electoral discontinuity, and Richard Waterman argued that "institutional realignment" in the House (though not the Senate) began in 1894.[16] At the state level, Republicans gained unified control over two-thirds of nonsouthern state governments.[17]

Thus, in 1894, the constituency bases of the parties began the shift that would accelerate over the next half-decade, with Republicans becoming more urban and labor-oriented and Democrats more rural.[18] This realignment would ultimately be based on the cross-cutting issue of whether the American future would be primarily industrial or agrarian. Under that issue were located several subsidiary issues, most important of which were currency, protection, and imperialism.[19]

Issue Development

Congressional majorities have three essential strategies available to them when faced with an opposing president: obstruct the president and slow the work of government, pass a raft of legislation to prove their value as a governing party, or confront the president with popular bills that he will likely be forced to veto because of principle or interest. Some combination of these strategies can be pursued simultaneously or sequentially.

The 54th Congress generally pursued the strategies of obstruction and confrontation with an eye toward depriving Cleveland of a record and exacerbating splits in the Democratic party. Students of the 54th Congress uniformly agree that it was "one of the least productive in American history," a verdict presaged by contemporary comment as well.[20] According to George H. Mayer, "Neither party could accomplish anything in the new Congress. The Republican majority possessed enough partisan spirit to harass Cleveland but not enough to pass a program of its own."[21] Indeed, it was questionable whether the Republicans actually wanted to pass a program of their own, since it might detract from Cleveland's responsibility; Republicans seemed "disposed to inaction."[22] Overall, the productivity of the 54th House fell considerably in comparison to the congresses immediately preceding and following it. The 51st through 53rd Congresses produced an average of 491 public laws; the 54th produced only 434 public laws, a number that grew again to an average of 498 in the next two congresses.[23] In short, the Republican majority possibly could not, and certainly did not, pursue a strategy of broad legislative accomplishment.

Instead, careful obstruction was the order of the day. The 54th Congress showed a substantial increase in partisanship over the 53rd Congress and most Congresses in the previous eight years. Party voting in the House of Representatives (calculated as a simple majority vs. simple majority) increased from 47 percent in the 53rd Congress to 70 percent in the 54th. That figure would increase further after the election of 1896, but the 54th Congress seems to have been the critical turning point (table 3.1). According to Pearl Olive Ponsford, "the presidential policy was undermined at every turn by a hostile Congress"—undermined, but not completely thwarted.[24] At least on the currency question, Republicans managed to position themselves in a way that preserved their (and Cleveland's) policy preference (gold) while still reaching out to silverites and exploiting Democratic division.

Aside from mere obstruction, the 54th Congress also pursued a policy of positive confrontation with Cleveland. Cleveland was already a prolific wielder of the veto pen, and his vetoes increased under the 54th Congress, both absolutely and as a proportion of public bills enacted.[25] Furthermore, the 54th Congress was much more confrontational in its veto override efforts. With the election of 1896, this confrontation almost completely subsided (table 3.2).

Despite this generally high level of confrontation, most of Cleveland's vetoes were applied to private pension bills and otherwise inconsequential public bills. Only on a few questions of substantial public policy did the veto come into play, including a major river and harbor improvements bill, a supplemental appropriations bill, and a tightening of immigration laws that was passed by Congress and vetoed by Cleveland after the November 1896 elections.[26]

Finally, the 54th Congress did succeed in positioning the Republican party for the 1896 elections. In the words of Arthur Wallace Dunn, "the Republicans sought to make campaign material at every opportunity."[27]

Table 3.1 Partisan Voting, 50th–55th Congresses

Congress	Years	Party Votes (%)
50th	1887–89	53
51st	1889–91	83
52nd	1891–93	43
53rd	1893–95	47
54th	1895–97	70
55th	1897–99	79

Source: Jerome M. Clubb and Santa A. Traugott, "Partisan Cleavage and Cohesion in the House of Representatives," *Journal of Interdisciplinary History* (Winter 1977): 382–83.

Table 3.2 Legislative Productivity and Presidential Vetoes, 53rd–54th Congresses

Congress	Bills Enacted	Vetoes	Vetoes (%)/Bills	Override attempts/successes
53rd	463	75	16.2	2/0
54th	434	86	19.8	10/5

Source: Data from George Galloway, *History of the U.S. House of Representatives*, 375–76; *Presidential Vetoes 1789–1988* (Washington, D.C.: GPO, 1989).

According to David Brady, three issues were particularly important in the realignment process: currency, tariff, and expansion. The 54th Congress contributed to the Republican reputation on all three, as well as introducing the lesser issues of immigration and rural postal delivery.

The tariff had long been a point of contention between Republicans and Democrats, with Republicans supportive of a protective tariff and Democrats preferring a more neutral and lower tariff limited to revenue purposes. Cleveland had come into office promising a reduction of the tariff, but the Wilson-Gorman Tariff produced by the Democratic Congress was so unsatisfactory to the President that he allowed it to become law without signing it. In the elections of 1894, the Republican party was "enabled to render increasingly vocal its contention that in Republican protectionism lay the key to the restoration of prosperity."[28] The 54th Congress reinforced the traditional party division on this issue when the House passed the Dingley Tariff bill, promising a return to the high protective tariffs of the Harrison administration.[29] The Dingley Tariff was later brought back successfully as the first legislative priority of the 55th Congress under McKinley. Although there were some divisions among Republicans on the tariff, the 54th Congress continued to hold forth protection as a key principle of the party: protectionism, which was the first item in the Republican platform of 1892, was also the first item in the 1896 platform.[30]

Currency was a more difficult issue, a cross-cutting issue that both parties had tried to straddle for many years. The 1892 Republican platform had been committed to a vague bimetallism, although congressional Republicans as a minority in 1893 had been instrumental in Cleveland's drive to repeal the Sherman Silver Purchase Act. In the 1894 elections, Republicans "handled the silver issue shrewdly."[31] Many became active in the American Bimetallic Society, while others remained silent or endorsed bimetallism without free coinage of silver. While not criticizing Cleveland's preference for gold (which most shared), they criticized Cleveland for the measures he had undertaken to prop up gold.

Republicans in the 54th Congress continued this general line of attack, defending the gold standard but criticizing and often obstructing Cleveland's specific policies.[32] His issuance of bonds came under attack, and measures that he proposed to strengthen the gold standard were delayed and sometimes destroyed.[33] House Speaker Thomas Reed prevented the bond bill of late 1895 from passing, prompting a contemporary critic to complain that "he preferred to force upon the President the necessity of saving the national credit in a more costly and less popular way."[34] This Republican approach was partially the consequence of divisions among Republicans, themselves, with a few silver Republicans and Populists holding the balance in the Senate, and partially a deliberate strategy to hold the center between the unpopular Cleveland and congressional Democrats.

In the end, the 1894 elections and Republicans in the 54th Congress did contribute to the realigning issue of currency, despite the partisan confusion on all sides. Speaker Reed, the single most visible congressional Republican, was a crucial figure in the defense of the gold standard.[35] Congressional Democrats, shorn of their northern industrial wing and chastened by the elections of 1894, became visible proponents of silver and inflation. Brady documents that, of all the relevant issue dimensions of the time, only on the currency question did the correlation between party voting and issue voting in the House substantially rise in the 54th Congress.[36] Thus, it was in the 54th Congress that the gold-silver split took on an identifiably partisan coloration, although this process was gradual both in Congress and in William McKinley's presidential campaign.[37] Whereas in 1892 both parties professed support for bimetallism, by 1896 the Republican platform was clearly committed to gold, and Democrats were clearly the party of silver.

While the third realigning issue of expansionism was predominantly dormant until 1898, congressional Republicans laid the groundwork on that issue, as well, prior to the 1896 presidential election. Much to Cleveland's consternation, the 54th Congress sought to "force the hand of the President on Cuban affairs."[38] This time the Senate took the lead, demanding presidential recognition of the anti-Spanish insurrectionists and their Republic of Cuba. As Henry Cabot Lodge argued at the time, "With an Administration which up to the present time has shown itself hostile or indifferent to the Cuban cause, the action of the two Houses of Congress had little practical value; but it served at least to call the attention of the American people more sharply to the condition of affairs in Cuba and to inform them more fully as to the facts."[39] Skeptics of expansionism also noticed the congressional shift after 1894, complaining that "one house or the other has been constantly in the throes of jingo debate."[40] Thus, Republican control of the 54th Congress served as an important transition toward a political environment in which expansionism was a major point of partisan contention. The Republican platform of 1892 did not mention Cuba, barely mentioned foreign policy, and only vaguely referred to the Monroe Doctrine; by 1896, the GOP platform declared, "We watch with deep and abiding interest the heroic battles of the Cuban patriots against cruelty and oppression . . . we believe that the government of the United States should actively use its influence and good offices to restore peace and give independence to the Island."[41] The 1896 platform also came out for control of Hawaii, construction of a Nicaraguan canal, purchase of the Danish West Indies, and a major naval buildup; even Turkish massacres in Armenia were mentioned and condemned. In contrast, the Democratic platform of 1896 extended sympathy to the Cuban people but did not call for U.S. action to liberate Cuba and avoided the other expansionist issues prominent in the Republican platform.[42]

Finally, the subsidiary issues of immigration and free rural postal delivery were pushed by the Republicans in Congress until they became at least minor campaign issues. Although their bill requiring immigrant literacy did not meet with Cleveland's veto until after the election, the issue did spark comment in both the Republican and Democratic platforms of 1896. Immigration had not been an issue in the 1892 Republican platform.[43] Likewise, the 54th Congress introduced free rural postal delivery in 1896 at least partially as an attempt to co-opt a popular Populist issue.[44]

Altogether, the 54th Congress helped to clarify each of the three issues that would be at the center of the realignment, though the third, expansion, did not come into its own until after the election of 1896. This clarification process was far from complete; the parties would not be fully sorted out on the currency question until the presidential nominating conventions and elections of 1896. Even the action that Congress took was limited in nature. The Dingley Tariff was written but not passed; gold was defended, but room for maneuver was maintained. Issue development in the 54th Congress was not exceptional in comparison with that in other post-midterm congresses; as we will see, many other congresses have developed a larger number of issues or developed them more fully. Yet it was significant. Above all, the issues the 54th Congress did help develop were realigning issues. And this issue framing was accomplished in the absence of major legislative achievement.

Leadership

The elections of 1894 contributed to a major leadership turnover in the Democratic party. Such well-known Democratic leaders as Richard Bland, Champ Clark, William Wilson, William Springer, and William Helman were defeated.[45] Democrats lost control of the governorship in eleven states, including New York, Pennsylvania, and Wisconsin; perhaps as important, only ten Democratic governors before 1894 remained in office after 1894, most in southern states or states that did not hold gubernatorial elections in 1894. Only a handful of Democratic officials who attended the 1892 national convention survived to attend the 1896 convention. As Paul Kleppner indicates, "repudiation opened the way for new leaders to seize control of the party, to nominate their own presidential candidate, and to craft a platform that challenged the bipartisan consensus on principles of political economy."[46] Thus, the elections of 1894 led directly to a fundamental reorientation of the Democratic party not only at the coalitional level but at the leadership level.

The strength of existing party leadership in the institutions of government might also be important in two ways: publicly effective leadership could help establish a positive party reputation in the electorate, and skilled party leadership would be more likely to take advantage of the new opportunities. In the 54th Congress, the Republican party leadership was clearly more adept than its primary competition, which was not the Democratic House leadership but President Cleveland, himself. Thomas Reed served as House Speaker, as he had in the 51st Congress, and continued displaying the tactical and strategic acumen that had made him legendary as one of the most powerful and influential of all House leaders. As "one of its greatest Speakers, and its greatest parliamentarian . . . Reed had made a reputation as a daring, resourceful leader."[47] When party cohesion seemed threatened, he preferred inaction to a risk of disunity. In general, he understood the importance of positioning the Republican Congress in a way to maximize the opportunity for victory in 1896.

Conversely, Cleveland was an exceedingly poor leader of his party. He "demanded recognition as party leader, yet he scorned the role of party manager. Prepared to instruct the Democratic members of Congress, he considered it beneath Presidential dignity to cajole or conciliate them."[48] Cleveland refused to offer patronage or Senatorial courtesy to Democrats from opposing party factions; his one major use of patronage—to help secure repeal of the Sherman Silver Purchase Act in 1893—while successful, was so heavy handed that it further hurt his standing as party leader.[49] He proved generally inflexible and inclined to view deviation from his positions as a betrayal of the party. The final break occurred in the spring of 1895. Silver Democrats issued a statement warning about the electoral and economic disasters inherent in continued adherence to the gold standard. Cleveland, rather than attempting to conciliate, responded with an equally bellicose letter that polarized the party beyond repair.[50] Thus, aside from the more substantive governmental consequences of Reed and Cleveland as party leaders, the nation was offered the public spectacle of a Republican party leadership that seemed, if not overly active, at least generally competent, and a Democratic leadership that was an utter failure.

Party Cohesion

Republican party cohesion, although strained at times by the currency question, continued on the generally upward path that it had followed throughout the period from 1861 through 1897.[51] House Republican cohesion was slightly lower in the 54th Congress than in the 53rd but was also slightly higher than it had been in the 52nd Congress. Democratic cohesion was on a more consistent upward path in the 52nd through 55th Congresses and was higher in the 54th Congress than Republican cohesion. Like partisanship, the cohesion of both parties was destined to increase further after the elections of 1896 (table 3.3).

House cohesion scores, however, do not tell the whole story of party unity. Indeed, in the 54th Congress they miss the most important point. While House Democrats had high cohesion, they were as a unit locked in combat against their own president. Thus, Grover Cleveland faced two problems: the large Republican majority in Congress and the fact that his own party in Congress was dominated by southern and populist-leaning (or, at a minimum, populist-pressured) members who had little philosophical reason to support him and even less political interest in supporting him.[52] In 1895, Hollingsworth estimates, at least 60 percent of Democrats in Con-

Table 3.3 House Party Cohesion Scores, 52nd–55th Congress

Congress	Years	Republican Cohesion	Democratic Cohesion
52nd	1891–93	79.6	76.2
53rd	1893–95	86.1	85.1
54th	1895–97	82.2	86.9
55th	1897–99	93.2	89.3

Source: Data from David A. Brady, *Critical Elections and Congressional Policymaking*, 80.

gress were pro-silver.[53] This change was a direct consequence of the intrapartisan compositional changes of 1894.

This division in the Democratic party, utterly masked by House party cohesion scores, was perhaps the worst enduring split between a president and his party in Congress in the history of the United States. A consequence of the elections of 1894, it was also exacerbated by those elections. Surviving congressional Democrats had no reason to follow the president who had produced such an electoral disaster, and, with the power that accompanied their new majority status, "Republican leaders were by no means averse to exploiting to the utmost the persistent disunity within the Democratic Party."[54] While the Republicans in the 54th Congress were not as cohesive as congressional Democrats (or as they themselves would be after 1896), and while there were splits in Republican ranks between the House and the Senate which are also masked by House cohesion scores, the Republicans as a national party were far more cohesive than the Democrats, when one takes all factors into account, and they were able to use their control of Congress in several instances to threaten Democratic party unity further.

The Election of 1930, the 72nd Congress, and the New Deal Realignment

Composition

The election of 1930, like the election of 1894, came in the midst of a terrible depression and significantly changed the political landscape in Washington. Democrats gained forty-nine House seats and eight seats in the Senate; thirteen vacancy elections prior to the convening of Congress in December 1931 led to a narrow Democratic House majority. The 1930–31 freshman class represented nearly one-fifth of the House.[55] Republicans retained a one-seat plurality in the Senate, which permitted them to organize the chamber, but Democrats combined with the one other Senator could block all action; together with a bloc of about a dozen progressive Republicans, Democrats had effective control of the Senate on many issues. Democrats also made significant gains at the state level in 1930, particularly in traditionally Republican strongholds in the east and midwest such as Massachusetts and Ohio.[56] Altogether, "the Democrats had ended the GOP supremacy without establishing their own."[57] Accordingly, Richard Waterman does not date the beginning of firmly entrenched "institutional realignment" in Congress until the 1932 elections.[58] Nevertheless, the election of 1930 presented the Democrats with a crucial opening and momentum to carry them into 1932.

That momentum, both partisan and more broadly ideological, was plainly evident. In the view of Arthur Schlesinger Jr., "The success of public power advocates in a series of states where private utilities were key issues—in Pennsylvania, where Gifford Pinchot became governor, in Wisconsin, which brought in old Bob LaFollette's younger son, Phil, in Oregon, in Washington, in Connecticut, in Maine, in Alabama—suggested a gathering revolt against business leadership."[59] News reports held that the election results "furnished encouraging evidence to Democracy's leaders that the sentiment expressed at the polls . . . presaged victory for their presidential ticket in the elections of 1932."[60] The *New York Times* editorialized that "the heavy blows dealt Republicans by the voters will be taken as a repudiation of President Hoover's leadership of his party." Republicans were struck down "by a revolution which is peaceful but none the less decisive and politically devastating."[61] As far as the newly elected 72nd Congress went, "the seeds of successful opposition have been scattered profusely upon this hitherto pleached political field."[62] Hoover, himself, who had claimed a public mandate in no fewer than nine issue areas in his 1929 inaugural address, made no attempt to explain the drubbing.[63]

Issue Development

Herbert Hoover, no great lover of Congress even when it was controlled by his own party, refused to call a special session in 1931, preferring to deal with the Depression in his own way without interference. When Congress did convene, it faced the same strategic choices that the 54th Congress had faced nearly forty years before. Contemporary analysts predicted that "the coming session will be full of politics; with moves and counter moves designed to have an effect on the Presidential election of 1932."[64] After a relatively non-partisan beginning by the 72nd Congress, this prediction was proven correct.

The initial plan of the Democratic leadership was to pursue a very different strategy toward the question of confrontation and productivity than the Republicans had done in 1895 and 1896. This plan was to cooperate with Hoover in a nonpartisan manner and allow him to bear the responsibility of proposing policy.[65] For the first three months of the 72nd Congress, this plan was effected, although not without some dissent by progressive Democrats. Hoover proposed and Congress approved a foreign debt moratorium, the Glass-Steagall Act to strengthen credit, and the Reconstruction Finance Corporation (RFC).

In March 1932, however, congressional Democrats rebelled against this strategy and their own leaders, first by restoring cuts that had been included in Hoover's government economy bill and then, more substantially, by rejecting Hoover's sales tax proposal and replacing it with greater taxes on wealth. From this point forward, congressional Democrats—in league with progressive Republicans—pursued the same essential strategy of obstruction and confrontation that had characterized the 54th Congress, although in a different incarnation. The 1930 election results (and the subsequent interpretation of those results) made the strategy possible; Democrats had to come to a decision, on their own, of whether, when, and how to exercise that option.

The overall productivity of the 72nd Congress declined, as it had in the 54th. The House in the 69th through 71st Congresses passed an average of 1,011 public laws per congress; the 72nd Congress produced only 516 public laws, a figure that jumped again to an average of 763 in the next two (New Deal) congresses.[66] Several important presidential proposals either were defeated or simply died in the 72nd Congress after February 1932, including Hoover's sales tax proposal, a proposal for government reorganization, and proposals for unemployment insurance, bankruptcy reform, and railroad reform. Extensive economy proposals were essentially gutted, producing only a small fraction of the proposed savings.[67]

Like the 54th Congress and Cleveland, the 72nd Congress and Hoover engaged in escalating confrontation, as measured by vetoes. The number of vetoes nearly doubled as a proportion of public bills enacted, although it never reached a very high absolute level (table 3.4).[68] Furthermore, while few vetoes in the 54th Congress were related to substantive policy disputes, in the 72nd Congress the bills vetoed were often of great significance. Perhaps the most important was Hoover's veto of the relief bill presented to him by Congress in July 1932. Congress confronted an unwilling president with a choice of adopting its relief policy or appearing indifferent to the suffering of millions of Americans; Hoover's opposition to federal relief

Table 3.4 Legislative Productivity and Presidential Vetoes, 71st–72nd Congresses

Congress	Bills Enacted	Vetoes	Vetoes/ %Bills	Override Attempts/Successes
71st	1009	19	1.9	3/1
72nd	516	18	3.5	3/1

Source: George Galloway, *History of the U.S. House of Representatives*, 375–76; *Presidential Vetoes 1789–1988* (Washington, D.C.: GPO, 1992).

"helped ensure that the measure would be perceived in partisan terms."[69] Indeed, "the essential difference between the Republican and Democratic approach to economic recovery and Depression relief was clarified in the public mind."[70] Hoover was also forced to make several other difficult vetoes, including a tariff reform measure, expanded spending on veterans, and Reconstruction Finance Corporation loans to farmers and ranchers.

While partisan voting in the 72nd Congress showed no increase over the 71st, quantitative assessments of partisanship do not entirely reflect reality. It seems probable that the intensity of partisan conflicts increased. Observers claimed that "at times legislative wheels were so completely mired in the swamp of unrestrained language that it seemed they would never turn again."[71] On balance, the behavior of Congress after February 1932 prompted some observers to conclude that "the Democrats did everything they could to embarrass the Republicans" with the purpose in view of winning the 1932 election.[72] Congress put Hoover on the tactical and strategic defensive, gutted a large part of his remaining program, thus depriving him of further legislative accomplishments, and presented to the American public an increasingly clear differentiation between the parties.

While some scholars downplay the effect of the 1930 elections and the 72nd Congress,[73] the 72nd Congress almost certainly contributed to the Roosevelt victory of 1932 and the subsequent realignment by introducing issues into the public debate that ultimately worked in favor of the Democratic party. Some of these issues were introduced through the confrontation process discussed above; other legislative proposals did not reach the president's desk but were also of symbolic importance. Above all, the whole social welfare issue dimension, so central to the New Deal realignment, either first emerged or expanded considerably during the 72nd Congress, just as the currency issue had first become a clearly partisan issue in the 54th Congress.[74]

More specifically, the 72nd Congress pushed forward the issue of federal relief in a way that substantially helped to frame the 1932 presidential election. Not only were congressional Democrats responsible for passage of relief, and not only did Hoover veto that bill (only to sign a revised version days later), but congressional Republicans stood with their president. While Democratic House Speaker John Nance Garner's name was attached to the original House relief bill, almost no House Republicans voted for it. Thus, unlike the currency issue, which had been muddled for some time by the Cleveland–silver Democrat split, the issue of relief provided a clear partisan division. Other relief-related questions included veterans support, such as House passage of the veterans bonus demanded by the bonus army, and extended RFC loans. The contrast between Democrats and Republicans, made clear by Congress, was also accentuated by Franklin Roosevelt's activism on the relief question while he was governor of New York from 1931 through 1932.[75]

The 72nd Congress also helped frame the issue of distribution of wealth, particularly when it rejected the sales tax in favor of much higher estate taxes and surtaxes on incomes over $1 million. As on the relief bill, there was a sharp partisan division on this issue: 75 percent of House Democrats opposed the sales tax, while 75 percent of Republicans supported it.[76] The redistributionist nature of the revised tax bill was noted frequently, and often positively, by the popular press.[77] House Democrats also passed the Goldsborough bill in May 1932, seeking an inflation of credit and currency—an implicitly redistributionist program.[78] Congressional Democrats began tentatively to establish a theme that might be called "people before balanced budgets." Legislatively, it was seen in the drastic scaling back of Hoover's economy bills, which started when House Democrats restored salary increases for government workers.[79] This theme could be seen during the debate over the sales tax, as well, when the argument was first heard that insisting on balanced budgets in times of economic distress might be unnecessary, if not dangerous.[80]

Finally, the House also attempted to appeal to labor by passing anti-injunction legislation. The Norris-LaGuardia Act of 1932, the sponsors of which were progressive Republicans, was crucial to limiting the use of court injunctions as a "weapon against the unions."[81] Labor would ultimately become a core element of the New Deal coalition.

The 72nd Congress, itself, became an issue in the presidential election of 1932. Congressional Democrats came under fierce attack from some editorial quarters for both the tax bill and the Garner relief bill, attacks that indicate the degree to which the nation's attention was focused on congressional action at that moment.[82] As one critic said, "While ordinarily Mr. John Citizen does not pay much attention to what is going on in Congress, in this year of hard times it has been brought home to him, as something like a revelation, that what Congress does actually affects his individual and personal pocketbook."[83] The Republican platform attacked "the vagaries of the present Democratic House of Representatives" and argued that "delay and the constant introduction and consideration of new and unsound measures has kept the country in a state of uncertainty and fear."[84] In his remarks upon accepting the renomination of the Republican party, Hoover thanked "patriotic" and cooperative Democrats while railing against "factional and demagogic opposition."[85] Early in the campaign, Hoover attacked the 72nd Congress for distorting needed public works into "porkbarrel non-productive works which impoverish the nation," planning to replace the protective tariff with a revenue tariff, refusing to reduce the budget or reorganize government, refusing to reform banking and railroad laws, and seeking to inflate the currency.[86]

The Democratic platform condemned the Hoover administration and proposed several principles that had already been part of the record of the 72nd Congress, including a stronger federal role in relief and public works, basing revenue on ability to pay, reducing the tariff, and providing farm loans and debt relief. At the same time, some principles were enunciated which seemed contrary to the record of the 72nd Congress, most notably a 25 percent reduction in federal spending and maintenance of a sound currency.[87] On balance, the Democratic platform of 1932 embraced the 72nd Congress and incorporated many of its themes while never explicitly mentioning it. Perhaps more importantly, Franklin Roosevelt chose as his running mate none other than Speaker Garner, who had unsuccessfully sought the presidential nomination. Garner's presence on the ticket was a powerful symbol of the Democratic commitment to more aggressive relief policies.

In contrast to Hoover, who attacked the 72nd Congress early in the campaign, Franklin Roosevelt did not make it integral to his campaign until late October, when he made a succession of speeches discussing it. On October 25th, Roosevelt claimed that Hoover had done nothing about the federal deficit until forced to do so by Congress. In an October 31st speech on unemployment, Roosevelt attacked Hoover for vetoing the relief bill in July; only on the insistence of Congress, Roosevelt said, had Hoover agreed to any form of relief. He reiterated this point in a November 3rd speech to the Republicans for Roosevelt League in New York, where he pointed out that Congress had to work for six months to convince Hoover of the need for relief. In both the unemployment speech and the New York speech, Roosevelt emphasized that the next Congress would surely be

Democratic and that Hoover, based on his record with the 72nd Congress, would be patently unable to deal with it constructively.[88]

Leadership

The most important effect of the 1930 election in thrusting forward new leadership was to place Franklin D. Roosevelt in the front rank of presidential contenders. Roosevelt, first elected governor of New York by the narrowest of margins in 1928, was reelected in a landslide; indeed, observers would later argue that "the event which more than any other made Roosevelt a candidate for the presidency was his re-election as Governor in 1930 by the great plurality of 725,000 votes."[89] At the same time, Huey Long was elected Senator from Louisiana, a result that worked together with FDR's 1932 presidential victory to push American politics significantly to the left.

As in the 54th Congress, the out-party in the 72nd Congress possessed an advantage in party leadership. Most crucially, Democratic House leadership proved considerably more effective over time than its Republican counterpart or President Hoover. The Democratic leadership, headed by Speaker John Nance Garner, was far from perfect; Garner, for example, made a major blunder in March 1932 by supporting Hoover's proposed sales tax when most Democrats opposed it, producing a short-lived runaway House. Throughout the early months of the 72nd Congress, Garner was criticized by progressive Democrats and the media for having no apparent plan. Nevertheless, Arthur Schlesinger Jr. credited Garner with persistence and "unlimited parliamentary astuteness . . . Whatever he did, he generally carried his well-disciplined followers with him."[90] After the sales tax fiasco, Garner accommodated himself rapidly to the more activist mood of the House Democrats. However, while Garner was clearly flawed, the House Republican leadership was in total disarray. Respected House Speaker Nicholas Longworth died in April 1931, creating a major leadership vacuum. Senate Republican leadership, which could conceivably have rallied the upper chamber to present an alternative to the Democratic House, was likewise of poor quality.[91]

For his part, President Hoover attempted to formulate strategy for the 72nd Congress independent of his party's congressional leadership, for whom he harbored contempt, if not hostility. He even alienated Senate Republicans by suggesting that they allow Democrats to organize the Senate, on the theory that Democrats would find control of both houses politically awkward.[92] Conflicts between Hoover and his party in Congress were reminiscent of Cleveland's in kind although not in degree. Thus, while both parties experienced some leadership problems, there was a substantial gap in leadership between the rising party and the falling party, as there had been at the time of the 54th Congress.

Party Cohesion

Party cohesion was, at times, a problem for both parties; party cohesion scores for Democrats and Republicans both fell from the previous Congress. The Democrats were clearly split between a progressive, activist faction and a faction more inclined toward caution. The Republicans, however, were more seriously split, consisting of at least three identifiable "parties": the Old Guard, the progressives, and a substantial group who stood in between.[93] Furthermore, Hoover was hobbled by the fact that Republican losses in 1930 had come disproportionately at the expense of members closely identified with him, just as Democratic losses in 1894 had disproportionately hurt Cleveland sympathizers. In Kansas, where there were two Senate elections simultaneously, the Republican incumbent perceived to be independent (Arthur Capper) won handily while the Republican incumbent perceived to be closely aligned with Hoover (Henry Allen) lost.[94] As an Iowan who had moved to California and never held elective office anywhere, Hoover did not possess a really solid regional base, although he had done particularly poorly only in the Midwest at the 1928 Republican convention. Ideologically, both parties shifted against him: according to Jordan A. Schwarz, "No election since 1922 so elated progressives . . . Whether wearing the Republican or Democratic label, it was a good year to be a progressive."[95]

Barbara Sinclair notes that the 72nd Congress saw a substantial increase in the populist-progressive score of both Democrats and, to a smaller extent, Republicans on the government management dimension; implicitly, this meant that Democratic cohesion on its dominant populist-progressive axis increased, while Republican cohesion on its dominant conservative axis declined.[96] Significantly, the most important turning point of the 72nd Congress, the rebellion against Hoover's sales tax proposal, was initiated not by Democrats but by progressive Republicans.[97] Clubb, Flanigan, and Zingale argue that Democratic cohesion lagged somewhat behind Republican cohesion after 1933, probably because the large majorities they possessed allowed for less discipline;[98] however, the situation was reversed in the 72nd Congress, where Democrats had a better party cohesion score than Republicans by 60 percent to 57 percent, the first time Democrats had enjoyed such an advantage since the 65th Congress (table 3.5).

Table 3.5 House Party Cohesion Scores, 70th–74th Congresses

Congress	Years	Democratic Cohesion	Republican Cohesion
70th	1927-29	64.6	65.1
71st	1929-31	67.5	68.1
72nd	1931-33	60.0	57.0
73rd	1933-35	68.2	70.2
74th	1935-37	64.4	68.0

Source: Data from David Brady and John Ettling, "The Electoral Connection and the Decline of Partisanship in the Twentieth Century House of Representatives," Congress and the Presidency 11 (Spring 1984): 22.

Congress and Realignment: Patterns

It is always difficult to postulate patterns in realignment, since there have been so few cases, and each case is surrounded with its own peculiar political, institutional, and social context. This difficulty is also inherent in any attempt to discover patterns in the two cases of pre-realignment congresses. Nevertheless, at least some limited conclusions can be drawn and tested against lesser examples of change at the presidential level.

First, the pre-realignment midterms brought about enormous compositional change in Congress. Both realignments were preceded by much larger than average presidential party losses in the midterm elections—an average loss of eighty-three seats in the House and seven seats in the Senate, compared to an average from 1894 through 1994 of thirty-five House seats and six Senate seats before non-realigning opposition presidential victories and thirty-one House seats and two Senate seats before opposition presidential defeats. These dramatic partisan shifts in Congress led in both instances to a strong sense that the out-party was coming up and the in-party was repudiated and on its way down. Intraparty compositional changes were also important, particularly in 1894 when the northern Democrats were virtually annihilated. And in both cases, partisan control of the House shifted against the president while either partisan or ideological control was more narrowly lost in the Senate.

Consequently, with a few exceptions, like the Wagner relief bills of the 71st and 72nd Congresses, the House of Representatives rather than the Senate was the driving force. In the 54th Congress, it was the House Republicans, not the more divided Senate Republicans, who pushed the Dingley Tariff and established the Republican party as the party of gold. In the 72nd Congress, it was the Democratic House that first revolted against the Hoover sales tax and that pushed the social welfare issue dimension to its further limits. Indeed, since the Senate was still nominally controlled by Republicans, disproportionate responsibility for establishing a Democratic record was in the hands of the House.

While a study of partisanship scores yields inconclusive evidence (they increased substantially in the 54th Congress but not in the 72nd), there is consistent evidence of hardened partisan attitudes and greater confrontationalism. Both of the pre-realignment congresses studied here exhibited a sharp decline in overall productivity compared to congresses immediately before and after. They utilized the strategy of conciliation and productivity either not at all (54th Congress) or for only a brief time (72nd Congress), and the political benefits reaped by the 72nd Congress clearly did not come from this period. Instead, both congresses ultimately pursued a strategy of obstruction and confrontation, although in somewhat different ways. The 54th Congress was simply unproductive in substantive terms, forced President Cleveland into an increasing number of vetoes, and increased its veto override attempts. The 72nd Congress did not confront President Hoover with a larger number of attempted overrides, but his vetoes did increase as a percentage of all public bills, and the vetoes that were forced on him were much more likely to be of a significant policy nature. The most important of these was the federal relief bill of July 1932, which was reported out of conference committee on the very day Franklin Roosevelt received the Democratic nomination for president.

Both the 54th Congress and the 72nd Congress succeeded to some extent in framing the issues that were ultimately at the center of each realignment. The 54th reemphasized the traditional partisan differences on the tariff; at the same time, the currency question first became a largely partisan issue in Congress, despite continuing division within both parties. The 72nd introduced in a major way the social welfare issue dimension and clarified the parties' positions on that dimension. Relief, distribution of wealth, a relative emphasizing of human needs over balanced budgets, and support for labor all emerged in the 72nd Congress, and the presidential candidates and platforms of both parties recognized and incorporated these issues.

In both eras, there was a significant leadership gap between the out-party and the in-party, especially if one takes into account the party leadership failings of the incumbent presidents. If Clubb, Flanigan, and Zingale are right about the general importance of leadership and performance in realignments, then it stands to reason that leadership will be crucial in the pre-realignment period as the rising out-party seeks to take advantage of favorable political circumstances.

When looking at the political system as a whole, the out-party exhibited an advantage in party cohesiveness. Congressional Democrats in the 54th Congress were slightly more cohesive than Republicans, but they were locked in a bitter struggle with their own president. In the 72nd Congress, both parties were divided, but the Republicans more so. These in-party splits were both cause and result of the midterm election results, and the newly advantaged party in Congress skillfully manipulated those splits for future legislative and electoral gain. The contribution of intraparty splits to this process may help confirm David Mayhew's observation that "innovative midterm elections" in general are connected with in-party factional division (although he does not list either 1894 or 1930 as such an election).[99]

Most realignment scholars argue that realignment is a process more than a single event, and Clubb, Flanigan, and Zingale contend that this process is highly reliant on the ability of the rising party to take advantage of its opportunity through effective leadership and performance. The new congressional majorities that preceded the elections of 1896 and 1932 were able to highlight a positive alternative of party leadership, highlight old policy differences and introduce new ones, exploit and exacerbate splits in the former majority, and embarrass the president both by denying him legislation he desired and by forcing him to veto popular legislation that he preferred to ignore. Such a role helps bridge the gap between what MacDonald and Rabinowitz call "structural" realignment and "performance" realignment.

Thus, while the 1894 and 1930 midterms registered existing dissatisfaction with the status quo—dissatisfaction that would surely have continued into the next presidential election—both congresses contributed in important ways to the public framing of the realigning issues. While the 1896 election results appear to be a simple extension of the 1894 results (a Republican landslide in both cases), that fact by itself could be equally consistent with 1894 playing an active role or a passive role in future events. And 1930 is very difficult to reconcile with the idea of the midterm election as merely a passive reflection of voter sentiment. The 1930 elections saw not a Democratic landslide but significant Democratic gains that nevertheless resulted in a rough congressional stalemate; indeed, even in 1930, the Republican share of the national two-party congressional vote was 54 percent.[100] Something changed between 1930 and 1932 which moved the electorate from ambivalence to overwhelming support for Democrats, and the new Democratic House was surely part of that change.

The role of these midterm congresses as the leading edge of realignment should not be exaggerated. Above all, events drove realignment. Realignment is the most powerful and most enduring partisan change, driven by the most dire of circumstances. The relative importance of those circumstances (depression) was surely greater, and hence that of midterm elections less, than in other less dramatic cases of partisan change. Consequently, realignment cases may provide a framework for considering change in general but may also delimit the lower edge of midterm effects in the preparatory category.

In some cases, such as the Republican attachment to gold in the 1890s, the issues were not as clear cut as they would later become. Whatever objective effect the 54th and 72nd congresses might have had on subsequent events, both came under considerable attack at the time for producing inaction and chaos.[101] No reliable opinion surveys are available to measure the ways in which these congresses might have contributed to shifts in mass public opinion. Of course, the long-term realigning issues in both cases were given salience only by the overwhelming short-term issue of depression, which would have been operative in the presidential elections of 1896 and 1932 with or without the preceding midterms. Most fundamentally, realignment is still ultimately dependent on presidential victories and successful presidential leadership. As MacDonald and Rabinowitz acknowledge, "congressional debate alone is not sufficiently visible to stimulate a mass realignment."[102] No one would argue that a new majority in Congress can single-handedly manufacture a realignment if other circumstances are not favorable.

Nevertheless, such majorities can contribute and have contributed to the onset of realignments under circumstances that were favorable but not preordained. Not only can midterm elections provide a crucial check on the president's party; they can also serve a preparatory function paving the way for later change, even contributing to the reversal of party dominance for a generation or more.

FOUR

Midterm Elections as the Vanguard of Change:

2. MORE PREPARATORY MIDTERMS

The pattern of pre-realignment congresses points the way to a broader analytical framework for midterm elections and midterm congresses in general, particularly those preceding less dramatic shifts of political power. The same factors that contribute to realignment contribute to changes on a smaller scale; the same effects are produced but are simply not as deep or as long lasting. Aside from realigning elections in 1896 and 1932, party control of the presidency has changed eight times since 1912, usually for more than one term—in 1912, 1920, 1952, 1960, 1968, 1976, 1980, and 1992. In six of those cases, the preceding midterm elections served functions that differed from pre-realigning midterms only in detail.

This chapter will examine those cases, using the pre-realigning midterms as a touchstone, and will draw from them some conclusions about the relationship of midterms with subsequent political change. That relationship depends on numerous factors, not least of which is the question of whether the opposition actually gains control of Congress, bolsters an already existing majority, or simply improves its position while remaining a minority. Yet, despite their variety in that respect and even though they range the gamut of seat shifts, from a very strong fifty-seven in the House (in 1910) to a mediocre fifteen (in 1978), the six midterm elections outlined here were each crucial in their own way.

1910 and the Rise of the Progressives

Republicans controlled both houses of Congress from 1894 through 1910 and the presidency from 1896 through 1912. This period of extended party control was sufficiently durable to be considered by most scholars to have constituted a period of realignment. Furthermore, after the Wilsonian interlude, Republicans regained control and held it securely until the onset of the Great Depression. That interlude, however, was of great importance. The decade of Wilsonian progressivism served as a crucial first step toward the establishment of the modern welfare state, the first of three waves of twentieth-century federal activism (the other two being the New Deal and the Great Society). While the election of Wilson in 1912 is often taken as the starting point of this progressive era at the federal level, such an interpretation does a disservice to the midterm election of 1910.

After 1900, Republican unity was increasingly strained by a split between the party's old guard and progressive (or insurgent) wings. Theodore Roosevelt managed to hold the wings together most of the time, but his successor, William Howard Taft, lacked Roosevelt's political dexterity. Elected in 1908, Taft spent his first two years making a series of mistakes that fueled the split and convinced progressives (largely in error) that he had abandoned Roosevelt's approach and had fully embraced the old guard.[1] On balance, Taft was an exceedingly poor party leader, unable to either mollify the progressives or crush them.

The midterm elections of 1910 proved to be a watershed for Republicans and the nation. The campaign served as a solvent rather than a glue for Republican unity. Taft, finally convinced that the insurgents were not only his enemies but enemies of the Constitution, "sought to read them out of the party by defeating them in the primaries of 1910."[2] Taft clubs, manned by party regulars, were formed to that end in Wisconsin, Iowa, Kansas, Nebraska, and Washington. Progressives in numerous states established clubs of their own with the purpose of defeating the old guard.[3] Theodore Roosevelt returned from his African safari, reentered politics by intervening in the New York state convention, and set out on a speaking tour supporting Republican candidates spanning the spectrum. Although claiming to seek unity, Roosevelt also contributed to the split, primarily through his radical "new nationalism" speech delivered in Osawatomie, Kansas.[4] Altogether, "the Congressional election of 1910 was one of those significant divides in American history which signalize a reversal of political trends before a complete transfer of power occurs."[5] For that reason, David Mayhew classed it as one of four "innovative midterms" in American history.[6]

The primaries and general elections both went strongly against the regular Republicans. In the primaries, forty-one Republican incumbents were defeated, almost all stand-patters, losing noted races in California, Kansas, Iowa, Minnesota, and Wisconsin.[7] The fall 1910 general election results were presaged by a March special election won by a Democratic candidate in a normally Republican Massachusetts district.[8] Taft's 6,000-word manifesto calling for Republican victory in 1910 fell on deaf ears. Democrats gained fifty-seven seats in the House and ten in the Senate, enough to give them outright control of the House and effective control, together with progressive Republicans, of the Senate. Similar Democratic gains occurred at the state level, where Democrats elected governors in New York and New Jersey for the first time since 1892, as well as in traditional Republican strongholds of Connecticut, Rhode Island, Ohio, and Massachusetts. Indeed, in the view of some observers, "the worst news for the Republicans and best news for the Democrats came from the states."[9]

Aside from the Republican loss of seats and congressional control, there were two other important consequences of the electoral results. First, between the primaries and general election, the composition of the Republican Party was shifted significantly in the progressive direction. Of the ninety-eight Republican congressmen who lost, only three were in the nine most progressive states (Wisconsin, Iowa, Kansas, Nebraska, North Dakota, South Dakota, Minnesota, California, and Washington). Conversely, twenty-six lost in just four predominantly stand-pat states (New York, New Jersey, Ohio, and Pennsylvania).[10] In short, "the regular forces met a veritable holocaust in the November elections."[11]

These results not only bolstered the numbers of the insurgents but vastly emboldened them: "When the results of the summer primaries and the November elections became known, the insurgents were ready to begin moving openly against the administration."[12] And indeed they did. Immediately after the 1910 elections, progressive Republicans met to draw up a declaration of principles and to call for a national meeting. That meeting was held on January 21, 1911, when the National Progressive Republican League was formed. At the opening of the April 1911 special session of Congress, forty-one House and ten Senate Republicans held their own insurgent caucus and demanded that the party leadership allot them committee assignments in their ratio to congressional Republicans (about one-fourth).[13] As well, "the outcome of the 1910 elections fixed the attention of Republicans on the presidential race to come."[14] After a then-unsuccessful overture to Theodore Roosevelt, progressives in early 1911 settled on Sen. Robert LaFollette (R-Wisc.) to carry the torch against Taft. After further intrigue, Roosevelt also entered the fray some months later. Thus, the 1910 elections hinged on an already existing Republican split, but they also stimulated and deepened that split.

Second, the 1910 elections helped to revive the Democratic Party to an extent well beyond that reflected in its numerical gain. The *New York Times* remarked, "What a wonderful and quick regeneration has been wrought in the Democratic Party in this year."[15] Above all, the election "went far to rehabilitate the Democratic party because it furnished it with a group of new reform-minded leaders," not least of whom was Woodrow Wilson, who became governor of New Jersey in a landslide victory and was immediately catapulted to the nation's attention as a prospective presidential candidate.[16] Taken together, the new Democratic governors "represented a bright new face that seemed to displace the received image of their party."[17] Furthermore, Democratic victories in 1910 pointed the way to a new Democratic Party and gave a glimpse of the possibilities fully grasped under Franklin D. Roosevelt two decades later. As Lewis L. Gould commented, "Politicians like Alfred E. Smith and Robert F. Wagner of New York, Edward F. Dunne of Illinois, and David I. Walsh of Massachusetts relied on urban machines for victory, but added a leaven of humanitarian sympathy and governmental activism that looked forward to the New Deal coalition."[18]

The 62nd Congress that resulted from the elections of 1910 was firmly in the grip of the Democratic–progressive Republican alliance. Often, the result was "legislative deadlock."[19] Vetoes doubled, and Taft, who had faced no override attempts in the previous Congress, faced nine veto override attempts in the 62nd, one of which succeeded. Most notably, Taft vetoed numerous tariff revisions and appropriations measures, an immigration measure, and Arizona and New Mexico statehood (on which he later relented). Overall legislative productivity also slipped.

When the outgoing 61st Congress refused to consider a reciprocal trade agreement negotiated by Taft with Canada, he called a special early session of the 62nd Congress in April 1911. Forced to rely on Democrats, Taft finally won passage of the agreement but only after three months of bitter wrangling. For their part, congressional Democrats joined with progressive midwestern Republicans on some issues and old guard easterners on others: "The only working principle behind Democratic tariff votes was to aggravate the divisive forces within the G.O.P."[20] The Democratic leadership also succeeded, perhaps not unintentionally, in agitating Canada (which had yet to ratify the agreement) by bold proclamations of how the agreement might lead to the "Stars and Stripes flying over Canada."[21] Fearful of a loss of sovereignty, Canadians rejected the agreement in a national referendum. Thus, Taft had deepened splits in his own party, been forced to rely on his partisan opponents, and lost several months in bitter bickering with nothing to show for it in the end.

At the same time, the 62nd Congress did pass numerous measures establishing a strong progressive record for Democrats in the next election and, not incidentally, serving as a foundation for Wilson's New Freedom program. As Mayhew pointed out, the 62nd Congress was responsible for the 17th Amendment (direct election of Senators), an eight-hour federal work day, a ban on hazardous phosphorous matches, creation of a federal Children's Bureau, establishment of the federal Department of Labor, and campaign-finance regulations limiting candidate spending.[22] In addition, the House's 1912 Money Trust Investigation was "the first Congressional investigation conducted in the 'grand manner' of modern times, and geared to the avowed purpose of proving and publicizing the need for major legislative enactments in new fields."[23]

Overall, the record of the 62nd Congress became an integral part of the Democratic campaign of 1912. The 1912 Democratic platform condemned Taft's tariff revision vetoes and devoted an entire section to highlighting congressional accomplishments, from liberalized House rules to the 17th Amendment to campaign finance reform to the eight-hour-day bill to the economizing appropriations bills. The Republican platform condemned the tariff revisions, although it also praised the campaign finance bill.[24]

When the 1912 elections were over, not only had Woodrow Wilson been swept into the presidency but Democrats had strengthened their control of the House and gained outright control of the Senate. The Democratic margin was 291–127 (with 17 Progressives) in the House and 51–44 (with one Progressive) in the Senate. The destruction of the Republican old guard, begun in 1910, was completed in 1912.[25]

1918 and the Return to Normalcy

Woodrow Wilson's New Freedom program received enthusiastic support from the Democratic majorities attained in 1912. In the midterm elections of 1914, Democrats lost fifty-nine House seats but held on to their majority and actually gained five seats in the Senate. In 1916, when Wilson narrowly won reelection, Democrats lost their House majority but maintained a plurality; they held effective control and organized the chamber through their alliance with Progressives and progressive Republicans. Thus, after eight years of progressive congressional control and six years of the Wilson presidency, the midterm elections of 1918 loomed large. The progressive wave, already slowed by the American entry into World War I, hung in the balance. Indeed, the very direction of America in the postwar world, both at home and abroad, would be shaped by the next Congress and the president who would be elected in 1920.

Coming as it did in the midst of war, the campaign of 1918 had the potential to be a highly charged affair. Democrats well understood the stakes involved, and the Taft and Roosevelt forces on the Republican side had reconciled. In a Wisconsin vacancy election held in April 1918, Wilson intimated that the Republican candidate was unpatriotic; he won anyway. As the larger campaign progressed, Democrats charged that a Republican Congress "would be a source of comfort to the Kaiser."[26] At the same time, Wilson conducted a largely successful purge of antiwar Bryanite Democrats.[27] Facing a public backlash, Wilson proclaimed on May 27 that "politics is adjourned."[28] Then, on October 24, in what Democratic leaders later almost universally viewed as an enormous blunder, Wilson again reversed course and issued a statement appealing for a Democratic Congress and arguing that the election was a referendum on his administration and party.[29] Republican leaders responded so quickly, attacking Wilson for divisive partisanship, that in many newspapers their response was printed in the same issue as Wilson's statement.[30]

Meanwhile, Republicans had shifted in late summer from an attack on the administration's prosecution of the war (which began going quite well) to an attack on Wilson's peace terms as enunciated in the Fourteen Points.[31] Henry Cabot Lodge and Theodore Roosevelt led the charge, criticizing Point III, calling for elimination of protective tariffs, and the President's internationalist and "utopian" conception of the League of Nations. "We are not internationalists," Roosevelt said. "We are American nationalists."[32] By October, as Germany staggered, Republicans were calling for unconditional surrender and professed to fear that Wilson would accept a result less than total victory. These "inflamed political passions at home" made it impossible for Wilson to accept when the Germans offered peace on the basis of the Fourteen Points on October 5, 1918.[33] The war dragged on for more than a month before an armistice was finally reached.

Sectionalism also played a major role in the campaign of 1918, with Republicans charging the administration with undue favoritism toward the South. As an overarching theme, Republicans promised "a speedy victory and a return to normal conditions."[34] On November 5, 1918, the Republicans gained nineteen House seats and six Senate seats—modest gains for midterm elections of the time. However, those gains were sufficient to take control of both chambers. Furthermore, Democratic losses were heaviest in the Midwest, the stronghold of Republican isolationism, meaning that the president's opposition was almost certainly more ideologically hostile after 1918. Because Wilson had staked his prestige on the outcome, Republicans could (and did) interpret the results as a mandate.[35] Furthermore, subsequent analysis has indicated that the 1918 election was "pivotal" in the post-1916 swing of the electorate back toward the Republicans.[36] Republicans did not lose control of either house of Congress again until 1930. Both Republicans and, to a lesser extent, Democrats gained fresh leadership: Democrat Al Smith was elected governor of New York, while Calvin Coolidge was elected the Republican governor of Massachusetts.

Numerous causes were cited for the Republican victory, including the success of Republican campaign appeals regarding the peace settlement, reconversion, and the South; superior Republican organization; Wilson's ill-advised October appeal; splits in the Democratic Party; poor Democratic turnout; and poor Democratic congressional leadership.[37] Altogether, "for all its narrowness and ambiguity, the outcome of the 1918 elections had major consequences."[38] The tide of progressivism was fully halted and the Wilson Administration emasculated. Furthermore, Herbert Hoover, who took the unusual step of backing Wilson's appeal for a Democratic Congress in 1918, later argued that the election results "damaged the confidence of the Allied statesmen in the President's ability to speak for the American people and the Congress."[39] They were right; ultimately, Wilsonian plans for a postwar international order were killed.

Domestically, the 66th Congress was characterized by "a desperate struggle marked by obtrusive partisanship on the part of the House of Representatives . . . a period almost barren of constructive legislation and administrative achievements."[40] House Democrats were led by Champ Clark, "never a strong leader" who "was nearly seventy and would himself be defeated for reelection to the 67th Congress."[41] Congress conducted bitter investigations of the administration's conduct of the war. Congressional productivity actually rose, but Congress ignored Wilson's most important legislative recommendations, including proposals for a budget system, simplification of income and profits taxes, assistance for returning soldiers and sailors, and efforts to gain greater commercial access to world markets. Wilson, who had vetoed only six measures of the 65th Congress, cast twenty-eight vetoes in the 66th Congress. The number of attempted overrides rose from three, all unsuccessful, to ten, of which four were successful.

The Republican Congress also made a major move in the direction of "normalcy," an idea promoted by a variety of names in the 1918 campaign and declared central by Sen. Warren G. Harding several months before he received the 1920 GOP presidential nomination. As Harding proclaimed in a May 1920 speech in Boston, America needed "not heroism but healing, not nostrums but normalcy, not revolution but restoration, not agitation but adjustment, not surgery but serenity, not the dramatic but the dispassionate, not experiment but equipoise, not submergence in internationality but sustainment in triumphant nationality."[42] Accordingly, "one by one, Congress abolished or diminished powers over the economy that the government had assumed during the war."[43] The 66th Congress repealed over sixty wartime laws, thus substantially curtailing the power of the presidency and restoring the nation to a footing more appropriate for peacetime.

In the Senate, Henry Cabot Lodge became both Senate Majority Leader and chairman of the Senate Foreign Relations Committee. The campaign of 1918 had already laid the groundwork for an attack on the president's peace plan. It was in this context that the battle over the Treaty of Versailles and the League of Nations was conducted. This battle was the pivotal political event of 1919 through 1920, and Woodrow Wilson lost. In retrospect, "the transfer of power to his enemies left Wilson in a hopeless position."[44] Three forces were in play: Wilson and most of the Democrats, backing the League; Lodge, seeking either to kill the League or to save it by modifying it to guarantee American sovereignty (historians still debate which is the accurate interpretation); and a group of twelve "irreconcilables," pledged to defeat it at all costs. In this contest, "Lodge was the better politician," understanding the centrality of organization to the task at hand.[45] When Wilson was struck down by stroke—a stroke brought on by a hectic pro-League speaking tour largely made necessary by Republican control of the Senate—the responsibility for piloting the measure devolved to Sen. Gilbert M. Hitchcock of Nebraska, the ranking minority member on the Foreign Relations Committee. It was said of Hitchcock that "no choice could have been more unfortunate," given his evident leadership failings.[46] In the end, Lodge's reservations, Wilson's obstinacy, and Hitchcock's weakness combined to doom the League. Leaving aside the question of Wilson's health, defeat of the League discredited the administration and ended any nascent hopes for a third term effort.

In sum, Republicans in the 66th Congress took full advantage of a leadership gap between Lodge on one hand and Wilson, Clark, and Hitchcock on the other, was obstructionist and confrontational toward the president, and established a legislative record that allowed Republicans to campaign as the restorers of prewar tranquility. Thus, the course of America after World War I was largely set by the 66th Congress: at home, a retreat from activism and wartime regimentation; abroad, a return to isolation. In this sense, the presidential election of 1920, which inaugurated a string of three consecutive Republican victories, merely ratified the return to normalcy that the elections of 1918 had already mandated.

1950 and the Eisenhower Interlude

The midterm elections of 1950 were not notable for large seat swings or a shift in partisan control of Congress. The Republicans gained twenty-nine House seats and six Senate seats—below average House gains and not enough to wrest majority status from the Democrats in either chamber. Nevertheless, 1950 was an important precursor to the Eisenhower era, "a final stage in the erosion of the New Deal majority" which "foreshadowed the Republican return to power in 1952."[47]

The elections of 1950 reduced the Democratic margin to two in the Senate and cut the Democratic House advantage by two-thirds. Indeed, observers noted that Republicans had "taken all but arithmetical control of the United States Senate" due to the large number of sympathetic Southern Democrats.[48] House Democrats had lost only 2 percent of their southern members, but 10 percent from the northeast and 37 percent from the midwest. Outside of the South, Republican Representatives outnumbered Democrats 196 to 126. Thus was established the congressional equilibrium that endured until the midterm elections of 1958. That equilibrium, in which neither party would gain a decisive advantage, was a central factor in the politics of consensus which dominated the 1950s. Along with their congressional gains, Republicans gained six governorships, giving them a 25-to-23 lead over Democrats.

In terms of policy, Harry S. Truman's Fair Deal was proclaimed dead. Contributing to this assessment were conditions surrounding the conduct of the campaign itself. Truman had imprudently predicted a Democratic landslide, magnifying the significance of the relatively modest Republican gains and turning Truman into the greatest loser of the election. Truman had suffered, in the view of *Time*, a "sharp and pointed rebuke."[49] Simultaneously, many Democrats had found it necessary to disassociate themselves from controversial elements of Truman's program, such as socialized medicine, the Brannan farm plan, and repeal of Taft-Hartley.[50] In the view of the *New York Times*, "No good reason remains, in the circumstances, for the President to insist upon his oft-repeated claim that he has a 'mandate from the people' for such measures."[51] While Truman argued that he was a victim of historical inevitability and local circumstances, Republicans claimed a sweeping ideological mandate.[52]

The 1950 elections saw a major effect on leadership in both parties. On the Republican side, Ohio Senator Robert Taft, the number one target of the Truman administration and its labor allies, won a huge reelection victory, positioning him for the presidential nominating race. Governors Thomas Dewey of New York and Earl Warren of California likewise won reelection, while Richard Nixon was elected Senator from California, a victory that propelled him toward the vice-presidential nomination of 1952.

Democrats, conversely, suffered a "series of conspicuous casualties."[53] Senate Majority Leader Scott Lucas of Illinois was defeated by Everett Dirksen (who later became Senate Minority Leader), Senate Majority Whip Francis Myers of Pennsylvania was likewise defeated, and Republicans laid low two major Democratic committee chairmen, Elbert Thomas (Utah) of Labor and Millard Tydings (Maryland) of Armed Services. Lucas was, hence, removed from contention as the Democratic presidential nominee in 1952 and was replaced as Majority Leader by Ernest McFarland of Arizona, who "was not much help to Truman on domestic issues ... [and was] himself in difficulty with his own constituents in 1952."[54] The road was thus opened for Lyndon Johnson to become the Democratic leader in the Senate after 1952. Analysts would later note that "the simultaneous defeat of four such important leaders weakened the power and prestige of the Democrats."[55]

A specific subset of Republican leaders would have a profound impact on the 1952 Republican nomination. New Republican Senator James H. Duff of Pennsylvania was instrumental in pushing the movement to draft Eisenhower.[56] Several of the new governors, such as Dan Thornton of Colorado, also provided important assistance to Eisenhower as individuals.[57] As a group, the newly powerful and newly invigorated Republican Governors Association played a decisive role in Eisenhower's convention victory by taking Eisenhower's side in a crucial credentials dispute only weeks before the convention opened.

Finally, the Republicans in 1950 began developing campaign issues that would be central in 1952. The battle cry "Korea, communism, and corruption" was tested in numerous congressional races in 1950, with a high degree of success. Failure by Truman to prevent the Korean War (and the loss of mainland China to communism) was a widespread issue. The internal security issue intensified with the convictions of Alger Hiss and others and with Truman's September 1950 veto (overridden by Congress) of the McCarran Internal Security Act. Tydings and Lucas both owed their defeats in no small part to their alleged obstruction of internal security efforts. They were beaten by Republicans "who repeated [Sen. Joseph] McCarthy's charges and who were aided by him in their campaigns."[58] And the corruption issue came to the surface with numerous scandals in the Truman administration and with the Kefauver organized crime hearings.

Meanwhile, the issues at the center of the Democratic campaigns, like Truman's medical plan and the Brannan plan, were seemingly discredited when their greatest champions—such as Senators Claude Pepper (Fla.), Frank Graham (N.C.), Elbert Thomas (Utah), Glen Taylor (Idaho), and Senate candidate Albert Loveland (Iowa)—lost in the primaries or general election. The new balance of forces in Congress guaranteed that no new programs could advance very far. Consequently, by 1952 Democrats seemed to be intellectually exhausted and running out of issues.[59]

After 1950, Republicans in the 82nd Congress pushed the "Korea, communism, and corruption" issues as far as they could. Predictions of legislative deadlock largely proved true, as legislative productivity fell considerably from the 81st Congress. According to *Congressional Quarterly*, "the 82nd Congress accomplished very little outside the realm of foreign and military affairs."[60] None of the Fair Deal programs central to the Democratic campaigns of 1948 and 1950 passed. Presidentially supported legislation on universal military training, restrictions on Senate filibustering, Alaska and Hawaii statehood, and federal fair employment practices failed, and the House repealed the twenty-one-day rule requiring automatic discharge of measures from the Rules Committee after twenty-one days. That change, both produced and made meaningful by renewed Republican strength, guaranteed that the conservative coalition in the Rules Committee could bottle up liberal legislation. The capacity of Congress to obstruct Truman's program was so complete that he was forced to back off substantially from his earlier posture; in his 1951 State of the Union message, he "departed radically from the Fair Deal tone of his earlier messages," concentrating almost solely on the war effort in Korea.[61]

Vetoes fell by two-thirds as a proportion of public bills enacted, a deviation from the normal pattern in such cases, perhaps because so few domestic measures of any sort were passed. Qualitatively, however, contention actually grew. Before the 1950 elections, "the Southern Democrats had co-operated with Republicans in limited warfare against the Fair Deal; but in the 82nd Congress the coalition made an all-out attack on the Administration, and conducted more than 130 investigations. Veteran Southern Democrats, who held most of the committee chairmanships, either took

the lead or stood politely aside while the minority brought forth information detrimental to the Administration."[62] Congress assailed Truman's conduct of the Korean War and growing evidence of scandal in the administration. Hearings were held on corruption in the Justice Department and
Bureau of Internal Revenue, while another set of hearings gave a platform
to fired General Douglas MacArthur. Extensive and often bitter investigations were also conducted regarding the administration's handling of internal security. McCarthy's influence grew, and his accusations were aimed
ever deeper in the administration. Truman was forced into another highly
visible veto with internal security implications when Congress passed the
McCarran-Walter Immigration and Nationality Act. Altogether, David
Mayhew calculates, Congress conducted five major sets of anti-administration hearings in 1951 through 1952, more than in any other Congress
from 1946 to 1990.[63] When Dwight Eisenhower received the Republican
nomination in 1952, congressional Republicans and rebellious conservative Democrats had already laid the groundwork for the campaign to dis-
lodge the liberal Democrats from national power.

1958 and the Coming of the New Frontier–Great Society

As 1910 had foreshadowed the era of Wilsonian progressivism and 1930
had foreshadowed the New Deal, the midterm elections of 1958 served as
the first wave of the coming of Lyndon Johnson's Great Society. After six
years of Dwight D. Eisenhower, the nation was at peace and had not slipped
back, as many had feared, into a postwar depression. Yet America in 1957
and 1958 had experienced the worst recession since the 1930s, with industrial manufacturing falling 25 percent and unemployment rising sharply.
Several other factors militated against the midterm success that some Republicans had predicted in 1957. The Soviets launched Sputnik, reopening
the question of American vulnerability in the Cold War; farm discontent
was on the rise; the modest gains Republicans had made in the South were
threatened by Eisenhower's firmness in the Little Rock desegregation crisis; and top presidential adviser Sherman Adams was forced to resign in
1958 due to scandal. Republican candidates also miscalculated public sentiment, attaching themselves closely to right-to-work initiatives in six states,
including Ohio and California.

Eisenhower, largely preoccupied with foreign affairs, did little to help
Republicans on the campaign trail; "when party candidates reached for his
coattails, they found no sign of a bold 'new Eisenhower'" that had been
promised.[64] To the extent that he took an active interest in the campaign,

he sought in a handful of televised addresses to turn the elections into a referendum on the "deficit-producing, inflation-inviting, irresponsible spending proposals of self-described liberal Democrats in the Congress."[65] As Ike argued, "only sturdy Republican resistance in Congress and my vetoes blocked over $5 billion of this spending."[66] Democrats, for their part, attacked the administration's management of the economy and national security and rode on the back of organized labor, which proved to be a crucial force in numerous races. In January 1958, in preparation for the upcoming campaign, Senate Majority Leader Lyndon Johnson gave his own State of the Union address before Eisenhower's address, calling for federal construction projects to alleviate unemployment and prime the economic pump.[67]

On election day, Republicans lost forty-eight House seats, thirteen Senate seats, seven governorships, and 686 state legislative seats. The Democratic majority in both the House and Senate was so large that only a handful of Republican defectors were required to override a presidential veto. The national House Republican vote fell to 43.7 percent. Democrats even won in Maine, where Edmund Muskie became Senator, and Vermont, where no Democrat had held a House seat for 116 years. Of seats they had previously held, Democrats lost only one district in the House and no seats in the Senate. A Republican National Committee study later concluded that of forty-nine districts where Republicans were ousted, unemployment was particularly high in thirty-eight.[68] All in all, "the Republicans suffered a disastrous defeat, second only to the debacle of 1936."[69]

Eisenhower blamed the disaster on a late campaign start by Republicans, defensively claimed that the results should not be read as a repudiation of the administration, and, in essence, accused voters of having been confused.[70] Rather generously, Democratic leaders went no further than arguing that voters wanted greater balance.[71] The media were not so kind. "If one generalization can be drawn from the election, it is that there has been a leftward swing," the *New York Times* opined. Democrats in 1958 capitalized on "the recession issue, the unemployment issue, the high cost of living issue, the 'right to work' issue, the foreign policy issue, and—possibly above all—on the Administration leadership issue."[72]

Despite the overwhelming magnitude of the Democratic victory, the immediate results fell short of the expectations (or fears) of analysts. In short, "the 86th Congress failed to produce the type of pro-labor, liberal legislation for which many observers had seen a mandate in the 1958 election returns."[73] The Republican–Southern Democrat alliance was weakened but still formidable. As a consequence, the most important piece of legislation to come out of the 86th Congress was the Landrum-Griffin Act, a labor bill opposed by the unions. By the end of the 1959 session, Eisenhower had won approximately twenty major legislative victories and had sustained no clear defeats.[74] When Democrats tried to use their numerical advantage to stake out a campaign position after the national party conventions of 1960, the effort failed miserably.

Nevertheless, the 86th Congress took small but important steps to establish a foundation for victory in 1960. The day after the election, Senate Majority Leader Lyndon Johnson announced a twelve-point legislative agenda that was largely at odds with the stated agenda of the administration. Eisenhower's vetoes increased slightly as a proportion of public bills enacted, the number of override attempts (and successes) grew considerably, and the Senate took a highly confrontational approach to confirmation of at least two of Eisenhower's appointments. Rejection of Lewis Strauss as Secretary of Commerce represented the first senatorial rejection of a presidential cabinet appointee since 1925.[75] Congressional productivity fell by one-fifth, and only 36 percent of the 411 proposals submitted by Eisenhower to the 86th Congress were enacted.[76] Out of the ranks of the bolstered Democratic Senate majority came four serious presidential contenders in 1960: John F. Kennedy, Lyndon B. Johnson, Stuart Symington, and Hubert Humphrey. At the same time, former Republican Senator William Knowland was knocked out of the presidential running by a defeat in his California gubernatorial bid.

The extension of Social Security to cover health care for the aged—the Forand Bill—became a major issue. The Democratic Advisory Council, consisting of the party's leaders outside of Congress, endorsed the proposal one month after the 1958 elections. Most northern and western Democrats, whose ranks had been so expanded in 1958, also supported the proposal. Scattered evidence indicates that the key shift in public opinion on Medicare occurred just after 1958.[77] And John F. Kennedy was one of the strongest supporters in the Senate of the Forand Bill, a fact which aided him in his quest for the presidency.

A second issue, national security policy, was also developed by Democrats in the 86th Congress. With the Sputnik launch of 1957, Democrats had accelerated their attacks on the administration for the supposed missile gap. The 86th Congress took up this call even more wholeheartedly. In 1960, Congress defied Eisenhower and added $600 million to the defense budget, emphasizing that "the area in which the President and Congress disagreed most violently was military policy."[78] After having supported Eisenhower on almost 70 percent of roll calls regarding defense in 1958,

House Democrats gave him only 32 percent support on defense issues in 1959. In 1960, that figure collapsed to zero.[79] Defense would become the first item in the 1960 Democratic platform.

Furthermore, the overall fiscal policy of the 86th Congress laid the groundwork for the New Frontier–Great Society. While disagreement over military policy may have been the most vehement feature of presidential-congressional relations, disagreement over spending was the most consistent. Congressional Democrats sought an additional $100 million for veterans' housing loans, $75 million for temporary unemployment compensation, $840 million for water pollution control, $565 million for an overall housing bill, and millions for school construction, centers for the elderly, and the Bureau of Reclamation. In 1960, a $750-million federal pay raise was passed over Eisenhower's veto, a veto that had been used successfully on many of the above projects. Congress also vigorously took up the issue of area redevelopment. Overall, Eisenhower calculated that the House had sought to add $1.26 billion and the Senate $1.86 billion to his budget proposals in 1959 alone.[80] In a time of recession and public unease with the status quo, such congressional action helped define the parties in a way that contributed to the Democratic message and victory of 1960.[81]

In a more thematic sense, Democratic victory in 1960 depended upon a promise to "get America moving again." Indeed, during 1960, congressional liberals "found a new issue—that of the need for a rapid rate of growth in the national economy—on which to base their call for increased social welfare legislation."[82] This theme was developed too late in 1960 to contribute to the legislative record of the 86th Congress, but it did much—combined with memories of the 1957–58 downturn—to elect Kennedy in November. Before the recession, Democrats and Republicans were rated roughly evenly on their ability to produce prosperity; not only did the recession, as one might expect, give the Democrats a large advantage (25 points) on that question, but the Republicans did not regain lost ground once the recession subsided.[83] Regarding both themes and more specific issues, political scientist James Sundquist noted that during Eisenhower's second term, a period dominated by the 1958 campaign and 86th Congress, "the party division became increasingly sharp and clear."[84]

Since partisan control did not change in 1958, one must look more deeply at questions of the size and composition of that majority and other more subtle effects, all of which "would reverberate across the political landscape for generations."[85] Most importantly, the election of 1958 swept into power a large and substantially unified class of Democrats. While important in the House, this shift was particularly crucial in the Senate, where

Democrats gained thirteen seats. The list of Democrats replacing Republicans in the Senate "reads like a 'who's who' of the Democratic coalition that would dominate the Senate for two decades," including Philip Hart of Michigan, Eugene McCarthy of Minnesota, and Thomas J. Dodd of Connecticut.[86] The Great Society surely owed much to the congressional sweep of 1964, but 1958 was also pivotal. Since 1950, the two parties had been locked in a tight struggle for control, with neither party holding a majority of more than thirty-five in the House or two in the Senate. The elections of 1958 demolished this equilibrium for the next decade. The 86th Congress saw the Democratic margin jump to 130 in the House and 30 in the Senate. At no time from 1958 until the midterm elections of 1966 did the Democratic margin fall below sixty in the House or thirty in the Senate. In the words of political analyst Rhodes Cook, "Democrats were able to live off the margin [won in 1958] for a generation"[87] (table 4.1).

While Republican losses were widely distributed between the two wings of the party (northeast and Midwest), almost all of the new Democrats were northern and western liberals, who began (as they did after 1932 and 1934) to significantly outweigh their southern brethren. All Democratic Senate gains and forty-seven of forty-eight House gains took place outside of the South. By some estimates, the party gained twenty-two seats from factory districts, greatly enhancing the lobbying power of the AFL-CIO, and fifteen from farm districts, whose representatives often gave support for other liberal programs in exchange for bountiful farm programs. Altogether, the shifting composition of the Democratic Party in Congress after 1958 made possible the move to the left that culminated in the Great Society.[88] In both House and Senate, victories by the conservative coalition declined in the 86th Congress.[89] Democratic liberals, having taken a large step toward seizing the upper hand, were energized beyond their numbers. As an outgrowth of the liberal momentum of 1958, the House Democratic

Table 4.1 Congressional Equilibrium, 1950–1958

Congress	Elected	Margin House/Senate
82nd	1950	D 35/2
83rd	1952	R 10/1
84th	1954	D 29/1
85th	1956	D 33/2
86th	1958	D 130/30

Source: Data from *Guide to U.S. Elections* (Washington, D.C.: Congressional Quarterly, 1975), 928.

Study Group (DSG) was formed in 1959 by liberal Democrats who wanted a vehicle to organize and promote their legislative priorities. Within three years, the DSG would play a major role in expanding the size of the House Rules Committee to prevent blockage of President Kennedy's program, and in 1965 the DSG spearheaded a successful attempt to strip two southern Democrats of seniority after they supported Barry Goldwater.[90]

Consequently, the 1958 elections had a profound impact on later civil rights policy and on the relative position of the two parties regarding civil rights. As Edward G. Carmines and James A. Stimson have pointed out, before 1958 Republican senators as a group were more liberal on race matters than Democrats; 1958 was a crucial turning point in the process of reversing that alignment. Ten of the eleven Republican Senators who lost to Democrats in 1958 were racial liberals, and all eleven of the Democratic victors were. As Carmines and Stimson said, the 1958 elections "must have been an important precondition in the struggle for control of the Democratic party that soon followed in the early 1960s."[91]

Liberals were also emboldened by the very terms over which the 1958 elections were fought out. It was Eisenhower who chose to make government spending a key issue and who made the "radical spenders" presidential target number one. In so doing, he guaranteed that the election results could be interpreted as a mandate for liberalism rather than just a protest against recession. This, of course, was neither the first nor last time that a president would contribute to the political momentum of his opponents by declaring the midterm elections to be a referendum.

Finally, the elections of 1958 contributed to splits in the Republican Party in numerous ways. Eisenhower's party leadership was called into question directly, and Republican National Committee (RNC) Chairman Meade Alcorn resigned. The repudiation at the polls led to a revolt by House Republicans against Minority Leader Joseph Martin; Charles Halleck of Indiana took Martin's place with the support of Gerald Ford and other young turks of the day. And the election results brought to the fore a rising philosophical split in the party between conservatives and liberals: the only two bright spots for the Republicans in 1958 were the reelection of Sen. Barry M. Goldwater in Arizona and the landslide election of Nelson A. Rockefeller as governor of New York. Six years later, the conservative icon Goldwater and the liberal standard-bearer Rockefeller would be the prime antagonists in a bloody nomination fight.[92]

The Martin-Halleck split was primarily tactical rather than philosophical in nature, and Republicans improved their position with the switch. Because of Halleck and new Senate Minority Leader Everett Dirksen, the

Republican congressional leadership was a match for their Democratic counterpart. The *New Republic* went so far as to argue in 1959 that "the dominant figure in the House was not [Speaker] Rayburn but Minority Leader Halleck,"[93] perhaps helping to explain why the expanded Democratic majorities did not immediately live up to expectations. Nevertheless, the split that produced the leadership switch was damaging, at least in the short run, and was dramatic evidence of the pressure placed on Republicans by 1958.

1966 and the Coming of the Republican Era

Eight years after the debacle of 1958 and only two years after the debacle of 1964, Republicans won gains in the midterm election of 1966 that ended the Great Society period and foretold the period of Republican presidential ascendancy which started in 1968. As in 1950, the congressional minority remained the congressional minority despite making significant gains. The opposition's ability to either embarrass the president or to establish a positive record of its own was therefore limited. Nevertheless, the elections of 1966 can fairly be said to have ended the Great Society era of activism and to have rejuvenated Republican presidential prospects in 1968. Republicans would go on to win five of the following six presidential elections.

Flush from the landslide of 1964 and the legislative triumphs of the Great Society, Lyndon Johnson looked forward to the onset of a period of consensus politics. By late 1966, however, the Johnsonian "consensus" was increasingly in trouble. Race riots had stirred predictions of a white backlash, the counterculture was beginning to surge to the surface, inflation was accelerating, public unease was growing about both the Great Society and the war in Vietnam, and Americans were beginning to find Johnson's autocratic personality irritating. Johnson's approval ratings fell from 66 percent in November 1965 to 44 percent in October 1966, and public support for the president's handling of a variety of issues including Vietnam, the economy, civil rights, the war on poverty, and taxes each fell by 19 to 27 percentage points.[94] Not least, Johnson had overseen a decimation of the Democratic Party machinery since 1964, having dismantled the central voter-registration drive, cut manpower at the Democratic National Committee (DNC) by 50 percent, and ended systematic communication with state party leaders.[95]

In the end, only two years after many pundits had declared them dead, Republicans made an extraordinary comeback at the polls, leading many of the same pundits to declare that "the Republican party reasserted itself as a major force in American politics."[96] Republicans gained forty-seven House seats, three Senate seats, eight governorships, and 557 state legislative seats. Republican governors controlled twenty-five states, the most since the early 1950s, and numerous analysts credited a large part of the House gains to candidates riding coattails of popular Republican gubernatorial candidates in California, Ohio, and Michigan.[97] The Republican share of the House vote (48.7 percent) was its highest since 1956, and Republicans actually won a majority of the national Senate vote. Only three high-level Republican incumbents seeking reelection were defeated (two governors and a Representative). Of forty-eight pro-Johnson freshmen House members elected in 1964, only twenty-one survived; altogether, Democrats held on to only fourteen of the thirty-eight districts they had wrested from Republicans two years earlier.[98] Ominously for Johnson, Democrats suffered proportionately much lower losses in the South than in any other region. In short, "in the space of a single autumn day . . . the 1,000 day reign of Lyndon I came to an end: The Emperor of American politics became just a President again."[99]

While Johnson blamed a combination of historical inevitability, local circumstances, and vague national discontent, Republicans asserted that the election results represented an anti-administration mandate and a desire on the part of voters for centrism and greater balance. House Minority Leader Gerald Ford declared, "I view this election as a repudiation of the President's domestic policies" and predicted that "it's going to be rough going for him around here. Congress will write the laws, not the executive branch."[100] Both the media and Johnson's fellow Democrats seconded the Republican version of events. The New York Times trumpeted that "the Republican Party has achieved a decisive national victory . . . the extent of the Republican gains and their almost uniform character across the country can only be interpreted as a serious setback for [the President]. The nation has, in effect, flashed a 'Caution—Go Slow' signal to the Johnson Administration."[101] Democratic interpretations of defeat also bolstered the new Republican confidence. California Governor Pat Brown's explanation was not atypical: "People think there's too much government. Maybe they feel Lyndon Johnson has given them too much. People can only accept so much and then they regurgitate."[102] Other Democrats in and out of Congress widely interpreted the 1966 elections as a repudiation of Johnson or a signal to slow down on civil rights and the Great Society.[103]

Republican gains more than wiped out the Johnson coattails of 1964 and "gave the opposition an effective veto against the President's grander legislative designs."[104] Furthermore, many of the Southern Democrats had survived by distancing themselves from Johnson, or even running against him. All seven Southern Democratic House incumbents who lost had been relatively pro-Johnson.[105] The electoral rebuke to Johnson also brought to the surface congressional resentments that crossed party lines; institutionally, many were prepared to take a stand against what they perceived as excesses of executive authority.[106] The President's friends and critics alike predicted an anti-LBJ Congress. As House Minority Whip Les Arends put it, "We have de facto control of Congress. The Democrats have de jure control. And that's the way we like it. The Democrats will have the responsibility. We will have the power."[107] If the post-1966 Republican–Southern Democrat bloc had been equally large before 1966, it could have stopped numerous Great Society measures.[108] The success rate of the conservative coalition doubled in the House and increased by half in the Senate in the 90th Congress.[109] Furthermore, the new House Republican leadership that resulted from a post-1964 revolt was strong and confident; the Democratic leaders, John McCormack and Carl Albert, were "uninspired and tired."[110]

The changed complexion of the 90th Congress did indeed stop or seriously slow the Great Society. Only days after the November 1966 elections, Lyndon Johnson said he would propose fewer measures and that he would seek to fund most existing programs at levels below their authorization. Congress in 1967 was characterized by stalemate, in which antipoverty budgets were cut, sometimes significantly, and only the Vietnam appropriation emerged completely unscathed. The administration's Social Security and antipoverty bills ultimately passed but only after the imposition of welfare restrictions and budget cuts. In 1968, a civil rights open housing bill passed to the surprise of many, and new housing programs were passed, but only after Republicans added provisions placing a new emphasis on private sector involvement. The administration's surtax also finally passed, but only after Johnson agreed to a $6-billion spending reduction and a ceiling on the number of federal employees, both of which he had previously opposed.[111] Otherwise, few new initiatives passed. Johnson was forced to concentrate on defending the programs he had already obtained. Congressional productivity fell, although vetoes did not rise—perhaps because the Republican–Southern Democrat alliance was stronger on the defense than on the offense.

Republicans were able to put forward ideas that were later embraced by Richard Nixon and helped define a positive, proactive Republican approach to problem solving. House Minority Leader Gerald Ford and Senate Minority Leader Everett Dirksen took a page from Johnson in 1960 by delivering an alternative State of the Union address, one of the main features of which was an emphasis on governmental decentralization.[112] With the blessing of the Republican leadership, Rep. Melvin Laird (R-Wisc.) proposed the program that later passed as general revenue sharing during the Nixon administration. The crime bill of 1968 was also notable in that Republicans were able to insert, for the first time in major legislation, a block grant proposal.[113] These proposals were tied together by the general theme of decentralization and states' rights elucidated by Ford and Dirksen, a theme that was important two years later and continues to reverberate three decades later. In that sense, the 90th Congress represented the first halting step away from the hypercentralization of the Great Society years. Johnson's nomination of Abe Fortas as Chief Justice of the Supreme Court was also killed in the 90th Congress, allowing Richard Nixon to appoint the Chief Justice and altering American jurisprudence. The Fortas controversy, not incidentally, also focused attention on the issue of liberal justices, another issue Nixon would use to great effect in 1968 and 1972.

The nature of the 90th Congress was not, however, at the center of why 1966 was so important. The election of 1966 broadly revitalized the Republican Party and established a solid nationwide foundation for the 1968 campaign and the Republican dominance at the presidential level for the next twenty years. It also had the effect of specifically helping future Republican leaders.

The 1966 Republican sweep not only changed the numbers but changed the mentality of Republicans toward 1968 and the image of Republicans held by voters. Republicans were able, for the first time in a decade, to say and to believe that the tide was moving in their direction. As *Time* put it, Johnson appeared "decidedly vulnerable," and the GOP had a "vastly improved outlook and buoyant spirits."[114] According to Stephen Hess and David Broder, "their 1966 successes had persuaded party members at all levels that the presidency could be won ... The mere expectation of victory in itself altered the whole psychological climate of internal Republican politics."[115]

As contemporary observers noted, the image of the party was immediately rehabilitated. A number of attractive new leaders gained power, including Gov. Ronald Reagan in California, Gov. Spiro Agnew in Maryland, Sen. Howard Baker in Tennessee, Sen. Charles Percy in Illinois, Sen. Mark Hatfield in Oregon, and the first black Senator since Reconstruction, Edward Brooke of Massachusetts. Simultaneously, Nelson Rockefeller was reelected governor of New York, and other Republican leaders were reelected handily, such as Gov. Rhodes of Ohio, Gov. Romney of Michigan,

Gov. Evans of Washington, and Sen. John Tower of Texas. As Hess and Broder remarked, "Suddenly, a party that had been bereft of leadership appeared to have a wealth of candidates from which to select its 1968 presidential nominee."[116] These figures spanned the ideological spectrum within the Republican Party, presenting the picture of a broadly based party.

Furthermore, the twenty-five Republican governors after 1966 sat in states with a large majority of the American population, including seven of the ten most populous states. Nationally, the Republican Party made gains in voters' party identification for the first time in twenty years. Much progress was made in restoring the Republican bastion in the Midwest, where nearly half of the House gains were made (twenty-two of forty-seven). Most Republican gubernatorial gains were recorded in the West (five of eight). And in the South, Republicans gained eight House seats and two governorships (Arkansas and Florida), almost winning a third (Georgia). Additionally, three Republican senators were elected or reelected in the South (Tennessee, Texas, and South Carolina). Of the sixteen contested districts where Republicans gained over twenty percentage points from 1962 to 1966, twelve were in Southern or border states, as were all sixteen Democratic districts that were uncontested in 1962 but saw Republican candidates receive more than 20 percent in 1966.[117] Contemporary observers contended that the GOP "went a long way" toward changing a "toe hold" in the South into a "firm foothold."[118] The Republican congressional strength gained in 1966 would remain stable for almost three decades, at about one-third of all Southern House members, until another spurt in 1994.[119]

Republicans in 1966 also made major inroads into the cities, particularly among ethnic blue-collar voters. These were the voters whom George Wallace had targeted in the northern primaries in 1964 and many of whom he would win as an independent candidate in 1968. After flirting with Wallace in 1964, they left the Democratic reservation for good in 1966.[120] In Chicago, for example, these voters deserted the Democrats en masse and were primarily responsible for Charles Percy's Senate victory over Paul Douglas. Analysts would later suggest that the Percy-Douglas race "marked the emergence of what would become known in the 1980s as the 'Reagan Democrat.'"[121] Thus, both geographically and demographically, Republicans in 1966 effectively put into practice much of the Goldwater Sunbelt strategy and set the stage for the Nixonian reiteration of that strategy in 1968. It was that coalition—Midwest, West, and South, bolstered by a growing share of blue-collar ethnics—that won not only that election but five of the next six.

Four of those five victories were won by two men, Richard Nixon and Ronald Reagan, who owed their success to 1966. The fifth was won by

George Bush, who entered the national political scene by winning a House seat in Texas in 1966 and later won the presidency on Reagan's coattails. Nixon had not even been on the ballot in 1966 but was strengthened immeasurably by the campaign. Nixon served as the chief Republican strategist and most energetic national campaigner. In so doing, he collected important IOUs from state and local party leaders and candidates: fifty-eight candidates, about two-thirds of those for whom he campaigned, won—a higher percentage than that recorded by any major political figure on either side.[122] He also rehabilitated his image as a winner and gained new respect by accurately predicting the 1966 results six months earlier.[123] Perhaps most importantly, Nixon was simultaneously inflated and martyred by the president of the United States when Johnson, only days before the election, launched a stinging attack on him as a "chronic campaigner" who was endangering American lives by criticizing the administration's Vietnam policy.[124] In response, the Republican Congressional Campaign Committee gave Nixon thirty minutes of network time it had reserved. Nixon later credited the broadcast for having "renewed my credentials as a national spokesman and a fighting campaigner. It also served to identify me with the Republican victory that now seemed certain in the election two days hence." When that victory was confirmed, Nixon declared it "an auspicious start" on the road to the White House. "It was gratifying," Nixon said, "to know that I had played a major part in this Republican victory— a prerequisite for my own comeback."[125]

For his part, Reagan, against expectations, won the governorship of California by over 1 million votes against incumbent Democrat Pat Brown. He supplanted Barry Goldwater as the hero of the conservatives, who immediately began touting him as presidential material. The significance of Reagan's win was largely overlooked at the time; more attention was paid to the up-and-coming moderates like Romney, Percy, and Hatfield. Yet, as Michael Barone would later note, Reagan's victory

> turned out to be a harbinger of American politics to come. . . . Reagan showed, in a state which contained one out of every ten Americans, that the old rule that conservative Republicans could not win in large industrial states was obsolete. He showed, even as Lyndon Johnson was seeking an ever bigger Great Society, that there was a demand in the political marketplace for a politician who would limit the growth of government. And he showed, even as Democrats were dabbling with theories about empowering the poor and speculating that they too would riot or commit crimes if they were victims of racial discrimination, that there was great

electoral power in the culturally conservative response of ordinary voters who wanted to see traditional American values honored and traditional American patterns of life followed.[126]

While Reagan's influence did not reach full flower until the 1980s, it was beginning to be felt as early as 1968. A halting campaign for the Republican nomination failed, but it forced Nixon to the right on a variety of issues. It is likely that Nixon owed his nomination to Barry Goldwater and Strom Thurmond, who held most of the South in line against the Reagan temptation. Over the long term, Reagan remade the image of conservatism, possessing, as Theodore H. White would later say, "all the Goldwater virtues and none of his flaws."[127] Thirty years later, the impact of Ronald Reagan on American politics had not subsided.

1978 and the Reagan Revolution

While 1966 went far toward setting the stage for Republican successes for the next twenty years, a subsidiary role was played by the midterm election of 1978, halfway through Jimmy Carter's presidency. Republican congressional gains were far below average—fifteen House seats and three Senate seats, leaving them well short of a majority. The GOP gained six governorships (including the important states of Texas and Pennsylvania) and controlled five of the seven most populous states, but Republicans were still outnumbered 32–18. There were widely mixed results in every region, leading the *New York Times* to call the results "as miscellaneous as any election in recent memory."[128] Yet the campaign and the election results had embedded within them a wide range of portentous consequences, many of which became clear only years later.

To many observers, the relatively low Democratic losses indicated that the Israeli-Egyptian Camp David II agreement of September 1978 had "brought the administration back from the edge of disaster."[129] However, the 1978 elections, despite the meager Republican gains, boosted Republican morale at a crucial time following Watergate, the election debacle of 1974, and the presidential loss of 1976. More tangibly, the 1978 elections gave the Republicans the opportunity to rebuild their party at the grassroots level. They gained about 300 state legislative seats, a crucial asset for candidate recruitment in higher-level races. Consequently, Republicans nearly tripled the number of states in which they controlled both legislative chambers from five to thirteen; they also held a majority in one house in eleven other states. As an added benefit of gains at the state level, Republicans believed they had obtained "gerrymandering insurance" for the upcoming redistricting process, a fact that RNC Chairman Bill Brock considered particularly significant.[130] While Republicans, themselves, complained throughout the 1980s that they had been treated unfairly in the redistricting process, there is little academic evidence to support that claim; the gerrymander insurance that they claimed in 1978 was probably more effective than they were later willing to admit.[131]

Furthermore, Republicans claimed an ideological mandate on the basis of numerous factors.[132] Nationally, 1978 marked the beginning of the nationwide tax revolt and the interjection of tax cuts into the national political debate. In June 1978, Proposition 13 passed overwhelmingly in California. Although a few Prop-13 imitations lost in statewide votes in November, twelve of sixteen tax and spending limitation initiatives succeeded. Indeed, the *New York Times* concluded that the only clear trend of the 1978 election was that the tax revolt was proven to be an "enduring national force."[133]

The tax issue was also interjected directly into the congressional elections, with debate centering on the Kemp-Roth proposal to cut personal income tax rates by one-third. Days before the 1978 election, the Steiger Amendment cutting capital gains taxes was adopted by Congress. Kemp-Roth put additional tax-cutting pressure on Democrats, and their response was evidence of the potential power of the proposal. That response consisted, by and large, not of condemnation but of co-optation and imitation. The Nunn Amendment was proposed in the Senate as an alternative, cutting both taxes and spending. Bill Bradley, facing a stiff challenge in New Jersey from supply-side Republican Jeffrey Bell, proposed his own $25-billion tax cut. Under electoral pressure from a tax-weary citizenry, both the House and Senate passed the Nunn amendment in October 1978, but opposition from the White House forced its removal in conference committee. In essence, the fight for significant across-the-board tax relief was waged and won in the crucible of the 1978 campaign; Ronald Reagan benefited from this revolution more than he created it.[134]

Indeed, observers noted at the time the degree to which the low partisan seat turnover masked a radical change in the agenda, a shift to the right that persisted through the 1980s and 1990s. As *Newsweek* argued, "The real message of the election returns was the ratification of a new and no longer partisan agenda for the nation—a consensus on inflation as the priority target and tax-and-spend government as the primary villain . . . [the Republicans'] real triumph was philosophic and often vicarious—the pride of authorship in a new politics in which Democrats talk like Republicans to survive."[135] One White House analyst remarked, "Everybody just collapsed toward the middle—and the middle moved toward the right."[136] Subsequent academic analysis seconded this notion, as scholars pointed out that "all prudent Democrats were careful to adjust their rhetoric and style to the mood of the voters—enabling the Democratic 'sponge' to absorb the Republicans' main issue so successfully."[137] Nearly two decades later, the conditions established in 1978 were still plainly operative, nowhere more so than in the presidency of Bill Clinton.

In more concrete terms, the 96th Congress was "considerably more conservative" than the 95th. Seventy-seven House freshmen swept in, almost all of them committed to tax and spending cuts regardless of party.[138] The "conservative coalition" reappeared in force in 1979, and "the post-Vietnam era came definitively to an end," with defense spending increases and calls for a more assertive anti-Soviet policy.[139] According to observers, the new alignment "laid bare a growing schism among House Democrats and brought out a new unity within the Republican Party."[140] Legislative productivity in the 96th Congress fell, and Congress passed fewer public laws in the year 1979 than in any single year since before the Second World War.[141] Indeed, House Republicans frequently put Democrats on the defensive with increasingly aggressive tactics; throughout 1979, "the House continually teetered on the brink of chaos, and occasionally fell over."[142]

The biggest change occurred in the Senate, however, where five prominent liberal Democrats were defeated, including Dick Clark of Iowa and Thomas McIntyre of New Hampshire. Ten new senators were regarded as more conservative than their predecessors, while only four were regarded as more liberal.[143] Altogether, Republicans won twenty of the thirty-five Senate races, their highest number since 1952. Surviving liberals in both parties moved to the right. Republican Charles Percy publicly repented of his waywardness on election eve; Democrat Frank Church turned hawkish on Cuba in 1979. As one White House staffer predicted about the liberals, "These guys are going to start looking at what happened to Dick Clark and start casting votes for their political futures instead of for what they think is right. And you can hardly blame them. How would you like to be Frank Church or George McGovern in 1980?"[144]

The Senate shift put into immediate jeopardy the ratification of the SALT II arms limitation treaty with the Soviet Union as well as Carter's plans for health reform and other social programs. McIntyre of New Hampshire was expected to be the administration's point man on SALT and was thought to be worth at least three votes. Although Carter pulled SALT II from consideration due to the December 1979 Soviet invasion of Afghanistan, it was already unlikely to be ratified. Overall, the Senate shift, though small in partisan terms, was enough to bring Democrats below the sixty votes needed to stop a filibuster and also to put Republicans within striking range of the majority status that they achieved in 1980. The mini-massacre of Senate liberals in 1978 turned out to be only a portent of the larger massacre of 1980; in retrospect, it is clear that the same trend and same factors were at work in both years.

The Senate majority and other Republican gains in 1980 were also owed to another feature of the 1978 midterm elections—the organizational maturing of the so-called New Right. New Right organizations—both secular and religious—were widely active and successful for the first time in 1978.[145] For example, Paul Weyrich's Committee for the Survival of a Free Congress gave substantial support to twenty-six nonincumbents, sixteen of whom won; lower-level assistance was given to twelve more nonincumbents, eight of whom won.[146]

Finally, the 1978 elections had important implications for the presidential election of 1980. Jimmy Carter would later complain that all of the agitation for tax cuts, which continued well into 1980, "was destroying confidence in the Democrats' ability to maintain a consistent economic policy."[147] Organizationally, David Broder remarked, "Carter now faces a Republican Party with a significantly stronger grass-roots base."[148] In contrast, in 1978 and throughout his presidency, Carter made virtually no effort to cultivate either the grassroots or elite base of his party, preferring to run a presidency that was almost as personalist as his 1976 campaign. Wilson Carey McWilliams argued that "for four years, Carter disdained the party and its organizations. He recognized that party loyalties—and especially, loyalties to party organizations—seemed to be attenuating, and he had no interest in reversing the decline."[149]

Several analysts have pointed to 1978 as a crucial juncture on the road to 1980. Michael Barone points out that Republican successes in 1978 were concentrated in small-town and rural areas, indicating trouble for Carter in 1980. Because of Carter's tacking to the left on the Panama Canal, abortion, and drugs, "the cultural segment of America which was most inclined to see Jimmy Carter as its kind of American had decided he was not; its members felt at the least disappointed, and in some cases betrayed ... the Carter Democrats had, unknowingly, lost their core cultural group, and had nothing to replace it with."[150] For his part, conservative columnist George Will argues that the 1978 midterm election was the point at which the Democratic Party first became clearly identified in the public mind as "the captive of grasping factions" and "a party most comfortable representing social casualties and professional victims."[151]

Yet the 1978 elections also almost certainly forced Jimmy Carter to the right on budget and national security issues; within days of the election, he signed a tax-cut bill he largely disliked and announced plans to increase defense spending and reduce the deficit.[152] This shift by Carter (and by much of the rest of the party) fueled the dissatisfaction of labor and the liberal wing of the party; as one "glum left-Democratic pro" complained to *Newsweek,* the elections represented a "total evaporation of the meaning of party."[153] Thus, 1978 contributed materially to Sen. Edward Kennedy's challenge from the left in 1980, a challenge that did much to damage Carter. Carter was also challenged by Governor Jerry Brown of California, who was a viable contender because he won reelection in 1978 by a margin of 1.3 million votes. For his part, Ronald Reagan campaigned hard for party candidates—as Nixon had done in 1966—and collected important IOUs, not least from Roger Jepsen in the first caucus state of Iowa (which Reagan lost anyway) and Gordon Humphrey in the first primary state of New Hampshire (where he won a crucial victory).[154]

The Weak Cases: 1974 and 1990

Two other midterm elections preceded a party shift in the White House, 1974 and 1990. Neither of these midterm elections had the impact on subsequent elections of the other six discussed above. Consequently, they are included in the normal midterm category (chapter 7) rather than in the preparatory category. Nevertheless, a brief discussion of them is warranted at this point to compare and contrast them with the preparatory midterms.

In 1974, Republicans lost forty-eight House and five Senate seats as well as being decimated at the gubernatorial level. Almost all contemporary accounts, as well as most subsequent academic accounts, held inflation, recession, and Watergate to be the factors driving the severe Republican losses.[155] The 94th Congress that resulted saw a decline in legislative productivity but cannot be said to have produced intensified confrontation with the president. The veto index rose slightly, veto override attempts remained stable (though at a level that was already high), and successful overrides increased; but it is difficult to imagine how the 94th Congress could have been more confrontational than the 93rd, which had drawn up papers of impeachment. An assault on seniority was launched by the reformist freshmen (the Watergate babies), who remained the dominant force in Congress for twenty years. Nevertheless, as Mayhew argued in denying 1974 the status of an innovative midterm, it produced "not much" otherwise.[156]

In 1990, Democrats made small gains of eight in the House and one in the Senate, dashing Republican hopes of a Senate comeback. The Republican disappointment was an early warning sign of the fallout of the Bush tax increase; in that sense, 1990 ended the long period of the saliency of the tax issue, just as 1978 had launched it. The Republican split of 1992 was foreshadowed (and perhaps stimulated) by the open declaration by Ed Rollins, chairman of the National Republican Congressional Committee, that GOP House candidates should not hesitate to publicly distance themselves from George Bush.

The results also had an effect in 1992 on the way that Democratic contenders were helped or hurt; Bill Clinton was helped by another reelection landslide while Bill Bradley and Mario Cuomo were hurt by surprisingly poor showings in their reelection wins. The latter two, of course, ultimately decided against running for president. And, although it was not clear at the time, Republicans positioned themselves well in the redistricting battle by winning the governorships of California and the Rust Belt states and doing unusually well in state legislative elections for a presidential party in a midterm year.

The two years following the 1990 midterm were highly contentious, as vetoes, override attempts, and successful overrides increased and legislative productivity fell. Indeed, George Bush was stymied almost completely. Bush's March 20, 1996, deadline for congressional action on his economic recovery plan was unceremoniously ignored (with no adverse consequences), and the 102nd Congress did such an effective job of stonewalling Bush that Bill Clinton was able to make an issue out of government gridlock. By the end of the 1992 campaign, the option of unified government was more strongly supported in the polls than it had been in many years. The behavior of Congress in this period clearly contributed to Clinton's 1992 victory. Nevertheless, this record of obstruction and confrontation, however important it may have been to 1992, was not significantly influenced by the 1990 elections. There was only a small partisan shift and no major change in the composition of either party in Congress. Democrats failed even to gain the intangible benefits of a perception of momentum, since the media tended to view the election results as a stalemate.

Midterm Elections as Preparation for Change

The significance of the preparatory midterms was surely not solely dependent on later presidential shifts. Many were crucial in their own right. The massive Democratic majorities that were created in 1958 would have been important even had Richard Nixon, rather than John Kennedy, squeaked through in 1960. Nevertheless, without the 1960 shift in presidential control, there would not have been a Great Society as we know it.

It is impossible to determine in advance from any given midterm election outcome what the ultimate consequences will be, except perhaps that the president's life will be made harder. To categorize some midterm elections as preparatory is a retrospective rather than predictive exercise. Nevertheless, the preparatory midterm category does help to illuminate several important probabilities, and the cases are similar enough to each other—and different enough from the average midterm—to represent a meaningful analytical category.

Not all midterm elections preceding shifts in presidential control contributed equally to those shifts. Furthermore, they fell on a continuum from a change in party control of Congress to a bolstered opposition majority to a bolstered opposition minority, with varying degrees and types of influence exerted in each case. Nevertheless, party shifts in presidential control have been significantly influenced by both the preceding midterm election campaign, itself, and the new political situation created by the results of the midterm election. This was true of the two realigning elections and six of the other eight presidential party shifts since 1894.

Composition

Partisan seat changes in the eight preparatory midterms were not uniformly high, and very high seat shifts were clearly not a prerequisite. Nevertheless, there was a clear pattern of very strong compositional change (table 4.2). Five of eight cases saw partisan seat shifts that were above average, and the average seat shift in the preparatory midterms was considerably higher than that of normal midterms (forty-eight House and seven Senate seats compared to thirty-three House and two Senate seats). These partisan seat shifts led to four cases of opposition takeover of one or both houses of Congress.

Furthermore, losses by the president's party and the commensurate gains by the opposition frequently affect party factions disproportionately, through both addition and subtraction. Pro-Cleveland Democrats and pro-Hoover Republicans were the chief victims in 1894 and 1930. In 1910, the composition of the Republican Party shifted significantly in the direction of progressivism. In 1950, and again in 1966, Republican gains were centered in the North (although some important gains were also recorded in the South in 1966), thus shifting the balance within the Democratic Party toward its Southern and more conservative members. The 1958 elections did much to change the composition of both the Republican and Democratic Parties, especially on the question of civil rights: Democrats became

Table 4.2 Compositional Change in Preparatory Midterms

Year	Partisan Seat Shift	Factional Composition Shift	Change in Chamber Control
1894	116/5	Yes	Partisan—H & S
1910	57/10	Yes	Partisan—H
			Ideological—S
1918	19/6	Yes	Partisan— H & S
1930	49/8	Yes	Partisan—H
			Ideological—S
1950	29/6	Yes	Ideological— H & S
1958	48/13	Yes	Ideological—H & S
1966	47/4	Yes	Ideological—H
1978	15/3	Yes	None
Total	47.5/6.9	8/8*	4/8 partisan (50%)
Normal Midterms	33.0/2.4	11/13*	3/13 partisan (23%)

*See table 1.6.

more liberal, while Republicans lost many of their civil rights liberals and became more conservative. Even in 1978, Senate Democrats lost five key liberals, while survivors were driven to the right by public sentiment. In all eight cases, the president's friends were hurt or his enemies helped across party lines. In five cases, changes in the factional composition of Congress placed the president's foes in operational control of one or both houses of Congress even though formal partisan control remained unchanged. These changes in party composition occasionally held significant implications for presidential nominations, as well. The infusion of moderate Republican governors in 1950 was a critical component in Dwight Eisenhower's nomination victory over Robert Taft two years later.

Plebiscitary Impact and Momentum

Intangibly, but not inconsequentially, midterm elections have provided psychological rejuvenation and a measure of momentum for the president's opposition. This was true, at least to some extent, in every case surveyed here. Furthermore, variations in this effect did not depend on the absolute degree of success in the midterm elections. Republicans, for example, were aided considerably by the boosts offered in 1966 and 1978, following the congressional bloodbaths of 1964 and 1974, even though they did not seize control of either house of Congress and in 1978 posted numerically mediocre gains. Even in low turnover years like 1918, 1950, and 1978, the president's partisan opponents claimed an anti-administration or ideological mandate.

During these midterm campaigns, presidents often walked directly into traps that further undermined their claim of popular grounding. Under the pressure of the campaign, Taft appealed for a Republican Congress and waged war against the progressives in 1910, Wilson appealed for a Democratic Congress in 1918, Truman predicted a Democratic landslide in 1950, and Eisenhower deliberately framed the 1958 elections as a referendum on the "radical spenders." In each case, losses in the midterm elections were more easily interpreted as a mandate against the administration and for an alternate course.

Issue Development

Midterm campaigns led to the development of issues that were later put to full use in subsequent presidential elections, like the "return to normal conditions" of 1918, "Korea, communism, and corruption" in 1950, Medicare in 1958, and Kemp- Roth tax cuts in 1978. Those campaigns also played an important role in establishing and solidifying party coalitions for the president's opposition. In the pre-realignment election of 1894, Republicans made substantial inroads among urban laborers, presaging their 1896 victory. Republican gains in 1918 pointed the way to an electoral coalition that lasted another dozen years. Similarly, Democrats bolstered their support among labor and farmers in 1958, support that was crucial in 1960. Republicans, for their part, fashioned the coalition in 1966 that won five of the next six presidential elections. In 1978, they took important steps toward reaffirming that coalition by chipping away at Jimmy Carter's rural and small-town support. These features of preparatory midterm campaigns— the testing of campaign issues and the use of those issues for coalition construction or maintenance—are also important features of the two-year governing phase between the midterm election and the next presidential election.

There is a clear pattern in the eight cases of post-midterm Congresses falling—often as a deliberate strategy—into low legislative productivity (table 4.3). In seven of the eight cases (all but 1918), productivity declined from the previous Congress, often to rise again in the next Congress. (This was also true in the two weak cases that contributed little else to the subsequent party shift). Overall, legislative productivity in the eight Congresses fell by an average of 21 percent, much greater than the average 5-percent decline for all post-midterm Congresses from 1894 through 1996. David Mayhew's study of legislative productivity, focusing not on all public bills but on "important" laws, indicated that the production of major legislation fell in all four of the preparatory Congresses since 1946 by an average

Table 4.3 Legislative Productivity and Vetoes, Preparatory and Preceding Congresses

Congress	Years Elected	Public Bills Enacted	Vetoes	Vetoes/Bills(%)
53rd	1892	463	75	16.2
54th	1894	434	86	19.8
61st	1908	595	13	2.2
62nd	1910	530	26	4.9
65th	1916	405	6	1.5
66th	1918	470	28	6.0
71st	1928	1,009	19	1.9
72nd	1930	516	18	3.5
81st	1948	921	79	8.6
82nd	1950	594	22	2.8
85th	1956	1,009	51	5.1
86th	1958	800	44	5.5
89th	1964	810	14	1.7
90th	1966	640	8	1.2
95th	1976	633	19	3.0
96th	1978	613	12	2.0
Avg. before midterm		730.6	34.5	4.7
Avg. after midterm		574.6	30.5	5.3

Sources: Data from George B. Galloway, *History of the House of Representatives* 2nd ed. (New York: Thomas Y. Crowell Company, 1976), 375-76; Robert Moon and Carol Hardy Vincent, *Workload and Activity Report: United States Senate, 1946-1992* (Washington, D.C.: Congressional Research Service, 1993), 15; *Presidential Vetoes, 1789-1988* (Washington, D.C. : GPO, 1989).

of 35 percent.[157] Deadlock was often the dominant theme, and the president was systematically denied major legislative accomplishments, whether or not his party still controlled Congress.

A pattern of increased contentiousness accompanied the legislative slowdown. The ratio of vetoes to public bills enacted increased in five out of eight cases, and confrontation as measured by veto override attempts and/or successes increased in five cases and declined in only one. On average, the proportion of bills vetoed grew by 13 percent in the preparatory Congresses. House partisanship scores also increased in five of the eight Congresses. When studying vetoes, veto overrides, and partisanship side by side—as alternative measurements of confrontation—we find that seven of the eight post-midterm Congresses demonstrated greater confrontation by at least one measurement, and five showed greater confrontation by two or more measurements. In addition, the 90th Congress, elected in 1966, was judged by almost all contemporary accounts to have been more

Table 4.4 Preparatory Congresses, Alternative Measures of Confrontation

Congress/ Elected	Vetoes/ bills	Veto Overrides	Partisanship
54th/1894	+	+	+
62nd/1910	+	+	-
66th/1918	+	+	+
72nd/1930	+	0	-
82nd/1950	-	-	+
86th/1958	+	+	+
90th/1966	-	0	-
96th/1978	-	+	+

Vetoes/bills= Did the index of vetoes to public bills rise or decline compared to the previous Congress?
Veto overrides= Did the number of veto override attempts and/or successes rise or decline compared to the previous Congress?
Partisanship= Did House partisanship scores rise or decline compared to the previous Congress?

confrontational than its predecessor. It is by no means clear that this qualitative assessment should be ignored (table 4.4).[158]

While the eight Congresses were generally caught up in legislative deadlock and confrontation, which themselves could become issues of presidential ineffectiveness, the out-party was consistently able to identify and develop a handful of other issues which would prove crucial in the next presidential election and often beyond. While some of these issues first appeared in force during the midterm campaign, they often arose during the congressional session, itself. The ability of the out-party to develop issues depended to some extent on whether it attained effective control of Congress, but even parties still in the minority were able to use the momentum and perceived mandate of the midterm election to push an agenda. As discussed in the previous chapter, the 54th Congress developed the realigning currency issue, and the 72nd Congress developed the social welfare issue complex. After 1910, the Democratic House established an important progressive legislative record on which to run, while the post-1918 Republicans developed the idea of normalcy both at home and abroad. After the "Korea, communism, and corruption" campaign of 1950, Republicans in Congress used their augmented strength to drive home those issues in the 82nd Congress. The post-1958 Democrats rode to power in 1960 largely on the issues of Medicare and defense and on the theme of "getting America moving again," which formed an important part of their congressional agenda. The post-1966 Republicans, still stuck in the minority, did not find issue development as easy but were still able to promote ideas of decentralization and judicial restraint which proved important in 1968. After 1978, strengthened Republicans (aided by events) kept tax cuts and national security before the public eye.

It would be a mistake to view too narrowly this tendency of midterm elections to alter the political balance and to affect policy. Aside from the implications for presidential campaigns and long-term party coalition building, the midterm elections surveyed here have been crucial to several periods of national policy. All three eras of twentieth-century federal activism have been bracketed not by presidential elections but by midterm elections. The era of Wilsonian progressivism began not in 1912 but in 1910 and ended not in 1920 but in 1918. The New Deal era began in a very real way in the 72nd Congress elected in 1930, and by most historical accounts it came to a close in 1938 (as we will see in chapter five). And the New Frontier–Great Society era can best be described as being bracketed by the midterm elections of 1958 and 1966. The League of Nations was killed by the midterm elections of 1918, and Harry Truman's Fair Deal was stopped by midterm elections not once but twice, in 1946 and 1950.

Leadership

Another factor often working to the benefit of the out-party was a gap in skilled party leadership. This gap has arguably been present in at least six of the eight cases. During the 54th and 72nd Congresses, the president's party was at a disadvantage in terms of leadership, especially if one factors in the leadership failings of the president, himself. The Republican leadership was in total disarray after 1910, with Taft a failure and congressional leadership rebuked in the 1910 revolt. In the 66th Congress, Henry Cabot Lodge clearly demonstrated superior political leadership skills in the decisive debate over the League of Nations. Republican leadership after 1966 was almost certainly stronger than Democratic, with the tired McCormack and Albert facing a confident Ford and Dirksen, and with Lyndon Johnson increasingly unpopular in his own party, the machinery of which he himself had decimated. And Jimmy Carter, by all accounts, was a weak party leader who, like Johnson, allowed the party to atrophy. In one other case, in the 82nd Congress after 1950, there was no discernible leadership advantage held by either side. Only in one case, the post-1958 leadership of the 86th Congress, was the out-party reportedly at something of a disadvantage, at least in the House. As mentioned in chapter three, leadership failings in the president's party can be important in two ways: substantively, it is more likely that the out-party will be able to successfully exploit its opportunities, and more intangibly, the out-party can present to the nation an image of relatively greater competence.

Furthermore, midterm elections have had an important role in the development of new leadership. This characteristic of midterms is not limited to preparatory elections but can be clearly seen in them. Woodrow Wilson became a prime contender for the presidency when he won the New Jersey governorship in 1910, and Calvin Coolidge gained the spotlight when he was elected governor of Massachusetts in 1918. Franklin Roosevelt was propelled by his landslide reelection of 1930. Richard Nixon was first elected to Congress in the 1946 midterm, gained a spot on the 1952 GOP ticket by winning a Senate seat in California in the 1950 midterm, and later was boosted in the 1966 midterm even though he was not on the ballot. Ronald Reagan and George Bush also owed their electoral entry into the national political scene to 1966. John F. Kennedy won reelection to the U.S. Senate, a necessary launching pad into the presidency, in 1958.

This leadership effect has in many cases taken years to bear full fruit. It has also been important below the level of the presidency. The Democratic class of 1958, for example, dominated the Senate for years. And, unlike most of the consequences of midterm elections discussed so far, the leadership effect has not been unidirectional, aiding only the out-party. Numerous important figures have emerged by swimming against the midterm tide. Al Smith was first elected governor of New York in the Republican year of 1918, Barry Goldwater and Nelson Rockefeller both won crucial elections in the Democratic sweep of 1958, and Bill Clinton was first elected governor of Arkansas in 1978, another Republican year. In short, midterm elections, because they favor the opposition party and because the president is not on the ticket to dominate analysis, are a ready source for the development of attractive new leaders, especially opposition ones. The leadership effect, like other parts of the general pattern described above, does not manifest itself evenly or identically in every crucial election studied.

Party Splits

Midterm election campaigns have often served as a solvent, exacerbating splits in, and otherwise weakening, the president's coalition. This occurred in 1894, when Cleveland and the silver Democrats battled; in 1910, when old guard and progressive Republicans bloodied each other; in 1950, when many Democrats repudiated key elements of the Fair Deal; and in 1966, when Southern Democrats were forced to run against Johnson to survive.

Furthermore, to an extent rivaling the impact of midterm campaigns, post-election changes have contributed to splits in the president's party. This was certainly true in pre-realignment elections, as shown in the previous chapter. It was also true after 1910, when Democrats used their effective control of Congress to exploit Republican splits, and to a lesser extent after 1950, 1966, and 1978, when conservative coalition voting grew. Furthermore, in most of the cases (1978 was an exception), the president's competence as party leader was questioned within his own party as a result of the election results, and in at least four cases the new political circumstances encouraged or provoked primary opposition to the president. In 1910 the insurgents were emboldened, in 1950 and 1966 Truman's and Johnson's prestige suffered considerably, and in 1978 Carter was forced to the right, making the Kennedy challenge more likely and more powerful. Interestingly, the importance of party disunity in this process—a factor Mayhew ranks as crucial in his analysis of "innovative elections"—does not show up primarily in terms of House party cohesion scores, which indicate at best a weak pattern. Of the eight preparatory cases, the out-party's House cohesion score was better than the presidential party's six times, but two of those cases were by less than one percent and, hence, arguably insignificant. More importantly, in seven of the eight cases (all but 1918), a qualitative judgment can reasonably be reached that the overall party cohesion—as opposed to merely House cohesion—of the rising party was superior. Much of the party conflict was not within Congress but between the president and his own party in Congress.

Conclusion

Some of the above factors—such as momentum, plebiscitary impact, and the introduction of new leaders—are clearly important but not decisive; these effects are common to most midterm elections regardless of future outcomes. What sets the preparatory midterms and Congresses apart? As was indicated in the previous chapter, several factors were particularly important in promoting change at the presidential level, starting with the above-average compositional change from which most of the other factors drew their power. Issue development, above-average gridlock, and the exacerbation of in-party splits were crucial, and superior out-party leadership was typical. That leadership superiority was not, strictly speaking, a product of midterm elections, but it was given greater salience, greater visibility, and often much greater power by midterm victories. All of these factors point to the Chubb, Flanigan, and Zingale model of realignment and, by extension, of political change in general—a model in which change is based on performance and leadership.

Altogether, midterm elections have frequently contributed to the results of subsequent presidential elections and even to the delineation of periods of partisan alignment or great policy change. The preparatory midterm elections studied in this and the preceding chapter demonstrate one of the most important roles of the midterm election: to serve as a balancing mechanism that guarantees the vitality of two-party competition. This check is not purely negative in nature; it is dynamic and creative, working by addition as well as by subtraction. It may close the door on the president and his party, but it opens other doors for his opponents to walk through.

The Calibrating Elections

MIDTERM THERMIDOR

Midterm elections have served as a precursor of change in policy and presidential control. Yet they have also served to blunt and redirect change. For all of the short-term forces at play, for all of the figures promising and to some extent delivering change, only two figures in the twentieth century wrought fundamental and long-lasting shifts in the direction of American government. Woodrow Wilson may have laid the foundation for the administrative state and Lyndon Johnson may have consummated it, but it was Franklin Roosevelt and his New Deal that produced an enduring paradigm shift and set the pace for federal activism in the twentieth century. Roosevelt transformed the debate from whether there should be federal activism to what kind and how much. Fifty years later, Ronald Reagan once again fundamentally transformed American politics, changing the debate from whether government should be slowed and decentralized to how and how much.

Neither the New Deal nor the Reagan Revolution was fully overturned, but both were ultimately slowed, stalled, stymied, and deflected by midterm elections in 1938, 1982, and 1986. These electoral defeats did not precede presidential defeats, nor did they reflect an outright repudiation of the president or his program by the American people. In each case they were, rather, events that tempered the course of the administration—and simultaneously helped to consolidate change due to the nature of the campaign run by the opposition. Hence the midterm as thermidor, bringing the revolutionary phase to a close without reinstating the *ancien régime*. In serving this calibrating function, these midterms set the parameters for future action and clearly shaped history in a variety of ways. Above all, they provide additional evidence for the notion that the most crucial role of midterm elections is to serve as an additional check on the executive while indicating that that role is nuanced.

1938 and the Rise of the Conservative Coalition

For the first six years of his presidency, Franklin Roosevelt dominated the political life of America. Democrats gained congressional seats in four consecutive elections—1930, 1932, 1934, and 1936—leaving the Democratic Party with gigantic numerical majorities in both houses. While those majorities did not always guarantee Roosevelt's success, he was seldom completely thwarted. His opposition, when not totally impotent, was resigned to a purely defensive posture.

Some cracks appeared in the Democratic contingent in 1935, when Roosevelt was forced to remove a controversial death sentence provision in his utilities bill. Larger cracks emerged in 1937, primarily as a consequence of the court-packing scheme opposed by many moderate and conservative Democrats. Throughout the first six years of the New Deal, "building under the surface even while the great measures thrashed their way through Congress was a deep bitterness toward the White House."[1] Nevertheless, even in 1938 the New Deal "still had some magic."[2] Not until late in 1938 and 1939 was Roosevelt's grip really loosened, and the midterm elections of 1938—both the primary and general elections—were central to that development. The court plan had split the Democrats, and the "Roosevelt recession" of 1937–38 further contributed to both the Democratic split and the resurgence of the Republicans. In the view of James T. Patterson, the recession "was a decisive event in the growth of congressional conservatism. It confused Roosevelt, making him indecisive and dilatory; it eroded more of the fabulous Roosevelt magic; it destroyed the unity and resolve of the New Deal coalition; and it caused some congressmen to grope toward a permanent bipartisan coalition."[3]

The growth of anti–New Deal sentiment in Congress, especially among Democrats, frustrated and infuriated Roosevelt. In response, he took an enormous gamble, choosing to work openly against a collection of conservative Democrats, mostly in the Senate. He campaigned hardest against Sen. Millard Tydings of Maryland, Sen. Walter George of Georgia, and Sen. Ed Smith of South Carolina. He also made known his displeasure with Sen. Guy Gillette of Iowa, Sen. Frederick Van Nuys of Indiana, and House Rules Committee Chairman John O'Connor of New York. Critics derided

Roosevelt's effort as a "purge"—a term with particularly dark connotations in the decade of Hitler and Stalin—and the intended victims defended themselves by attacking outside interference in local politics. In the end, only in the case of O'Connor did the president's efforts succeed; all his other targets won anyway, some (like Tydings) by embarrassingly large margins. Other New Deal supporters, such as Sen. James Pope (Idaho) and Rep. Maury Maverick (Texas), lost their primaries to conservatives, although several incumbent liberals, like Claude Pepper (Florida) and Alben Barkley (Kentucky), won in tough races.[4] In a few states, including Iowa, Idaho, and Indiana, Republicans helped thwart the president with "clandestine but well-organized support of conservative [Democratic] candidates."[5]

Analysts still dispute the long-term consequences of the purge attempt. Some argue that, in the long run, Roosevelt gained by clearly identifying the national Democratic Party with the cause of liberalism; while he may have lost battles, "he won the war for control of the ideological character and policy agenda of the Party."[6] The short-term consequences, however, were clear enough. The purge not only seriously damaged Roosevelt's prestige but "intensified the liberal-conservative split within the Democratic party."[7] Thus, while the split had already existed, the 1938 primaries and Roosevelt's determination to influence them sent the opposing blocs beyond the point of no return. Conservative Democrats were simultaneously affronted by Roosevelt's efforts and emboldened by his failure.

The fall elections carried, if possible, even worse news for Roosevelt. Public opinion showed a definite turn away from further liberalism, as a Gallup poll indicated in August 1938 that 66 percent wanted Roosevelt to pursue more conservative domestic policies.[8] Republicans, sensing their first real opportunity since losing congressional power in 1930, ran tough campaigns with new and attractive candidates. Rather than frontally assaulting the New Deal, they criticized its administration and its tendency to centralize power, a tendency allegedly illustrated by the court-packing plan, the executive reorganization plan (also defeated), and the attempted purge. They also argued, as the country suffered a recession within the depression, that six years of Roosevelt plans had failed. Democrats, for their part, often ran away from (if not against) aspects of the New Deal. This phenomenon was not confined to Democrats who had already evidenced disaffection; even many relatively liberal members sought to put some distance between themselves and the White House.

Roosevelt privately admitted to expecting losses of one Senate seat and sixteen House seats.[9] In the final event, as Raymond Moley would later say, Republicans "staged a comeback of astounding proportions."[10] Democrats lost six seats in the Senate, seventy-one seats in the House, and about a dozen governorships, including Pennsylvania, Michigan, and Ohio. Progressive governors Philip La Follette of Wisconsin and Elmer Benson of Minnesota also fell, and they attributed their losses to "a national reaction against the New Deal."[11] Thomas Dewey nearly upset New York's Democratic governor, Herbert Lehman, thus propelling Dewey to the front rank of presidential contenders. Republicans Leverett Saltonstall, John Bricker, Harold Stassen, and Robert Taft took a new place in the national limelight. Across the country, the Republican House vote nearly matched the Democratic vote, 47 percent to 48.6 percent, while no House Republican incumbents lost.[12]

While Democrats still maintained wide margins of control in both houses of Congress and the statehouses, the 1938 elections proved a decisive point in the consolidation of the conservative coalition in Congress. The liberal bloc in the House had been cut in half, while conservative Democrats had escaped "relatively untouched."[13] While Democrats lost no seats in the South or border states, their representation fell by one-third in the Northeast and by almost half in the Midwest. If Republicans stuck together, only fifty Democratic defectors were needed to stop legislation; the House elected in 1938 contained at least thirty anti–New Deal Democrats and another fifty who were "not at all enthusiastic."[14] Conservatives also regained control of the House Rules Committee, despite the defeat of O'Connor. In the Senate, only one conservative Democrat (Augustine Lonergan of Connecticut) lost, while six New Deal Democrats lost. The new Senate was split about evenly between pro– and anti–New Deal factions.[15]

Republicans reveled in their new competitiveness. Sen. Arthur Vandenberg (R-Mich.) called the election results "an amazing defeat for the Roosevelt party and program" and a "victory for Republicans, for Jeffersonian Democrats, for constitutionalism, and for free enterprise."[16] At the same time, *New York Times* reporter Arthur Krock held that

> the New Deal has been halted; the Republican party is large enough for
> effective opposition; the moderate Democrats in Congress can guide
> legislation; the third-term movement has been strongly checked; Federal
> relief money in elections has been overcome by voters in several States;
> the White House circle, which invented the court bill and the "purge," has
> been discredited . . . the sit-down strike and the Democratic-C.I.O.
> alliance have been emphatically rebuked; the Farm Belt has revolted; the
> country is back on a two-party system . . . and legislative authority has
> been restored to Congress.[17]

Krock maintained that "voters of the nation were moving to reverse the long and crescent trend in favor of the President and the New Deal" and freely predicted that "the effect will surely be to stiffen Democratic resistance in Congress to New Deal programs and agents."[18]

These predictions were borne out. The administration did win a few victories—for example, on currency, trade, and transportation questions.[19] Nevertheless, as Patterson says, "The administration was in trouble from the first day of the session."[20] The 76th Congress showed hostility toward Roosevelt from the very beginning. Almost immediately, congressional committees began investigating subversion, Works Progress Administration electioneering, Frances Perkins' Labor Department, the National Labor Relations Board, and other topics damaging to the administration. Nominations were blocked or stalled, executive reorganization was curtailed, and the Hatch Act and Smith anti-subversion bill were enacted despite Roosevelt's concerns. Overall, vetoes increased sharply, both in absolute numbers and as a proportion of public bills enacted. Congress also reasserted its control over appropriations. Roosevelt's $875-million emergency relief bill was cut by $150 million. A self-liquidating public works project bill was killed; the administration's housing bill was killed; the Federal Theater Project was eliminated; the undistributed profits tax was repealed. In short, "by 1939 coalition leaders in Congress had left their defensive posture of '37 and '38 and had moved openly to the attack."[21] The administration read the tea leaves; 1939 was the first year since Roosevelt took power that no new reform legislation was proposed to Congress.[22] Altogether, if Roosevelt, himself, was not finished after 1938, "his domestic reform program was. Except for some minor unfinished business it was time to audit the New Deal books."[23] Aside from a consolidation and expansion of Social Security, no major New Deal measure passed Congress after 1938.[24]

Yet 1938 was better interpreted as a call to restrain and limit the New Deal than as a call to reverse it. At best, the election results produced "stalemate."[25] The stalemate created by the elections of 1938 was the dominant feature of American political life for most of the next twenty years. Mayhew consequently classified 1938 as one of his four "innovative midterm elections" in that it brought to congressional power a new coalition that triggered a new policy era.[26] To the *New York Times,* the 1938 elections provided evidence for the notion that Americans were moving to the middle of the road. Roosevelt's opposition had gained but was forced to "reorient itself and adopt to its own the purposes of the party in power." While the results "constitute a sharp reversal for the Roosevelt Administration," the administration could still claim to have "accomplished a fundamental change in the American point of view."[27] And indeed, if no further measures were passed, it was also true that none of the major accomplishments of the New Deal were reversed as a consequence of 1938. The 1938 elections can, thus, be said to have blunted the sharpest edges of the New Deal and to have restored a rough equilibrium in American politics—both ideologically and institutionally—after a period of breathtaking change and executive dominance.

1982/1986 and the Reagan Revolution

When Ronald Reagan assumed office in 1981, he was the first president since Roosevelt to promise to fundamentally change the direction of the federal government rather than just the pace of its growth. Challenging New Deal assumptions about the role of government, he came to the presidency pledged to cut taxes, reduce the domestic functions of government, ease the burden of regulation, reverse the seemingly inexorable trend of centralization, and emphasize the role of individual and community responsibility, while retaining a basic safety net of social services.

In Reagan's first two years, he exerted effective control over Congress—Republicans controlled the Senate, while a coalition of Republicans and conservative, mostly Southern, Democrats maintained a working majority in the House. Reagan's mastery over Congress was never as complete as Roosevelt's had been—even in his first year, Social Security reforms and a second round of budget cuts proposed in September 1981 were unceremoniously rejected by Congress. Nevertheless, victories in 1981 through 1982 established his image as a legislatively successful president and put into effect large parts of his program, including a major tax cut and the largest domestic spending cuts (mostly reductions in the rate of increase) in American history. The 97th Congress, spurred by the Soviet invasion of Afghanistan, also approved the Reagan defense buildup, giving the administration almost everything it wanted to restore American military capabilities. In the words of Albert Hunt, Reagan "dominated the capital to degree not seen since Lyndon Johnson's pre-Vietnam salad days."[28] These successes set both the substantive parameters and the tone for the remainder of Reagan's presidency.[29] Over the long term, it is clear that Reagan transformed the American debate much as Roosevelt had done. By 1996, a Democratic president with activist inclinations was forced to proclaim the end of the era of big government after dickering with a Reaganite Congress over how fast to reduce government and cut taxes.

Yet the natural equilibrium of American government could be overcome only for a short while. The Depression gave Roosevelt six years; the Carter stagflation and Afghanistan gave Reagan less time than that. The process of checking Reagan, however, was accomplished not in a single midterm election, as in 1938, but sequentially, in a pair of midterm elections that deprived him of effective House control in 1982 and of partisan control of the Senate in 1986. Ultimately, Reagan's initial successes gave him "a political momentum that lasted until the mid-term elections of 1986."[30]

In 1982, Republicans expressed hope that they might reverse the historic midterm trend and actually gain enough seats to win outright control of the House. Indeed, in June 1981 Republican National Committee chairman Richard Richards flatly promised a House takeover. Republicans also harbored hopes of additional Senate gains, since Democrats were forced to defend twenty-one of the thirty-three Senate seats up for election. Just as Franklin Roosevelt was undone by the "Roosevelt recession" of 1937–38, however, Reagan and the Republicans were stymied by the "Reagan recession" of 1981–82.

The central campaign themes of 1982 revolved around the economy, which faced the deepest recession since the Great Depression.[31] Democrats blamed the failure of Reaganomics, while Republicans blamed Jimmy Carter and pointed to the compensating decline in inflation. "It's not fair, it's Republican" was the Democratic slogan, while Republicans urged the nation to "stay the course." Despite the attempt to fashion a national Republican campaign theme, Republican candidates, under enormous pressure due to the recession, degenerated into a cacophony of voices, seeking to distinguish themselves and gain some distance from the White House. As observers pointed out, this breakdown represented a "radical departure from Republican strategy in 1980"; now it was "every candidate for himself."[32] Inevitably, these fissures appeared on the floor of Congress, where Republican unity dissolved on issues like the balanced budget amendment and on an important appropriations veto override vote. In the view of Democratic pollster Peter Hart, the latter "cut the ground out from under their national message."[33] Democrats, for their part, vowed not a reversal of the Reagan program but rather what they called a "midcourse correction."[34] Mann and Ornstein noted that

> often just as important in a campaign is the message that could be sent—but is not. In 1982, few candidates called for restoring every budget cut made in 1981 and adding more federal dollars for good measure, for increasing taxes over and above what they were in 1980, or for cutting

national defense in real terms. The overall agenda of the campaign virtually *assumed* acceptance of the notions that we should cut back and streamline the role of government, reduce the tax burden to relieve citizens and enhance economic growth, and keep our country strong enough to avert an outside threat.[35]

When the votes were counted, Republicans had lost twenty-six House seats and gained one Senate seat. They had also lost a net of seven governorships and 177 state legislative seats. Voter turnout edged upward for the first time in years, and subsequent analysis indicated that the economy had been the primary factor mobilizing voters.[36] Democrats, as one might expect, did particularly well in high- unemployment areas.[37]

A debate immediately ensued over whether the results should be considered bad for the Republicans or good. GOP losses exceeded the average since World War II for a party's first midterm election. Thirteen of the twenty-six Republican losses were suffered by freshmen seeking their first reelection, a figure representing 25 percent of all House Republican freshmen. While Republicans picked up one in the Senate, the lack of significant gains in a year when two Democratic seats were contested for every one Republican seat did not bode well for the party's ability to hold on in 1984 and 1986, when the ratios would be reversed. (Indeed, Republicans did lose the Senate in 1986.)[38] More generally, Republicans were often privately depressed over their inability in both House and Senate to capitalize on what they had thought would be an important chance to solidify the gains of 1980; instead, they faced "an election of missed opportunity."[39]

On the other hand, the Republicans did hold on to control of the Senate, the first time they had maintained control of either chamber of Congress for two consecutive elections since before the New Deal. When taking economic conditions into account, the Republican House losses were much smaller than might have been predicted. The president's party had lost forty-eight House seats in the two previous recessions (1958 and 1974), neither of which had been as deep as the 1981–82 recession; statistical analyses based on economic performance predicted 1982 Republican losses at upwards of sixty seats.[40] Furthermore, there were indications that a significant portion of the Democratic gain—by estimates ranging from five to as many as fifteen seats—was owed to Democratic successes in the post-1980 redistricting wars.[41] Indeed, nine of the thirteen House Republican freshmen who lost had been adversely affected by redistricting.[42] Thus, perhaps as much as one-half of the Democratic gain was baked into the 1982 elections.

Why did the Republicans lose so many fewer seats in 1982 than one might have anticipated given the state of the economy? Reagan himself remained widely popular, and a large portion of the electorate accepted the Republican interpretation that the recession was a product of failed Democratic policies of the past. In preelection polls and election-day exit surveys, voters were roughly evenly divided in their evaluations of Reagan and in their views of who was responsible for the economic mess; the decline of inflation apparently aided the Republicans, too.[43] Furthermore, Samuel Kernell and Gary C. Jacobson advanced the theory that "strategic politicians" made decisions on whether to retire from Congress, run for reelection, or challenge an incumbent based on information of 1981 and early 1982, when Reagan was on a roll and long before the recession reached its trough. Consequently, the Republicans had an unusually strong coterie of candidates, while many potentially strong Democrats stayed out of the race in a mistaken fear that 1982 would be a "bad year."[44] Compounding this factor was the superior allocation of resources by the Republicans; Democrats, looking back to the slaughter of 1980, dedicated disproportionate resources to protecting their incumbents instead of helping their challengers.[45] In any event, the elections of 1982 were ambiguous and admitted to a variety of interpretations, both because of the results and because of the terms on which the campaign was fought.

Nevertheless, a consensus quickly emerged on two points. First, "few observers, if any, saw the election as a widespread repudiation of President Reagan, the Republican Party, and current policies."[46] Instead, journalist David Broder referred to the elections as a "caution sign in the way of President Reagan's effort to redirect American government onto the conservative track."[47] *Time* claimed the message was to "keep on course—but trim the sails," while the *New York Times* held that Reagan got "a message to go with the flow . . . The flow is to the center."[48] The Democrats' "midcourse correction" theme, while perhaps necessary for their success, also reinforced this interpretation and, thus, limited the impact of that success. Democrats claimed an anti-administration mandate and a mandate for balance but no more sweeping ideological mandate.[49]

Second, Ronald Reagan would face a much different and more difficult Congress, particularly in the House. The entry of eight-one newcomers to the House "meant a clear shift in votes, perhaps twenty-five or more on any given issue, away from the more 'conservative' policies favored by President Reagan—enough to change many vote outcomes."[50] A *New York Times* survey indicated that the House class of 1982 would be significantly less favorably disposed to Reagan's agenda, and it was clear from the outset that the Democratic leadership had regained effective control of the House.[51] The president's coalition was damaged by more than the twenty-six-seat Republican loss. Moderate northeastern Republicans (the so-called Gypsy Moths) fared poorly in 1982, making it less likely that they would stick with Reagan on tough votes in the future; the Northeast lost 27 percent of its Republican representatives, far more than any other region. More conservative Republicans were shaken into greater independence by the loss of many of their compatriots and the near defeat of House Minority Leader Robert Michel of Illinois. Republican failures in Virginia and North Carolina (which the GOP had heavily targeted) convinced many Southern Democrats that they did not need to fear the effect of Reagan in their districts. No pro-Reagan, Southern Democrat, "Boll Weevil" was defeated, but other relatively liberal Democrats also did quite well in the South. Overall, "the twenty-six-seat increase reassured Democratic leaders that the President's popularity was not transferrable to congressional Republicans."[52] As one analyst said, "To prevail in the House in 1983, Reagan would have to make major concessions."[53]

In the Senate, Republicans gained a seat and only five seats changed hands—the smallest turnover in seventy years. Yet, even in those circumstances, it was clear that life would be more difficult for the president. Two relatively conservative Democrats on the Senate Armed Services Committee (Virginia's Byrd, who was technically an Independent, and Nevada's Cannon) were replaced by two liberals (Kennedy of Massachusetts and Bingaman of New Mexico). Republican Senator Harrison Schmitt of New Mexico, one of the few incumbent Senators to lose in 1982, was replaced as chairman of the appropriations subcommittee on Labor, Health, and Human Services by liberal Republican Lowell Weicker.[54] As in the House, northeastern Senate Republicans survived numerous close calls, making them more disposed to assert independence from Reagan. And in both the House and Senate, the Democratic Party's liberal base was a significantly larger proportion of the party than before 1982.[55]

It is important not to overstate the effect of 1982. Reagan's coalition in Congress had begun slipping before the elections, as Roosevelt's coalition slipped noticeably in 1937 through 1938. Thus, to some extent, the 1982 elections ratified a new equilibrium as much as they created one.[56] Nevertheless, that equilibrium *was* ratified, and the 1982 elections made it impossible for Reagan to regain the mastery he exerted in 1981. His congressional support scores declined steadily, although he did win important victories from time to time on issues like contra aid and tax reform. Yet, as one could predict by closely examining the content of the 1982 campaign, the

Reagan policies adopted in 1981 were modified but not reversed; "the 1981 legacy dominated presidential-congressional policy politics in the 98th Congress"—and beyond.[57] And for another four years, Reagan was able to use continued Republican control of the Senate as a launching pad for new initiatives and as a last bastion of defense.

The Gramm-Rudman-Hollings deficit reduction plan came out of the Republican Senate in 1985; the tax reform package of 1986 was spurred largely by the Senate Finance Committee, which took dramatic action at key points in the process; Strategic Defense Initiative funds were protected and contra aid was kept alive by Senate support; and the Rehnquist and Scalia Supreme Court battles were won by the administration. Thus, despite loss of his working majority in the House, Reagan had an important legislative ally in the Senate. All of that came to an end, however, when Democrats regained control of the Senate in 1986.

The battle for Senate control was the central political story of 1986. The large Republican class of 1980, swept in on Ronald Reagan's coattails, would have to win on its own. There were roughly twice as many Republican seats in contention as Democratic seats, and many of them were vulnerable. Thus, both parties concentrated unprecedented firepower on the Senate races. Reagan, himself, undertook a massive campaign effort, traveling thousands of miles for Republican Senate candidates.[58] However, the Republicans did not adopt a national theme as in 1980 or 1982, a decision many of them later regretted.[59] Instead, the campaign was widely dismissed as possessing "no gravity . . . issues flared across the political sky and disappeared, as sudden and distant comets."[60] As a result, the midterm elections of 1986 reverted to the more common pattern of overwhelming localism.[61]

The common pattern of presidential losses also reasserted itself, at least in the Senate, where Democrats took control, not to lose it again until 1994. In a reversal of 1980, Republicans lost eight seats, including six freshmen Senators elected in 1980, many by very small margins. Accordingly, Democrats won nine of the eleven races decided with 52 percent of the vote or less; a hypothetical shift of 32,000 votes in selected races would have kept the Senate in Republican hands. Indeed, the Republican seat loss came despite the fact that Republican Senate candidates actually polled a slightly higher proportion of the vote nationwide than they had six years earlier.[62] In the House, Republican losses were held to five, well below average, a result potentially explainable by a variety of theories: national conditions were good for Reagan and the Republicans, House Republican exposure was low, and the small Republican gain recorded in 1984 was consistent with small surge-and-decline effects. And Republicans did quite well at the gubernatorial level, gaining eight statehouses and putting the GOP at its highest level (24) in seventeen years—also attributable, at least in part, to the much larger number of governorships Democrats had to defend. Thus, in some respects, the election was a return to normalcy, an event that balanced out the abnormal Republican Senate gains of 1980 and the abnormal Democratic statehouse gains of 1982.[63]

Consequently, the elections of 1986—even more than those of 1982—carried a mixed and confusing message. Ticket splitting reached new heights, as several southern states simultaneously deposed incumbent Republican Senators and elected new Republican governors. Whether one should emphasize the Senate shift or the gubernatorial shift as a signal of forthcoming trends—or whether one could reasonably divine any trend at all—remained an open question. And observers pointed out that Republican losses were shared by conservatives, moderates, and liberals, as were Democratic gains.[64]

Nevertheless, as in 1982, some points were fairly clear. To an even greater extent than in 1982, the reversal of Reaganism was not a Democratic theme. "Fine-tuning" was the order of the day, and "most Democrats made sure that they did not appear to be campaigning against the President."[65] Indeed, *Newsweek* noted that Democrats had won "largely by sounding their own version of Reaganite trumpets."[66] Writing in the *National Journal,* analyst Ronald Brownstein said that "notable in its absence was the dispute over government's role that Reagan provoked but that both parties welcomed in the last three elections."[67] The unwillingness of Democrats to frontally challenge Reagan was traceable both to Reagan's personal popularity and to a more general satisfaction that did not leave much room for angry denunciation. As Brownstein remarked, "The very disengagement of the voters testified paradoxically to the strength of Reagan's basic political message . . . the polls capture a general sense of wellness against which the deliberations of Congress or the fulminations of politicians seem remote and obscure."[68] Against this background, however, were several more specific consequences of the 1986 elections, none of them good for Reagan or the Republicans. Any talk of realignment was clearly fanciful, at least for the time being; the Republican beachhead in the legislative branch was annihilated, and previous gains among southerners and younger voters were not sustained. Reagan's prestige, so forcefully put on the line in his campaign for a Republican Senate, was seriously damaged. His campaign had proven "a bold gamble that clearly backfired."[69]

Legislatively, for all practical purposes, the Reagan administration ended in 1986. Any residual notion of a presidential mandate flowing from the 1984 landslide was extinguished, and Democrats claimed a counter mandate.[70] Loss of Republican control of the Senate "propelled the Democrats into a more aggressive posture"[71] both in the Senate and the House, where Speaker Jim Wright took the offensive. Of course, added to loss of the Senate was the Iran-Contra scandal, which broke days after the midterm elections, and the lame-duck status of the president, who could not run for reelection. It is difficult to disentangle the relative impact of those three factors, a complication compounded by the possibility that the Iran-Contra hearings would have been less damaging had Republicans still controlled the Senate. Taken together, though, they "rendered presidential leadership something that existed only in memory."[72]

A few measures of note passed in Reagan's last two years, including ratification of the Intermediate Nuclear Forces Treaty and a welfare reform measure that was much heralded at the time but turned out to be largely ineffective. On balance, the last two years of the Reagan administration saw the president's congressional support scores fall below 50 percent for the first time. The decline in congressional support was about three times greater after 1986 than it had been after 1982, at least partially reflecting the importance of Senate control to the Reagan agenda.[73] Indeed, Reagan's 1987 congressional support score of 43.5 percent, calculated by *Congressional Quarterly,* was the lowest on record for thirty-five years; even Senate Republicans supported him only 64 percent of the time.[74] As soon as the 1986 returns were in, one newsmagazine held, correctly, that Reagan was "newly diminished, in the twilight of his presidency."[75]

The Reagan Revolution was not only economic and not only aimed at short-term legislative gain. It was, at its heart, a constitutional revolution in the broadest sense. It aimed to revise and relimit the role of government in American society. Thus, it aimed to change not only the elected branches but the federal judiciary, the branch least democratically accountable and arguably the most prone to arbitrarily centralize at the expense of state and local government. Many scholars view the Reagan administration's impact on the federal courts to have been its most significant long-term legacy.[76]

Yet that impact was not as great as Reagan's supporters had hoped or his opponents had feared, largely because of the outcome of the midterm elections of 1986. Specifically, the Supreme Court nomination of Robert Bork, who might well have been confirmed in 1986, faced disaster in 1987. Virtually all observers agreed that Bork hurt his own cause in a variety of ways, and many also argued that he was hurt by lack of a concerted conservative defense to match the drubbing he took in the public relations wars at the hands of liberal organizations. Yet Democratic control of the Senate and the 1986 elections, in particular, were crucial in several respects. First, the two-and-a-half-month delay of the Senate Judiciary Committee hearings gave opponents time to marshal their forces and orchestrate the anti-Bork campaign. That decision was made by Judiciary Committee Chairman Joseph Biden and would almost certainly not have been made by Strom Thurmond, the South Carolina Republican who preceded Biden. Overall, the nine-to-five vote against Bork in the Judiciary Committee was probably the decisive moment. Contemporary news accounts stressed that Chairman Biden was "a chief architect of Bork's defeat."[77] Second, a bloc of four southern Democratic Senators first elected in 1986 moved against Bork, prodded by Bennett Johnston of Louisiana. Those Democrats had been elected by deftly constructing a coalition of blacks and moderate whites, and civil rights organizations were highly successful in mobilizing southern blacks to pressure the new Senators.

Finally, in raw numbers, the Bork defeat cannot be understood without reference to the results of 1986. Of all major committees in the Senate, the Judiciary Committee suffered the greatest decline in conservative coalition success scores, falling from 63 percent in 1985 to 49 percent in 1987.[78] On the floor, Bork lost fifty- eight to forty-two, meaning that a switch of eight votes would have confirmed him. Among the "no" votes were eleven Democrats first elected in 1986, nine of whom had taken Republican seats.[79] In the words of administration lobbyist Tom Korologos, "there weren't enough conservatives left to win."[80]

At the time, it was not clear how important the defeat of Bork would be. In his place, the Reagan administration successfully appointed Anthony Kennedy, a California jurist who was allegedly a solid conservative but less prone to controversy than Bork had been. Indeed, in his first few years, Kennedy tended to vote on the conservative side, including a vote in the majority on the 1989 *Webster v. Reproductive Health Services* abortion case in Missouri. However, by the early 1990s, Kennedy was straying with increasing frequency, reversing in the 1992 *Planned Parenthood v. Casey* decision his *Webster* position in favor of overturning *Roe v. Wade* (his would have been the fifth vote to overturn) and also providing the decisive vote declaring unconstitutional the use of religious invocations at high school graduation ceremonies. By the mid-1990s, he was firmly ensconced in a three-person moderate bloc that also included Sandra Day O'Connor and David Souter, the little-known New Hampshire jurist who was seemingly chosen by George Bush primarily with the purpose in mind of avoiding another "Borking." Thus, liberal positions on a closely divided Supreme Court arguably gained not one but two votes (Kennedy and Souter) on numerous crucial issues owing to the failure of the Bork nomination. It is, of course, impossible to say with certainty what would have happened had Bork been confirmed. He, too, might have shifted leftward, like Kennedy, and the Souter nomination might have gone to someone equally nondescript and malleable; but those prospects, especially the former, seem unlikely. The federal judiciary, which was a nonissue during the campaign of 1986, was thus profoundly affected by the outcome of those elections.

Midterm Elections as a Barrier to Change

The elections of 1938, 1982, and 1986 point to an important role for midterm elections in a period of change. Under the right conditions, midterm elections have served as a mechanism for slowing the pace of change without overturning it completely. The three elections were notable for the degree to which the president's opposition was forced onto his field of play. By and large, Republicans in 1938 did not call for a reversal of the New Deal, nor did Democrats in 1982 and 1986 call for much more than trimming what they perceived to be the excesses of Reaganism. Furthermore, Roosevelt was reelected twice after 1938, and Harry Truman was elected once in his own right on a New Deal platform; Reagan was reelected after 1982, and his protégé, George Bush, was elected after 1986.

Nevertheless, the midterm elections in question did soften the sharp edges of change. Both presidents were facing coalitional troubles in Congress before the crucial midterms, Roosevelt in 1937 through 1938 and Reagan from the fall of 1981 onward. But the midterm elections formalized and added to their difficulties. The onset of the midterm campaigns, themselves, also stimulated their pre-election difficulties, as opponents seized on potential campaign issues and erstwhile supporters sought electoral cover. The opposition regained confidence, and the media proclaimed the president checked (though not repudiated). The aura of a popular mandate surrounding the president was diminished, if not ended. Roosevelt and Reagan were forced to seek new coalitions in a much more difficult legislative environment. Not only did their parties lose seats, but the composition of their own party and often of the opposition party became less friendly. Of the five chambers effectively dominated by the president in these three midterm years, only one shifted party hands (1986 Senate), but the president lost control of three others in factional terms (1938 House, 1938 Senate, and 1982 House). Adding to the damage inflicted in the midterm elections, both Roosevelt and Reagan saw their prestige hurt by close identification with their party's—or, in the case of Roosevelt, a faction of their party's—fate, especially in 1938 and 1986.

Table 5.1 Legislative Productivity and Presidential Vetoes Before and
After Calibrating Midterms

Congress	Year Elected	Public Bills Enacted	Vetoes	Vetoes/Bills (%)
75th	1936	788	117	14.8
76th	1938	894	167	18.7
97th	1980	473	15	3.2
98th	1982	623	24	3.8
99th	1984	664	20	3.0
100th	1986	713	19	2.7
Avg. before midterm		641.7	50.7	7.9
Avg. after midterm		743.3	70.0	9.4

Sources: Data from George B. Galloway, *History of the House of Representatives* 2nd ed. (New York: Thomas Y. Crowell Company, 1976), 375-76; Robert Moon and Carol Hardy Vincent *Workload and Activity Report: United States Senate, 1946-1992 (Washington, D.C.: Congressional Research Service, 1993), 15; Presidential Vetoes 1789-1988 (Washington, D.C.: GPO, 1989).*

Legislative productivity actually rose after each of the three calibrating midterms, clearly distinguishing them from preparatory elections and indicating that the elections had not brought governing to a standstill. Yet vetoes rose in two of the three cases, and presidential policy initiatives slowed drastically in comparison to earlier periods of presidential aggressiveness (table 5.1). It is little exaggeration to say that the New Deal ended in 1938, at least in the sense of an era of legislative accomplishment. The most important programs, of course, remained and were later expanded upon. And the Reagan Revolution slowed considerably after 1982 and was finished after 1986, although its legacy also survived.

Every revolution has a thermidor. The revolutions of the 1930s and 1980s were no exception. Their thermidors were carried on the wings of midterm elections that gave the American people the opportunity to shift the political balance of power without actually ejecting from office popular presidents or removing from the White House the party promoting change. Midterm elections can thus be seen as instruments permitting a more nuanced calibration than would be possible in a presidential system with completely coterminous congressional elections or in a parliamentary system. Midterm elections can provide a check that falls well short of reversal.

SIX

The Dogs That Did Not Bark

EXCEPTIONS THAT SHAPED HISTORY

Out of all the midterm elections from 1894 through 1998, three stand out as exceptions to the general anti-administration trend. These twentieth-century exceptions to the midterm rule should remove any doubt about either the catalytic potential of midterm elections or their potential to stymie presidents. In 1934, Franklin D. Roosevelt's Democrats actually gained seats in both houses of Congress; in 1962, John F. Kennedy's Democrats gained three Senate seats and held House losses to four, the lowest figure since the Civil War era. In both cases, the exceptions to the midterm rule were touted as evidence of a national mandate in favor of the administration. More tangibly, the ability of the president's party to avoid even average midterm losses measurably strengthened him (and, in Kennedy's case, his successor) in his fight for an extensive legislative program of reform. Thus, the midterm elections of 1934 and 1962, far from being nonevents, were central to the ultimate successes of the New Deal and the New Frontier–Great Society—what could be called creative exceptions. By indirection, they also clearly demonstrate the importance of the midterm check. There were three major expansions of the federal government in the twentieth century, and two of them coincided with occasions on which the midterm check was not present to some degree. In the absence of these rare exceptions, it seems likely that the New Deal and New Frontier–Great Society would have taken a markedly different (and more limited) course. And, while it is too early to assess the long-term importance of 1998, the short-term impact confirms many of the lessons of 1934 and 1962.

The Great Exception: 1934

The midterm elections of 1934 were the only instance in the century from 1894 through 1994 of a midterm election in which the president's party did not suffer a net loss of seats in the House of Representatives.[1] While this fact is frequently noted by political historians, the actual significance of the election of 1934 is seldom remarked upon. The Democratic gain of nine seats in the House and ten in the Senate guaranteed legislative and political momentum for Franklin D. Roosevelt and the New Deal. It also foreshadowed Roosevelt's landslide reelection in 1936 and contributed to the overwhelming congressional majorities attained by Democrats throughout the 1930s. While the presidential election of 1936 is rightly given credit among many scholars for solidifying the New Deal alignment, the midterm elections of 1934 share in that accomplishment; indeed, 1936 might not have looked the same without 1934.

The 1934 elections took place in a highly charged atmosphere. The short-lived consensus of 1933 had given way to acrimony and resurgent opposition. As Edgar Eugene Robinson pointed out:

> Although the President was not personally a candidate, to an unusual degree the campaigning of 1934 was done in terms of the issues raised by [Roosevelt's] Presidential leadership. He was charged with unconstitutional action, with general usurpation of power, with a shifting policy on both taxation and debts, and with a general willingness to push the nation into later bankruptcy in his vigorous desire to build broader bases for political action through public expenditure.[2]

These criticisms came from three major sources: business interests such as the U.S. Chamber of Commerce and National Association of Manufacturers, defeated Republicans like former President Herbert Hoover, and disenchanted Jeffersonian Democrats, including former Democratic presidential nominees Al Smith and John W. Davis, who feared the concentration of governmental power represented by the New Deal.[3] The latter group was centered in the American Liberty League, formed in August 1934.

Along with this general critique of the Roosevelt Administration, social security proposals were a key issue. Roosevelt had announced in June 1934 that he would submit to the next Congress an ambitious program including social insurance, housing, and development of natural resources.[4] Those proposals were supported by most Democrats and by the Democratic machines, and served as a specific line of demarcation with the Republicans.[5] Most Democrats welcomed an election revolving around the issue of Roosevelt and the New Deal.[6]

Conditions of 1934 and early 1935 indicated that the nation was reaching a critical turning point. While the economy had improved from its low point in 1932–33, it had not recovered beyond 1931 levels and was still much weaker than in 1929. Whatever recovery had occurred seemed stalled. A wave of increasingly militant industrial strikes had unsettled the nation even further. In the words of New Deal historian William E. Leuchtenberg, "As the country weathered the crisis but failed to achieve prosperity, dissatisfaction mounted."[7] To James MacGregor Burns, Roosevelt had "aroused consciousness of the need for change without bringing about fundamental or enduring transformation."[8] For his part, after two years in office Roosevelt seemed unusually dispirited, his confidence shaken.[9] Finally, America faced a variety of demagogues—starting with Huey Long, Father Charles E. Coughlin, and Dr. Francis E. Townsend—whose following might have grown exponentially without an amelioration of national circumstances. In retrospect, both the elections of 1934 and the Congress that resulted determined the direction, and perhaps survival, of the New Deal. The campaign proceeded without the benefit of modern opinion polling, and the concerted anti–New Deal campaign waged by business "gave some Democrats pre-election jitters."[10] Vice President John Nance Garner anticipated House losses of thirty-seven, while others both in and out of the party guessed that losses would be much higher.[11] Meanwhile, "Republicans and other New Deal opponents eagerly awaited the 1934 congressional elections, believing that stalled recovery would render Democratic candidates especially vulnerable."[12]

Nevertheless, when the votes were counted, the national verdict was clear: the New Deal would go forward (and leftward), with bolstered strength in both houses of Congress for pro-Roosevelt Democrats and assorted left-wing minor parties. Never before had Republicans held such a low percentage of the House; never had either party attained such a great margin in the Senate. Republicans retained only seven governorships to thirty-nine for the Democrats and two for minor left-wing parties. Some of the most vehement anti–New Deal Republican leaders were swept aside in traditionally Republican strongholds like Pennsylvania, Indiana, and Ohio; in the view of the *New York Times,* the election "literally destroyed the right wing of the Republican Party."[13] Meanwhile, outspoken New Dealers both inside and outside the Democratic Party—like Vito Marcantonio (N.Y.), Maury Maverick (Tex.), Ernest Lundeen (Minn.), and Tom Amlie

(Wisc.)—won.[14] Also swept in with the Democratic tide was Harry Truman, who defeated an incumbent Republican to win a Senate seat in Missouri. Democrats made major inroads into demographic Republican bastions, as well; in a shift that portended much for the future, Democrats began to do quite well among black voters in cities such as Kansas City, Pittsburgh, and Chicago. These gains would be solidified in 1936.[15] It was significant that 1934 saw not only a net Democratic gain in the House but a large gross turnover of both Republican and Democratic seats; the parties were sorting themselves out as part of the realignment process. Overall, the electoral cohesion of what became the New Deal coalition increased considerably in 1934.[16]

The *New York Times* said that "no President halfway through his term ever won such an overwhelming popular endorsement ... [the results were] an individual triumph for the President."[17] To columnist Arthur Krock, the election results represented "the most overwhelming victory in the history of American politics . . . There has been no such popular endorsement since the days of Thomas Jefferson and Andrew Jackson."[18] Historians like William Leuchtenberg have since seconded that contemporary view: "If there was an issue in the campaign, it was Roosevelt. The election was a thumping personal victory for the President ... The election almost erased the Republican Party as a national force . . . [with] no program of any substance, no leader with a popular appeal and none on the horizon."[19] This endorsement was crucial to the continuance of the New Deal. There were four notable consequences flowing directly from the midterm elections of 1934. They made possible the Second New Deal; they ensured the reelection of Franklin Roosevelt; they laid the foundation for the long-term Democratic coalition; and they forestalled the rise of radicals and demagogues.

Had the Democrats in 1934 suffered midterm losses that were average for the period 1894–1930, they would have lost forty-five House seats and three Senate seats instead of gaining nine in the House and ten in the Senate. The Democratic advantage in the House would have been 265–162 instead of 319–103; in the Senate, their advantage would have been 56–36 instead of 69–25. These hypothetical majorities would seem at first glance to be sufficiently large, but in fact such a shift could have been enough to stall or significantly weaken subsequent New Deal measures. Indeed, as we have seen in chapter 5, the 76th Congress, elected in the midterm elections of 1938, did stall, weaken, and destroy most of Roosevelt's substantial proposals—and is considered to be the Congress that saw the maturation of the potent conservative coalition—with a Democratic advantage of 261–

164 in the House and 69–23 in the Senate. Thus, it is very possible that the conservative coalition would have made its appearance in force after 1934 instead of four years later; indeed, there were halting efforts to form such a coalition even then—efforts stymied by electoral failure and overwhelming liberal numbers.[20]

Added to the numerical effects of an average seat loss given the large number of Southern Democrats, Roosevelt and New Dealers would have had to contend with the psychological effects on Congress of a perceived mandate against the administration. Republicans would have felt at least partially vindicated; Jeffersonian Democratic opposition to Roosevelt would have been emboldened; Democratic bosses and party leaders who were privately ambivalent—and, at the beginning, there were many—may have had second thoughts out loud. The Democratic Party was accustomed to being the minority for most of the previous forty years. Its control of the presidency and Congress were only recently obtained—and not because of an upswell of support for Democrats but because Republicans were in power when the Depression began. Midterm congressional losses of even average magnitude for the time could easily have shaken Democratic confidence and had catastrophic effects for Roosevelt's program and Democratic unity in 1936.

Instead, Roosevelt's leadership was endorsed. Consequently, "the Democratic sweep in the election of 1934 created a favorable climate for new federal action."[21] Indeed, many read the election returns not just as an endorsement of Roosevelt but as a plea for even greater reformism. As Robert S. McElvaine pointed out, "The congressional elections of 1934 saw victories by some thirty-five men who were clearly to the left of the President."[22] Henrik Shipstead of the Farmer-Labor Party won the governorship of Minnesota; under the Progressive Party banner in Wisconsin, the LaFollette brothers won the governorship (Phil) and U.S. Senate seat (Bob Jr.); and in California, Upton Sinclair made a credible run at the governorship, winning 800,000 votes while his allies in the End Poverty in California (EPIC) movement won thirty legislative seats. Bob LaFollette told Roosevelt that the returns indicated a popular upswell for more dramatic— and enduring—change than had yet been forthcoming. Roosevelt reportedly agreed.[23] Thus, the elections of 1934 both permitted and arguably demanded the Second New Deal.

In short, "the legislative harvest of 1935—the Second New Deal—produced some of the most important and long-lasting achievements of the Roosevelt Administration."[24] The following measures were part of that harvest:

- The Social Security Act. Probably the most enduring legacy of the New Deal, it passed in 1935—boosted by the mandate of 1934
- The Wagner Act, or National Labor Relations Act of 1935, guaranteeing collective bargaining rights to labor. The Wagner Act has since served as the linchpin of national labor law (though modified in the 1947 Taft-Hartley Act). Before the 1934 elections, Roosevelt had blocked consideration of the Wagner Act; it was subsequently put on the administration's "must" list.[25]
- A $4.8-billion Emergency Relief Appropriations Act in 1935, the largest to that point in American history. This appropriation created the Works Progress Administration and funded it with $1.5 billion, also earmarking large sums for a new Resettlement Administration and rural relief.
- The Wheeler-Rayburn Public Utility Holding Company Act of 1935, which applied a new level of antitrust scrutiny to public utilities.
- The Banking Act of 1935, which restructured and centralized the Federal Reserve Board: "To a greater extent than ever before, the 1935 law established government control of credit and currency."[26]
- The Revenue Act of 1935, which established a federal estate tax and corporate tax and raised the personal income tax rates in the highest brackets.
- The creation of the Rural Electrification Agency by executive order in 1935, confirmed in legislative statute the next year.
- The Robinson-Patman Federal Anti–Price Discrimination Act of 1936, outlawing numerous discriminatory pricing strategies often used by large companies to undercut competition.
- The Walsh-Healey Act of 1936, establishing minimum standards in federal labor contracts. This act served as the opening wedge in the drive for a Fair Labor Standards Act with nationwide application, which was ultimately successful in 1938.

Furthermore, the momentum of 1935 brought initiation or invigoration of other less notable measures like youth and farm credit programs, protection of natural resources, and the Guffey Bill establishing a coal code.[27] Undergirding this avalanche of measures was a decided antibusiness turn in the tone and ideology of the Roosevelt Administration. That turn was a two-fold consequence of 1934: not only did the Democratic victories bring renewed confidence to the administration, but the strong anti–New Deal campaign waged by business prior to the elections greatly contributed to the polarization.[28]

In retrospect, much of this legislative harvest appears to have been effortless, but in fact numerous obstacles were presented despite the gigantic Democratic majorities. Republican opposition to the Social Security Act was much stiffer than the 371–33 margin of final passage indicated; every congressional Republican but one voted at least once to recommit the bill and remove old-age insurance from it. Senate Finance Committee Chairman Pat Harrison had to hold up the legislation for some time waiting to secure the one additional vote needed to get it out of committee.[29] The Wheeler-Rayburn utilities bill was initially defeated before being significantly moderated and subsequently passed. The Robinson-Patman anti–price discrimination bill experienced initial difficulties, and both the Revenue Act and the Banking Act had to be weakened by several degrees to attain passage. It is not difficult to imagine a less sanguine outcome for Roosevelt if Democratic majorities had been half their actual size, as would have been the case if Democrats had sustained average losses in 1934. Indeed, it is not difficult to imagine a less sanguine outcome for Roosevelt even if there had been no midterm election at all: popular support for his legislative program was crucial to its passage, but without the 1934 elections, that support would have remained unregistered.

The three other consequences of 1934 flowed from the introduction and passage of the 1935 legislative program. The Second New Deal halted the president's slide and tempered public dissatisfaction. Indeed, it is not farfetched to argue that "the energies of this second New Deal . . . ensured Roosevelt's reelection."[30] If one examines the 74th Congress along the same lines as the preparatory congresses, the patterns remain similar, although a mirror image, with the advantages usually held by the out-party accruing instead to the president's party. As in the previous Congress, party cohesion scores slightly favored the Republicans, probably because the Democratic majority was so large and unwieldy. But on questions of partisanship, leadership, productivity, and issue development, the pattern held in reverse. Partisanship in the 74th Congress fell from that in the 73rd, probably because many Republicans, shellshocked by 1934, signed on to New Deal measures. There was indeed a substantial leadership gap, with the presidential party holding an advantage: Democrats had Roosevelt and Rayburn, while House Republicans were led by the "ineffectual and disorganized" Bertrand H. Snell.[31] Legislative productivity rose from 539 public laws enacted in the 73rd Congress to 987 in the 74th Congress.[32] And the 74th Congress used that productivity to develop campaign issues to help the president in 1936. Needless to say, Social Security, labor reforms, rural electrification, and other measures from 1935 received prominent attention in the Democratic platform and Democratic campaign of 1936.[33] To no small degree, the issues developed in 1935 have defined the Democratic Party ever since.

Thus, the 1934 elections and the Second New Deal helped—indeed, were probably necessary—to cement the New Deal coalition into place. As Arthur M. Schlesinger Jr. observed, "A flood of Democratic votes gushing from traditionally non-Democratic sources washed the traditional Democratic party into the discard" and helped make it "predominantly a northern and, to a new degree, an urban party."[34] Of sixty-nine Senate Democrats, only twenty-four were southern; of 322 in the House, only 108 were southern.

Particularly powerful in maintaining this trend was the impact of the 74th Congress on labor. Labor was "one keystone of the emerging Democratic coalition,"[35] and two of the three measures judged most responsible for molding the long-term loyalty of labor to the Democrats were the Social Security Act and the Wagner Act.[36] In short, "what had been in 1932 an anti-Republican vote was becoming by 1934 a pro-Democratic—or, at least, pro-Roosevelt—vote . . . The legislation of 1935 completed the identification of the cause of labor with the New Deal."[37] Subsequent analyses seem to confirm that the class basis of the party coalitions did not develop until the period between the 1932 and 1936 presidential elections.[38] Thus, not only did the 1934 elections and subsequent legislation contribute mightily to the reelection of Roosevelt in 1936, but they made a major if not decisive contribution to long-term Democratic successes in American politics. In that sense, 1934 was as much a part of the realignment process as 1930, demonstrating the permeability of the midterm categories under some conditions.

Finally, the Second New Deal succeeded in largely preempting and co-opting the forces of radicalism and demagoguery which threatened to continue growing in the absence of vigorous action. The Social Security Act took the wind out of the sails of the Townsend plan, while the Wealth Tax Act and rich baiting undercut Huey Long. This consequence of 1934 continues to be a subject of debate. Many on the left have since complained that Roosevelt acted out of political necessity rather than conviction, that the Second New Deal was only a halfway measure that was designed primarily to forestall more fundamental change, and that it (unfortunately) succeeded in that design. Many on the right have pointed out that if the Second New Deal succeeded in containing radicals and demagogues, it did so only at the cost of moving significantly in their direction, introducing an unhealthy degree of radicalism, class warfare, and demagoguery into the mainstream of American political discourse. Whatever truth there may be in either (or both) of these critiques, most Americans seemed to welcome the program and the peace that it promised. In that sense, the safety of the American Republic in the midst of Depression might be traced not to 1932 but to 1934.

Altogether, the midterm elections of 1934 must be counted as among the most momentous of the last century. Like the elections of 1894 and 1930, the elections of 1934 not only foretold but contributed to the victory of the winning party's presidential candidate two years later. They led to one of the most important congresses in American history, a Congress that fundamentally changed the relationship of citizens to the national government. They, probably more than the elections of 1936, led to the solidification of a new party alignment that lasted decades. Even average Democratic losses in 1934 could have changed the picture in any of these respects.

The Great Exception Redux: 1962

As the exception of 1934 played a crucial role in the New Deal, a smaller-scale exception in 1962 played an important, although largely overlooked, role in the New Frontier–Great Society era of federal activism. John F. Kennedy won election to the presidency in 1960 by one of the narrowest margins in American electoral history. He showed no coattails, as Democrats lost twenty House seats—about two-fifths of their 1958 gains. While some Democrats such as Senator Paul Douglas acclaimed the 87th Congress,[39] most observers viewed it as an obstructionist body. Most of the president's program stalled; Medicare lost fifty-two to forty-eight in the Senate, agriculture controls lost by a handful of votes in the House, and several other measures failed. Clearly, even if 1958 represented a beginning for what ultimately became known as the Great Society, the victory would be won only in stages.

Having already watched most of his program fail, Kennedy was forced to contend with midterm elections in 1962. In those elections, there was but one question and one issue. The question was whether Kennedy could beat the anti-administration history of midterm elections. In his view, "History is so much against us, yet if we can hold our own, if we can win five seats or ten seats, it would change the whole opinion in the House and in the Senate."[40] Against the advice of Arthur Schlesinger and others, Kennedy undertook a vast and avowedly political national campaign tour, willingly gambling his prestige on the outcome.[41] The issue was Cuba, raised by Republicans with increasing vehemence starting in late August 1962. The potential power of the Cuban issue was clear. Before the missile crisis, some Republicans even believed that the forty-four-seat gain necessary for House control was within reach, and once the crisis broke in late October there was talk within the administration of how American retreat would likely lead to a Republican House and/or impeachment.[42] Having planned a 19,000-mile campaign trip, Kennedy was forced by the crisis to stop after 5,500 miles.[43] Nevertheless, the resolution of the crisis aided Kennedy and the Democrats, rallying the public behind the president and depriving the Republicans of an issue. While Republicans criticized Kennedy's noninvasion pledge right up to election day, the attack did not resonate.[44]

By November, most analysts expected a ten-to-fifteen-seat Republican gain in the House. The 1962 midterms would be "one of the most inconclusive midterm elections in years," one journalist predicted.[45] The final results, however, led to talk of a presidential mandate. Democrats lost only four seats in the House, the smallest loss (excluding the Democratic gain of 1934) by any presidential party since 1866. Furthermore, they actually gained three Senate seats and suffered no net loss of governorships (although they did lose Pennsylvania, Ohio, and Michigan), the only time from the 1920s until 1986 that the president's party was not set back in statehouses. Vermont elected a Democratic governor for the first time in 109 years. Some of the president's strongest critics were defeated, such as Senator Homer Capehart of Indiana and Representative Walter Judd of Minnesota. Richard Nixon was defeated in the California gubernatorial election, leading most analysts to declare his political career over, and new liberal Democrats came to the fore. Birch Bayh won in Indiana, Gaylord Nelson in Wisconsin, and George McGovern in South Dakota. Candidates on both extremes fared poorly: all four avowed members of the John Birch Society in the House lost reelection bids, while all but a handful of seventeen "peace" candidates nationwide "sank without a trace."[46]

Interpretations at the time were not uniform. The president, himself, said he was "heartened" by the results.[47] A few commentators called the election a standoff, and several pointed out that passage of Kennedy's program was far from assured. Nevertheless, Kennedy was generally conceded to have won a victory. In the view of New York Times correspondent Tom Wicker, who had earlier predicted an inconsequential midterm, "Democrats have scored a remarkable midterm election success. The outcome of Tuesday's election demonstrated support for President Kennedy's Cuban policies and warded off a Republican threat to his legislative strength . . . The President emerged with greater prestige—and political strength."[48] In Arthur Schlesinger's opinion, "the President's personal mandate was triumphantly refreshed."[49] Others would, either contemporaneously or after the fact, call the elections a "clearer mandate," an "indication of confidence," a "big negative victory with some positive overtones," and a "victory for the Administration to rank with victories of 1902 and 1934."[50] Democratic National Committee Chairman John M. Bailey also compared the results to Franklin Roosevelt's earlier success, saying "President Kennedy has received a midterm vote of confidence which will affect our country's destiny as greatly as did the F.D.R. midterm victory in 1934."[51] Unnamed sources at the Republican National Committee said simply, "We were nicely clobbered."[52]

There were several elements to Kennedy's victory. Developments in the Senate, where it was believed that the new Democratic members could put Medicare over the top, were important. Because Democratic House losses were concentrated in the South, they did not necessarily indicate a loss of voting power for the president. To the contrary, observers estimated that Kennedy had actually gained eight to twelve supporters in the House between the general election and the primaries, where at least two anti-Kennedy Southern Democrats had lost to more favorable Democrats.[53] Furthermore, the brightest and most energetic of the new members in both the House and Senate were pro–New Frontier. Consequently, it was possible for Kennedy supporters to speak of a quantitative and qualitative move to the left coming out of the 1962 elections.[54] Connected with this compositional change of the congressional Democratic Party was the rise of southern Republicanism, which was felt in a major way at the congressional level for the first time in 1962.[55] Four years later, in the midterm elections of 1966, this trend would blossom, not necessarily to the benefit of the national Democratic Party. For the time being, however, Democratic control was secure enough that factional composition was more important than raw numbers.

An image of momentum for Kennedy was projected as a result of the 1962 elections and the subsequent dominant media interpretation. Conversely, Republicans were assumed to have stalled in their drive to regain control of government. Wicker remarked that "the Republicans had lost rather than gained momentum in the incipient race to win back the White House in 1964."[56] The effect of these assessments on the morale of each party cannot be quantified but was surely important.

Finally, as in 1934, the Democrats gained an important victory for the future just by not losing the seats that a president's party usually loses. Of course, the twenty-seat Democratic loss in 1960, despite Kennedy's presidential victory, meant that fewer Democratic seats were exposed and that surge-and-decline effects would be less likely to rob the Democrats of seats in 1962. Nevertheless, even the modest twenty-seat Republican gain expected by many would have seriously jeopardized the New Frontier (assuming that many of those gains would have come at the expense of northern Democrats) and might have made Lyndon Johnson's task much more difficult, even after his 1964 landslide.

It is impossible to untangle the effect of Kennedy's assassination on the passage of the Kennedy-Johnson program, but there is significant reason to believe that the midterm of 1962 was an important turning point even before the assassination. As James Sundquist pointed out:

> The Democratic program was unblocked in 1963 and 1964 by a Congress substantially the same in makeup as the one that had blocked the program two years earlier. The most profound influence upon the new Congress was, of course, the assassination of the President and the country's reaction to that tragedy. Nevertheless, the ice-jam of stalled legislation had been thawing in the months before Dallas.[57]

On issues ranging from education aid to wilderness protection to tax reduction to civil rights, legislation had begun moving. In fact, Kennedy was the only president from 1953 through 1996 whose average *Congressional Quarterly* support score actually rose after a midterm election.[58] This improvement, significantly, was even evident among conservative Democrats.[59] In the view of Sundquist, the Democratic House leadership of Speaker John McCormack and Majority Leader Carl Albert was also much more effective in the 88th Congress than in the 87th Congress, when they were first becoming accustomed to their new roles.[60]

Overall, "the considerable progress of the Kennedy program prior to November suggests strongly that most of what happened would have happened—more slowly perhaps, but ultimately—if Kennedy had lived."[61] In Sundquist's view, Kennedy's relative success in 1962 "superseded" the narrow presidential victory of 1960, providing him with greater prestige and a new and more potent mandate.[62] The same could not be said if Democrats had suffered the average midterm loss in 1962, restoring the pre-1958 equilibrium in the House.

The Creative Exceptions and Political Change

In previous chapters, we have seen how midterm elections have often served as a check on the incumbent president and (sometimes simultaneously) as a harbinger of political change. In those cases, the out-party gained seats and sometimes gained control of Congress, then used those gains to stymie the president and lay the groundwork for a takeover of the presidency. Yet, as can be seen in this chapter, midterm elections have on occasion served the cause of change not by stymieing the president but by strengthening him. In 1934 and, to a lesser extent, in 1962, the president's party beat history and gave momentum to the president and his program. The midterm exceptions of 1934 and 1962 were integral components of the New Deal and New Frontier–Great Society eras. Thus, not only were all three of this century's eras of federal activism bracketed by midterm elections, but two of the three were propelled midway through by midterm elections that were unusually favorable to the president's party. And, just as heavy losses have often foretold or contributed to presidential defeats, the in-party's victories in 1934 and 1962 preceded landslide victories by the party's incumbent president two years later.

There are several strands holding together the two exceptions as mirror images of the preparatory elections. In both cases, the success of the president's party provided it with intangible momentum and demoralized the opposition; the president's popular mandate appeared refreshed rather than diminished. The very act of registering and revealing voter preferences strengthened the president's hand. In both cases, the composition of the president's party was shifted to some degree in a manner favorable to the president. At the same time, some of the president's most bitter opponents in both parties were defeated and removed (at least temporarily) from public life. In both instances, the in-party's gains—in 1934, in the House and Senate, and in 1962, in the Senate—were important but were outweighed by the losses that did not happen. Even average losses in those years could have killed the Second New Deal and the New Frontier–Great Society. Instead, majorities were maintained which made possible major legislative accomplishments. Even Lyndon Johnson, helped tremendously by the influx of new Democrats in 1964, achieved much of Kennedy's agenda before the 1964 elections. Those accomplishments, aided by relatively strong congressional leadership, solidified the presidential party's electoral coalition for the next presidential election. Thus, the dogs that did not bark—the midterm losses that did not happen—have been a key but largely overlooked element of American political history, leaving open the question of how many other presidential initiatives might have made history, for better or worse, in the absence of the check imposed through the midterm pattern.

A Note on the Exception of 1998

Since this is primarily a study of the consequences of midterm elections, and the full consequences of the 1998 midterm elections are not yet manifest, only a few preliminary remarks can be offered here. Nevertheless, those elections clearly must be placed in the exception category. Given virtually any theory of midterm elections, one should have expected modest Republican gains—gains because of the historical midterm pattern, modest because of the president's high approval rating, the good economy, the president's short 1996 coattails, and relatively low Democratic exposure. That the GOP lost five House seats, a governorship, and a number of legislative seats and chambers, while making no Senate gains, was a surprise, especially in the context of overheated expectations of large scandal-driven gains only a month before.

The 1998 elections were anomalous in more ways than one. Not only was the result a dramatic reversal of the historical trend of midterm elections, but the elections themselves were held under unprecedented circumstances. Only twice before had U.S. presidents been faced with impeachment, and neither instance coincided with an election. Impeachment was an electoral wild card, and it is reasonable to believe that it was the decisive factor in the unusual outcome, probably by mobilizing core Democratic constituencies like blacks and labor.

The impact of impeachment on the 1998 elections was, however, probably more complex than was commonly recognized and more dependent on the strategic choices of political actors. House Democrats, who benefited from public weariness with the scandal, were also successful at distancing themselves from the president; most voted for releasing the Starr Report, and all but five voted for some form of impeachment inquiry. Republicans, for their part, made numerous blunders, ranging from public release of the president's grand jury testimony to insisting on an open-ended inquiry to running anti-Clinton television ads in the week before election day. They compounded their errors by negotiating a bad budget deal in early October, which probably had the effect of simultaneously dispiriting their base and persuading the Democratic base that Bill Clinton was still sufficiently capable of "delivering the goods" that it was worth their while to save his presidency.

In a broader sense, if the presidential-penalty theorists are right, impeachment reversed the normal midterm election equation. Under normal circumstances, a vote for the president's congressional opposition is a vote for balance, a vote to check the president. In 1998, it was a vote to provide Congress with a license to overthrow him. This changed dynamic raises several interesting theoretical questions, among them whether Richard Nixon would have avoided his fate if the midterm elections of 1974 had been held in February, when only 38 percent of poll respondents favored impeachment.

Even in the small category of exceptions, the 1998 elections are unique in that they took place in the president's second term (1934 and 1962 were first-term midterms) and in that it was much more difficult to interpret them as a public mandate for a comprehensive presidential program for change (since it would be difficult to argue that Bill Clinton in 1998 had such a program). Nevertheless, the 1998 elections help to illustrate by way of exception how midterm elections generally work against a president. As in 1934 and 1962, the 1998 results seemed to promise a reversal of the typical anti-administration midterm effects across the board. The composition of Congress improved for the president. The president and his supporters claimed a "vindication" and popular mandate against impeachment or, to put it another way, in favor of continuance of the president's leadership;[63] Republicans, who had hoped to claim a counter mandate, were silenced, except for the debate they had among themselves over who was to blame for the defeat. Outside observers claimed to see an election-driven shift in momentum; analysis in the *New York Times* called the elections "a crushing disappointment to the giddy hopes of the Republicans and an unexpected elixir to the recently ailing Democrats."[64] Democratic operatives, who a few weeks earlier had feared annihilation, began arguing that a Democratic recapture of the House in 2000 was highly likely.[65]

Republican divisions were exacerbated, leading to a shake-up of House leadership, including the resignation of House Speaker Newt Gingrich, and a challenge to RNC chairman Jim Nicholson. The Democratic gubernatorial victory in California raised the prospect of a redistricting disaster for Republicans, although they continued to hold a two-to-one advantage in governorships nationwide. Several strong potential challengers to Al Gore, such as House Minority Leader Richard Gephardt and Senator Bob Kerrey, removed themselves from contention for the 2000 Democratic presidential nomination; on the Republican side, only Texas Governor George W. Bush benefited from the election results. And it was clear that Democrats had outmaneuvered Republicans on issues from impeachment to Social Security to education, leaving no reason for Republicans to hope that 1998 would serve as a foundation for issue development in 2000. The narrow and diminished Republican House majority also made it more difficult for congressional Republicans to formulate a distinctive legislative program. Instead, Democrats believed that administration priorities that had seemed dead in Congress might be alive after all. Days after the election, White House spokesman Joe Lockhart said, "We are trying to use the political capital we have gained to move the agenda items we were pushing in the campaign. We think the message from the voters it that the Republicans ought to come with us."[66]

All in all, any Republican victory in 2000 would have to occur without any of the benefits usually gained by the out-party in the midterm election. Democrats, on the other hand, seemed invigorated and united by the elections. And while a historic program offered by Bill Clinton may not have been ushered in by the exception of 1998, his presidency may well have been saved by it; in November 1998, no item was higher on Bill Clinton's agenda than survival. Had Democrats lost the six Senate seats typical in a president's sixth year, only half a dozen Democrats would have had to defect to remove him from office. That the election results did not stop impeachment in the House, as many had expected, was a testament to the contingent nature of election consequences, to the mistakes and miscalculations of the administration, and to the strength of many of the charges arrayed against the president. Nevertheless, House Republicans were forced to vote for impeachment in the face of electoral evidence that most Americans did not want it, and to vote for it without the benefit of the bipartisan cover that might well have developed if the normal midterm pattern had continued in 1998. Thus, while it cannot be said with certainty what the ultimate consequences will be of the exception of 1998, it can be said that, all other things being equal, Bill Clinton and his party were significantly better positioned—and Republicans significantly worse off—than they would have been had there been no midterm elections of 1998 or had the midterm elections of 1998 followed a typical course.

SEVEN

Normal Midterms

Some midterm elections may precede and contribute to a long-term change in presidential control—perhaps even a realignment—but most do not. Some midterm elections may play a calibrating role in times of great change, but most do not—if for no other reason than that there are so few periods of great change. Only twice in the century from 1894 to 1994 did midterm elections propel change by violating the anti-administration rule. What about the rest?

Of the twenty-six midterms from 1894 to 1994, thirteen do not easily fit into any of the categories of preparatory, calibrating, or exceptional elections. This group—1898, 1902, 1906, 1914, 1922, 1926, 1942, 1946, 1954, 1970, 1974, 1990, and 1994—could be called normal midterms, both because more midterms fit in this category than in any other and because these midterms, in a sense, comprise the default category. Most did not precede a change of party in the White House, and the two that did (1974 and 1990) contributed little to the shift. Many of the thirteen are mired in obscurity, and those that are known—like 1946—are known largely for their ultimate futility, producing "sound and fury, signifying nothing." Yet these normal midterms are hardly irrelevant; indeed, they frequently hold enormous import.

At a minimum, even in normal midterms presidents face a less friendly Congress. In terms of seat losses, the president's party lost an average of thirty-three House and two Senate seats in normal midterms. Those figures are roughly the same as the average for all midterms in this period (thirty-five House and three Senate seats), and are certainly enough to mean that the president is often caused serious problems. Results in normal midterms ranged from high losses of seventy-five House and twelve Senate seats to a low of ten House seats lost and seven Senate seats gained by the president's party, but every normal House midterm and eight of thirteen Senate midterms featured a loss by the president's party to some extent. Furthermore, the regional analysis presented in chapter 1 indicates that there was an anti-administration trend in factional terms in eleven of the thirteen normal midterms (see table 1.6). On three of thirteen occasions, the president's party lost formal control of both houses of Congress (1946, 1954, and 1994) and on at least three others (1922, 1926, and 1942) lost working control of one or both houses.

As was also discussed in chapter one, presidential and congressional explanations for midterm election results are an important element of the midterm equation, and of the capacity of midterm elections to serve as an added check on the president. In three of the six normal midterms since the end of World War Two, the president was forced to acknowledge that the election results represented some sort of referendum on national conditions; in four of the six, the president was put on the defensive to the extent of blaming history and/or explicitly denying that the results were a referendum against his administration. And in five of the six normal midterms since 1946, the congressional opposition was able to claim a counter mandate of some sort, whether partisan, ideological, or anti-administration (see Appendixes B and C). The threat posed to the president's plebiscitary authority clearly extends to normal midterms.

Anti-administration interpretations are likely to be supported by journalistic analysis, even in normal midterms. A review of election analysis by the *New York Times* shows that three-fourths of normal midterm elections from 1898 through 1994 were described in terms that presented the results as a rebuke for the president and his party (see Appendix E). This tendency of journalistic sources to interpret the elections in anti-administration terms both undercuts the president's position and undoubtedly provides some degree of important though unquantifiable political momentum to his opponents.

Normal midterms, however, are much more likely than preparatory midterms to produce congresses in which legislative productivity increases. Productivity changed little, falling from an average of 622 public laws enacted per session to 609 (2.1 percent); six of thirteen congresses following normal midterms actually saw legislative productivity rise (including six of eleven that did not precede an opposition takeover of the presidency). Furthermore, confrontation increased less consistently after normal midterms than after preparatory elections. Vetoes as a proportion of public bills enacted increased in eight out of thirteen congresses following normal midterms (compared with five of eight preparatory congresses), but total vetoes and the proportion of all post–normal midterm public bills that were vetoed were essentially unchanged. The only indication of greater confrontation, on average, was found in the total number of override attempts and override successes, which increased considerably after normal midterms. In particular, the proportion of successful overrides more than doubled (table 7.1). Thus, normal midterm congresses follow a course of general obstruction and of confrontation less consistently than do most preparatory congresses, although there is still roughly a fifty-fifty chance that presidents will be plagued by them.

The transfusion of new leadership is effective in normal midterms, and those midterms have frequently exerted significant influence on policy. A brief review of the normal midterms between 1894 and 1994 can help to illustrate this point.

1898

Republican losses under William McKinley were a bearable twenty-one seats in the House, leaving them with a narrow twenty-two-vote margin. Republican Senate gains, part of the aftershock of the 1896 realignment, made possible the ratification of the Treaty of Paris, ending the Spanish-American War. Nevertheless, House Democrats were invigorated by a gain of fifty seats, mostly at the expense of the Populist contingent, leading at least some journalists to view the results as a censure of the administra-

Table 7.1 Legislative Productivity and Presidential Vetoes Before and
After Normal Midterms, 1896–1996

	Public Bills	Vetoes	Vetoes/ Bills (%)	Override Attempts/Successes
Congresses prior to normal midterms	8,087	361	4.5	44/9 (20.5%)
Congresses after normal midterms	7,923	362	4.6	65/27 (41.5%)

Source: George B. Galloway, *History of the House of Representatives* 2nd ed. (New York: Thomas Y. Crowell Company, 1976), 375–76; Robert Moon and Carol Hardy Vincent, *Workload and Activity Report: United States Senate, 1946–92* (Washington, D.C.: Congressional Research Service, 1993), 15; *Presidential Vetoes 1789–1988* (Washington, D.C.: GPO, 1992); *Presidential Vetoes 1989–1994* (Washington, D.C.: GPO, 1994).

tion. Clearly, Democrats had moved further in the direction charted in 1896 of incorporating the populist movement into the Democratic Party.[1]

1902

Theodore Roosevelt's first midterm election saw a net Republican loss of sixteen House seats, leaving the GOP with a thirty-vote margin.[2] The *New York Times* perceived a "strong current of opinion" against Republican policies, although historical accounts generally hold the elections not to have harmed Roosevelt significantly. Indeed, the vote, taken in the midst of Roosevelt's experiment of personalizing the presidency, may have helped to confirm that institutional direction.[3]

1906

In Roosevelt's second midterm, Republican losses of twenty-eight House seats led the opposition to rejoice that "the Democrats had begun the road back" from a dismal showing in 1904.[4] Beneath the partisan surface, it was also clear that progressivism as a force was gaining strength in both parties. Within the Republican Party, "the oligarchy blamed Roosevelt for Progressive agitation and brought his legislative program virtually to a standstill in 1907 and 1908."[5] Overall, some scholars have pointed to 1906 as the beginning of the Democratic–A.F.L. alliance and the first step toward Woodrow Wilson's ascendancy.[6]

1914

Woodrow Wilson's Democrats lost fifty-nine seats in the House. At the same time, Progressive Party congressional candidates, while polling a much smaller number than in 1912, still gained enough votes by one estimate to deprive Republicans of House control.[7] Republicans were thus both emboldened and encouraged to draw Progressives back into the fold, laying the groundwork for the full recovery of the Republican Party after the catastrophe of 1912.

1922

Warren Harding's Republicans lost seventy-five House seats and eight Senate seats. Furthermore, as one analyst argued, "the election issues crossed party lines, and the blow that the conservative Harding administration had suffered was far more serious than the surface facts seemed to indicate."[8] The president's friends and allies disproportionately became victims, while his intraparty critics were emboldened and organized around Sen. Robert LaFollette (R-Wisc.). The Teapot Dome investigation was launched, and the stage was set for LaFollette's unsuccessful third-party presidential candidacy in 1924.

1926

The 1926 midterm elections deprived pro-administration Republicans of a working majority in the Senate. Consequently, the McNary-Haugen farm bill, which had been introduced every year since 1924, finally passed Congress, inviting Calvin Coolidge's veto in 1927 and again in 1928. In the view of scholars, the McNary-Haugen bill—while never enacted over the president's veto—"set the stage for the adoption of parity in later agricultural policy, swung American society to the principle of government farm aid, and contributed to altering the partisan loyalties of farmers."[9]

1942

The midterm elections of 1942 strengthened the conservative coalition in Congress. Despite nominal Democratic control, Congress in 1943 through 1944 "carried out a retroactive revenge against the New Deal," passing the Smith-Connally Anti-Strike Act over Franklin Roosevelt's veto and abolishing the National Resources Planning Board, which had recommended a major postwar expansion of the welfare state.[10]

1946

Republicans regained control of Congress for the first time since 1930, reorienting postwar policy and putting an end to Harry S. Truman's Fair Deal.

1954

Democratic gains, while small, were sufficient to make Democrats the majority in both the House and Senate after a two-year hiatus. They would not surrender majority status in the Senate until 1980 and in the House until 1994.

1970

The midterm election pattern held in the House, where Democrats picked up a modest twelve seats. Richard Nixon's social issues campaign, focusing on law and order themes, seemed to backfire, producing no electoral gains but significantly increased partisan polarization between the White House and Congress—in short, a "sharply-divided, distrustful, adversary government in Washington."[11]

1974

The influx of liberal Democrats in 1974 probably sealed the fate of Indochina; when North Vietnam violated the Paris Peace Accords and launched a full-scale invasion of the South in spring 1975, Gerald Ford did not have the votes to continue military assistance to Saigon. That class of Watergate babies subsequently dominated the House for twenty years.

1990

Despite strong Republican hopes of a comeback in the Senate, Democrats made modest gains in both houses. Republican unity began to crack around the tax issue, and George Bush continued to confront large and recalcitrant Democratic majorities.

1994

Republicans gained control of both houses of Congress in one of the most dramatic midterm elections in American history. They stymied most of Bill Clinton's agenda, forced policy to the right on a wide range of issues, and also inadvertently helped guarantee Clinton's reelection in 1996.

On balance, even normal midterms can pose numerous difficulties for presidents, ranging from substantial seat losses to increased confrontation with Congress to a palpable shift in political momentum and diminution of his previous electoral mandate. While there is an even chance of increasing legislative productivity, there remains a strong possibility that less friendly Congresses will attempt to obstruct the president's agenda and/or displace it with their own. Even when midterms have little or no effect on long-term partisan control of the institutions of government, they can end up having significant influence on policy. And the very fact that midterm elections are scheduled can affect a president's calculations, as well as the calculations of his congressional co-partisans and his opponents, in ways that generally encourage presidential caution and, failing that, stymie him anyway.

Some of the limits and complexities of the role of normal midterm elections and midterm congresses can be seen by reviewing in detail the elections of 1946 and 1994. Both were what one might call high-octane normal midterms, with above-average seat turnover and a shift in party control of both houses of Congress. Indeed, so many things about 1994 were extraordinary that calling it normal might strike some as implausible, except that it so clearly does not fit into any of the other categories. In the end, despite much contemporary speculation to the contrary, neither 1946 nor 1994 led to a change in presidential control. Yet, despite that failure, and the added failure of the congressional change of 1946 to sustain itself in 1948, both midterms launched substantial policy change. These two midterms were the most dramatic of the normal midterms but failed to reach a higher level of impact. Thus, 1946 and 1994 serve as examples of the potential significance of normal midterms as well as examples of why normal midterms do not go further; the 80th and 104th Congresses can illuminate the range of effects of midterm elections both through their failures and through their triumphs.

1946 and the "Do-Nothing" 80th Congress

The famed 80th Congress resulted from a Republican gain of fifty-five House seats and twelve Senate seats in the midterm elections of 1946. Southern Democrats suffered no net House losses, while Democrats in the Northeast, Midwest, and West suffered losses in excess of 40 percent. The 1946 elections brought not only a change in congressional control but a change at the state level and a turnover in leadership. The Republicans gained three governorships, a relatively small number but enough to give them control of more than half of the states (twenty-five of forty-eight) for the first time since before the Depression. Scores of Democratic New Dealers fell, although John F. Kennedy was first elected to the House; numerous future Republican leaders joined Congress, such as Representative Richard M. Nixon and Senators John Bricker (Ohio), William Jenner (Ind.), Joseph McCarthy (Wisc.), and John Williams (Del.). Thomas Dewey, first elected governor of New York in 1942, was reelected by a margin of 680,000 votes in 1946, giving strength to his presidential campaign.[12]

Observers could seriously ask whether the elections of 1946 would "foreshadow a major political realignment from which the GOP would emerge again as the dominant national party."[13] At the very least, many considered the 1946 election results to be the death knell of the Truman administration. Democratic Senator William Fulbright of Arkansas went so far as to suggest that Truman appoint a Republican secretary of state and then resign, an action that would have placed the Republicans in control of the presidency. Yet not only did the Republican takeover of the 80th Congress not precede realignment, it did not precede a presidential victory of any sort, and the Republican congressional majority was, itself, swept back out of power in 1948.

Along the dimensions that were discussed in regard to the preparatory congresses, the 80th Congress exhibited some similarities and several crucial differences. In terms of party cohesion, although both parties had their splits, congressional Democrats had much greater difficulty maintaining party cohesion than did the Republicans—consistent with the pattern of preparatory congresses.[14] House Democratic defectors on major votes, mostly from the South, consistently numbered at least thirty and sometimes as high as sixty; similar problems existed for the Democrats in the Senate. House Republican cohesion scores were substantially better than Democratic scores, although as the 80th Congress proceeded, splits between liberal and conservative Republicans widened (table 7.2).[15] The Republicans were also plagued by the split between their presidential party and their congressional party, which Harry Truman skillfully exploited by challenging a special session of Congress to implement the Republican presidential platform of 1948, but this split was hardly worse than the concerted liberal campaign to dump Truman and the subsequent three-way split at the presidential level in the Democratic party in 1948.[16]

However, the 80th Congress exhibited a different pattern of party leadership, of partisanship, of productivity and confrontation, and of issue development than preparatory congresses. The gap in party leadership which typically hurts the in-parties was not evident in the 80th Congress, with both sides fairly evenly matched. The House Democrats boasted Sam Rayburn, while Harry Truman, himself, conceived and effectively executed a political strategy that turned back the Republican tide and reestablished Democratic supremacy in 1948. While Truman did not adequately coordinate with the Democratic congressional leadership for the first portion of the 80th Congress, he remedied that shortcoming starting in April 1948.[17] This occasional breakdown in communications could not be compared with the hostility felt toward Cleveland by his party or the contempt often shared between Hoover and his party.

For their part, the Republicans utilized the considerable talents of Senators Robert Taft and Arthur Vandenberg, but House Speaker Joseph Martin was best described as workmanlike, attaining his successes by establishing priorities on which substantial intraparty consensus already existed.[18] And at critical junctures in the last half of 1948, Thomas Dewey failed his copartisans in Congress: "Strong leadership from their presidential nominee was not forthcoming" at a time when the whole party needed to stand together to meet the challenge of the special session.[19]

Perhaps surprisingly, given the mythology surrounding the 80th Congress, there is little evidence of an across-the-board increase in confrontation. Partisanship did not increase, with party voting actually falling to a trough of 45 percent (see table 7.2). There was no increase in the number of vetoes from the 79th to the 80th Congress (indeed, the proportion of public bills vetoed by Truman fell), although there was an increase in veto override attempts and a high level of override success (table 7.3).

The 80th Congress was also inclined to try to establish a large legisla-

Table 7.2 Partisan Voting and House Cohesion Scores, 78th–82nd Congresses

Congress	Years	Party votes (%)	Democratic Cohesion	Republican Cohesion
78th	1943–44	49.4	59.9	73.0
79th	1945–46	48.1	64.4	69.4
80th	1947–48	44.8	65.1	76.1
81st	1949–50	50.9	63.0	67.6
82nd	1951–52	64.1	61.8	65.2

Source: Data from David Brady and John Ettling, "The Electoral Connection and the Decline of Partisanship in the Twentieth Century House of Representatives," *Congress and the Presidency* 11 (Spring 1984): 22.

Table 7.3 Legislative Productivity and Presidential Vetoes, 79th–80th Congresses Public Bills

Congress	Public Bills Enacted	Vetoes	Override Vetoes/Bills (%)	Attempts/Successes
79th	734	76*	10.4	4/0
80th	905	75	8.3	8/6

Source: Data from *Presidential Vetoes 1789–1989* (Washington, D.C.: GPO, 1992).
*Franklin Roosevelt vetoed two bills in the 79th Congress before his death; the remaining 74 were cast by Truman.

tive record and pursued a high level of conciliation and cooperation with the president on foreign affairs issues throughout the congressional term. It was the Congress of aid to Greece and Turkey, the Marshall Plan, and the National Security Act. In contrast to most of the preparatory congresses, productivity in the 80th Congress, measured by public bills enacted, was substantially greater than the averages of the congresses immediately preceding and succeeding it, despite the moniker of "Do-Nothing" Congress affixed by Truman (see table 7.3).

The 80th Congress did obstruct most of Truman's agenda (such as inflation control measures, housing programs, and an increased minimum wage), and Truman vetoed much of the Republican agenda, including tax cuts and the Taft-Hartley labor legislation. (Both vetoes were ultimately overridden.) Both obstruction and confrontation produced crucial campaign issues, but most of them worked to Truman's benefit because public sentiment was more often on his side. The novel feature of this presidential-congressional conflict was the degree to which it was manufactured by Harry Truman. Truman's advisers, led by Clark Clifford and James Rowe, outlined in late 1947 what was to become Truman's legislative strategy: "Its tactics must . . . be entirely different than if there were any real point to bargaining and compromise. Its recommendations tailored for the voters, not Congressmen; they must display a label which reads 'no compromise.'"[20] Truman himself later said of the "Turnip Day" session, "I knew that the special session would produce no results in the way of legislation."[21] In the words of political biographer Cabell Phillips, Truman was "too much of a fighter not to know that an offense is the best defense."[22]

Thus, in contrast to the preparatory cases, confrontation in the 80th Congress was limited and was largely the product of a deliberate strategy by the president to embarrass Congress and differentiate himself from it.[23] That differentiation proved crucial to Truman's reelection. While apparently not swaying independents, it solidified and mobilized his partisan base; for a Democrat in 1948, that was enough. Subsequent analysis showed that a strong labor and farm vote was responsible for Democratic victory in 1948.[24]

Although the 80th Congress utterly failed to serve as the precursor of a more enduring electoral alignment in American politics, it can hardly be considered a mere blip. The 1946 elections did have lasting importance in other ways. Legislatively, taxes were cut significantly, the 22nd Amendment limiting presidential terms was forwarded to the states, and the Taft-Hartley Act passed, fundamentally altering labor relations (and, as an important side-effect, eviscerating communist influence in the union movement).

Despite Truman's 1948 victory and the Democratic reconquest of Congress, Taft-Hartley was never repealed.

The election results also persuaded Truman to declare the end of World War II hostilities and to surrender many of his wartime emergency powers before the 80th Congress even convened. Indeed, sensing the political tides, Truman decontrolled meat three weeks *before* election day 1946. The Office of Price Administration was likewise disbanded and with it the highly centralized wage and price administration system. Truman also proposed a balanced budget.

Finally, the 80th Congress laid the groundwork for a postwar policy of active American engagement in the world. A Democratic Congress would also have almost certainly adopted the key pillars of containment, but Republican control of Congress meant that Republicans had obtained a proprietary interest in a policy of engagement. They became, of necessity, partners in the construction of that policy. Few accomplishments in American politics in the twentieth century bore greater import than the end (at least until 1972, when the parties' positions were reversed) of the partisan division on internationalist-isolationist lines. As David Mayhew has observed, the 80th Congress may have been "a classic example of up the hill and down again," but judging it against a more modest standard of normal politics, it was "quite a successful two years."[25]

Altogether, the 1946 elections jolted American politics away from the hypercentralization produced by the twin crises of Depression and World War II. If the 1938 midterm elections killed the New Deal, the 1946 elections drove the nails in the coffin. Before 1946, liberals could hope that New Deal activism had only been interrupted by war and could be resumed in a new era of peace; 1946 signaled the end of that hope—although the New Deal coalition lived on for two or three decades more—and the onset of a period of substantial convergence in the center. In the words of Michael Barone, the Democratic victory of 1948 "did little to overturn the economic settlement made by Taft's 80th Congress and its rather conservative predecessors."[26] From 1946 until the mid-1960s, American politics was more or less settled on domestic caution and anticommunist internationalism.[27]

Indeed, Truman won in 1948 and carried the Democrats back into control of Congress not merely because of his success in executing a strategy of contrived confrontation but also because he knew when to confront and when to accommodate. The significance of the 80th Congress lay not only in its use by Truman as a foil to rally partisan Democrats; it forced him to take steps he would not otherwise have taken in order to soothe the public discontents that had exploded in 1946. If the Democrats possessed the stronger base (as surely they did), Republicans won in 1946 because short-term forces worked overwhelmingly in their favor. Those forces centered on public concern over inflation, demobilization, and excessive union power; unhappiness with high wartime taxes; and fears of permanent, powerful, regimented, and centralized crisis government. The isolationism of Republicans in the 1930s had at its root the fear that American entry into war could save freedom abroad only at the cost of losing it at home. When Americans visited the polls in November 1946, it was yet an open question whether those fears would become realized. If the post-1946 years appear in retrospect to be so normal, it is largely because of 1946 itself.

Despite Truman's generally well-deserved "give 'em hell" reputation, he—unlike Cleveland, Hoover, and Wilson—did not rigidly choose to defend an untenable position. And whatever he did not change, Congress changed for him. Altogether, the climate of public concern was altered in a way that would have been much less likely had Democrats retained control of Congress and no sharp break had been made with the New Deal–wartime regime. In no small way, Harry Truman won in 1948 because the 80th Congress drove him to more defensible ground. As Barone argues, voters in 1946 "wanted what the Republicans wanted, and what they delivered after they won."[28] But once they delivered, the road was again open to Harry Truman. In a sense, he won in 1948 by losing in 1946. The surprising point is not that he won, or even that he won by confronting the Republicans, but that he was able to confront them successfully—able to refocus public attention on the issues that cut his way—only because he and Congress had already removed the issues that posed the greatest dangers to him. In this respect, Truman's victory bears an uncanny resemblance to Bill Clinton's half a century later, although Truman's victory was a more complete one for his party.

The "Earthquake" of 1994

One of the most compelling political stories in America in the 1990s revolved around the Republican takeover of Congress in the 1994 midterm elections. Republicans hoped that 1994 would be 1894 all over again, the precursor to a more general realignment that would find completion in a presidential victory and solidification of long-term control of government. Democrats hoped that 1994 would be another 1946, a fluke that would be quickly reversed with a Trumanesque recovery and sweep in the next election. As it turned out, 1994 was neither 1894 nor 1946 but something in-between.

There was one essential prerequisite for the Republican takeover of Congress in 1994: a Democratic president. As Thomas Mann pointed out in the late 1980s, "Republicans probably must lose a presidential election in order to position themselves to take a majority of the House seats." The midterm curse makes it "virtually impossible for a party to strengthen its position in the House at the same time that it occupies the White House."[29] When Bill Clinton won the presidency in 1992, that condition was fulfilled. Democrats were then fighting not only the traditional tide of midterm patterns but the more recent tendency of voters to take only brief respites from divided government. That tendency soon reasserted itself, driven in no small part by miscalculations made by Clinton himself. Throughout his first two years in office, Clinton belied the New Democrat image on which he had run in 1992. A large tax increase was proposed, culturally liberal positions like gays in the military were espoused, and health care reform appeared to many voters to entail a giant new government bureaucracy. Welfare reform, the centerpiece of Clinton's New Democrat agenda, was effectively shelved.

Clinton, who had won with only 43 percent of the popular vote, started in a precarious position that only grew worse. His standing in Washington was adversely affected by a series of odd-year and special elections. Only weeks after election day, Republican Paul Coverdell beat incumbent Democrat and Clinton ally Wyche Fowler in a Georgia Senate runoff. In steady succession through 1993, Republicans won every major race, from a special Senate election in Texas to mayoral races in Los Angeles and Jersey City to a triple victory in November: on one day in November 1993, Rudolph Giuliani beat New York City Mayor David Dinkins, George Allen won the governorship of Virginia, and Christine Todd Whitman beat incumbent New Jersey Governor Tom Florio on the basis of antitax sentiment.

News commentary invariably presented this triple Republican victory as a major blow to Bill Clinton, who was forced to defend himself by claiming, "I don't know anybody who's out there who believes that all these elections are any more than a referendum on what people want for their mayors and their governors."[30] Republicans gained momentum and confidence going into the midterm elections, confidence that also had the effect of stiffening their spines in the legislative battles of 1994. Peter Roff, political director of Newt Gingrich's GOPAC, later held that the political tidal wave of 1994 "was created earlier—in fact, just weeks after Clinton and Gore took office. The seismic realignment that caused the eventual Republican takeover of Congress began with a series of political eruptions in 1993, from Los Angeles to Trenton."[31]

There were three important consequences of the midterm campaign of 1994. First, as in many of the other cases, the campaign became intertwined with congressional action on a number of fronts. The crime bill of 1994 became a debacle for the administration, despite its ultimate passage, when it was delayed and almost killed in no small part owing to election-year pressure by the National Rifle Association. More important by far, however, was the fate of the health care reform initiative, which foundered and died when public opinion turned against it and congressional Democrats lost their nerve. Preferring to face a disappointed president rather than an infuriated electorate, the Democratic leadership admitted temporary defeat and went home to campaign. This attempt to appease the voters failed, but it was central to the collapse of health care reform in 1994.

Second, House Republicans campaigned on the basis of the "Contract with America," a document outlining the prospective program of a new Republican majority and signed by over 300 candidates in September 1994. The contract was an attempt to explicitly nationalize the elections—that is, focus the electorate on national issues rather than on local concerns. In general, the strategy worked.[32] While only a minority of voters were familiar with the contract, considerable majorities supported the substance of each of its elements, and Republican candidates hammered consistently on those themes. The nationalization of the elections, in general, and the contract, specifically, were important not only to the outcome of the elections but to their aftermath. By putting forward a positive program before the elections—no matter how many or how few people knew its details—House Republicans put themselves in a position to claim a mandate for action.

Bill Clinton contributed the third crucial element of the campaign by responding directly to the contract and accepting the Republicans' challenge to turn the election into a face-off over those national issues. In the waning days of the campaign, Clinton and administration spokesmen frontally attacked the contract as a reversion to the "flawed policies and easy promises" of Reaganism and indicated that they accepted the election as a national referendum.[33] Just as Republicans set themselves up to claim a mandate for the contract, Clinton set himself up to suffer a greater loss of prestige than was necessary. He was, of course, hardly the first president to make that mistake.

While analysts had expected significant Republican gains, very few had anticipated the full extent of the carnage inflicted on Democrats nationwide. Republicans gained fifty-two House seats and eight Senate seats, putting them in control of both houses of Congress for the first time in forty years. By all indications, the Democratic congressional contingent became more liberal and the Republicans more conservative. Republicans also gained eleven governorships, knocking off such Democratic stalwarts as New York Governor Mario Cuomo and Texas Governor Ann Richards, placing the GOP in control of thirty governorships (including seven of the eight most populous states). Republicans gained approximately 500 state legislative seats and 19 legislative chambers, giving them rough parity with Democrats for the first time in years. Not a single incumbent Republican senator, governor, or representative lost a bid for reelection. Immediately, explanations for the electoral explosion were forthcoming from a variety of sources. Virtually all agreed that Bill Clinton's mandate from 1992, such as it was, was exhausted. Analyst William Schneider, for example, said simply, "It was Bill Clinton, stupid. A massive anti-Clinton coalition came together and produced the revolution of Nov. 8."[34] The *New York Times* echoed that the national election results were "a powerful body blow to Bill Clinton and a repudiation of his party's conduct in Congress."[35]

Clinton's interpretation of the 1994 elections utilized at least seven distinct (and occasionally contradictory) arguments, more than any other postwar president, running the gamut from accepting partial responsibility to blaming the voters for not adequately understanding his program. His explanation of 1994 as a call for smaller government committed him more fully than before to a centrist course. He argued that the voters deliberately sought divided government, paving the way for his reelection campaign, which was built largely on the theme that divided government should deliberately be chosen again—that he should be reelected to check the Republican Congress. Clinton's interpretation—that voters were not repudiating him but that he was at least partly responsible for Democratic defeats and that voters did desire a change—became the essence of what was later known as triangulation, a middle course between surrender to Congress and uncompromising defense of the status quo.[36]

The Republicans stressed an ideological mandate and talked of "revolution," which energized congressional action and made a credible case for superseding the president's plebiscitary claim to power, which was already weak.[37] At the same time, it also inhibited the use of tactical compromise and incremental change and unwittingly laid a rhetorical groundwork for Bill Clinton's campaign charging Republicans with extremism. The predominant interpretation expressed by congressional Democrats in 1994— that the elections represented a reaction against Clinton's leftward tilt in 1993 through 1994—undermined Clinton's 1992 mandate but also gave him the political breathing room to reposition himself to the right.[38] Thus, on balance, the interpretive process heavily damaged any claim Clinton might have had to govern on the basis of popular mandate, although he did squeeze some longer-term benefit out of some of the interpretations that were offered.

Because of the contract, Republicans had a ready-made program to rally around. For the first three-and-a-half months of the 104th Congress, Congress was clearly in command of the agenda, and House Speaker Newt Gingrich rivaled the president in the public eye. The night before the bombing of the Alfred E. Murrah Federal Building in Oklahoma City, President Clinton was reduced to pleading for his relevance: "The Constitution gives me relevance, the power of our ideas gives me relevance . . . The President is relevant, especially an activist President."[39] Even after the bombing, which catapulted Clinton back into public consciousness, the momentum of Congress continued driving events. There were two primary consequences of the 104th Congress: it shifted national policy significantly to the right, and it helped reelect Bill Clinton president of the United States.

The policy direction of the 104th Congress was unmistakable. Unfunded mandates imposed by the federal government on state and local government were restricted. The Freedom to Farm Act mandated a gradual phase-out of the system of agricultural controls dating back to the New Deal; communications legislation likewise mandated a more free-market approach in an area of enormous significance to the modern American economy. Tens of billions of dollars in reductions were achieved in discretionary domestic spending, and over 200 government programs were abolished. Clinton, himself, was forced to adopt in principle the objective of a balanced budget within a clear time frame; before the summer of 1995, Clinton's budgets had foreseen and accepted deficits in excess of $200 billion indefinitely. Health care reform, at least as envisioned by the administration, was dead. Finally, much to the consternation of Clinton's liberal allies, welfare reform was passed and signed, fundamentally transforming and decentralizing the federal welfare system and ending its status as an entitlement. This policy direction was bolstered by the sympathy of the nation's governors, particularly regarding welfare reform.

At the same time, the Republican takeover of Congress helped reelect Bill Clinton. As one presidential adviser put it in early 1996, "If the President wins re-election, it is in no small part due to our losing the Congress."[40] First, it forced to him to the right on a variety of crucial issues, thus allowing him to co-opt those issues and resume the New Democrat posture that had been so important in 1992 and so implausible in 1993 and 1994. Clinton moved in the direction of a balanced budget, proposed new tax cuts of his own, eased up on regulatory enforcement, signed welfare reform, issued guidelines clarifying the role of religion in schools, dumped Surgeon General Joycelyn Elders, agreed to mend (but not end) affirmative action, and even declared in his 1996 State of the Union Address that "the era of big government is over."

Second, relieved of the responsibility of governing, Clinton was free to use the 104th Congress as a foil through well-managed confrontation on selected issues like Medicare. Although the two partial government shutdowns of late 1995 and early 1996 were as much Clinton's responsibility as the Republicans', he succeeded in imposing his interpretation of those shutdowns as the dominant one. A combination of Republican missteps and his own political dexterity allowed Clinton to benefit from that confrontation in the long run, although at the time the verdict was not so clear.[41] Furthermore, the aggressive posture of Congress helped Clinton to solidify the liberal base of the Democratic Party, a base that before 1995 he could by no means take for granted. In this sense, Clinton's strategy was a reprise of Truman's: confront where confrontation was useful, yet adapt by moving to more defensible ground. For Clinton, confrontation with the 104th Congress was important, but at least as important was his ability to co-opt Republican themes and defuse the anger of 1994. Had Clinton imitated Grover Cleveland and Herbert Hoover, rigidly refusing to give ground or to acknowledge the depth of the electorate's concerns, he could easily have joined them in the graveyard of repudiated presidents.

Clinton's recovery, like his pre-1994 descent, was speeded by odd-year and special elections. Republicans won a difficult special election for a California House seat in October, but Democrats did well thereafter. State elections in Kentucky and Virginia in November 1995 seemed to indicate a stalled Republican tide. And the special Senate election in Oregon in January 1996, narrowly won by Democrat Ron Wyden to fill Sen. Robert Packwood's seat, gave an enormous boost to Democratic morale. That these elections went in favor of the president's party, in contrast with the general tendency of state midterm and special elections, might be ascribed to the fundamental basis of that tendency, which is to register a reaction against those who are perceived to be in charge. Most of the time, that is the president; through at least early 1996, it was congressional Republicans. In any event, 1995 through 1996, no less than 1993, demonstrated the potential impact of special elections and odd-year state elections to set the tone for the more important contests to come.

In contrast to the preparatory congresses, the president's opposition in the 104th Congress displayed neither superior party cohesion (both parties had high levels of cohesion) nor superior party leadership. Senate Majority Leader Bob Dole was a steady hand but lacked the charisma that is so needed in the communications age and was frequently outmaneuvered by Senate Democrats, especially in the critical days of early 1996. In particular, Dole's mishandling of the minimum wage fight was highly damaging to the Republicans. Newt Gingrich, as Speaker of the House, enjoyed remarkable success in maintaining party discipline and utilizing the contract as a tool to seize temporary control of the agenda, but his immaturity led to numerous mistakes and miscalculations. By early 1996, he was one of the most unpopular political figures in America. President Clinton was not, perhaps, more mature than Gingrich—indeed, numerous commentators drew parallels between the two men as equally self-absorbed baby boomers—but he proved considerably more adept at framing the debate with the public at large. Democratic congressional leaders (Sen. Thomas Daschle, S. D. and Rep. Richard Gephardt, Mo.) were often frustrated and sometimes infuriated by the White House, but in the end they climbed on board the President's New Democrat Express and played their roles serviceably. Indeed, Daschle's Senate strategies went far to forcing Bob Dole on the defensive and out of the Senate.[42]

The pattern of most preparatory congresses has been an increase in confrontation with the president, obstruction of the president's agenda, and low legislative productivity. The 104th Congress followed that script in certain respects until the summer of 1996, when it was abandoned altogether. In one sense, though, Republicans departed from the script from the very beginning. They hoped and expected from the opening days of the 104th Congress that they would implement large portions of the "Contract with America," a positive program of major legislation covering areas as widely separated as tax cuts and missile defense, deregulation and tort reform. Indeed, much of 1995 was spent in furious action trying to implement the contract. This action stands in stark contrast with most of the preparatory congresses, which were characterized by more or less complete stalemate and a willingness by the president's opposition to leave in his hands the responsibility of governing.

On the other hand, confrontation was a major feature of much of the 104th Congress. Very high levels of partisan voting characterized most of the first session and much of the second. Clinton, who had vetoed no bills at all in the 103rd Congress, cast seventeen vetoes in the 104th, only one of which was successfully overridden. And perhaps the defining moment of the 104th was its titanic budget war with Clinton, which was never really resolved until the 105th Congress. Obstruction was likewise the policy of the 104th through 1995. Clinton, who had enjoyed a legislative success rate of 86 percent in 1993 through 1994, saw Congress approve only 36 percent of his proposals in 1995—a record low since *Congressional Quarterly* began tabulating figures in the Eisenhower administration.[43] Overall, legislative productivity fell by over one-fourth in the 104th Congress.

In the summer of 1996, however, congressional Republicans reversed course and jettisoned confrontation and obstruction in favor of building a legislative record. Conciliation became the order of the day. Deals were struck on the minimum wage, welfare reform, and health insurance reform. At the same time, legislation that could have passed and would have presented Clinton with very difficult veto choices was quietly allowed to die; bills mandating missile defense, banning racial preferences, and cutting taxes were all shelved. The ultimate manifestation of this new strategy was a fiscal-year 1997 appropriations love-fest a month before election day, in which Republicans gave Clinton virtually everything he asked for—and, in some cases, more. By the end of 1996, Clinton's success rate with Congress had reached 55 percent.[44] This shift was the result of a calculation by Republicans that confrontation had gone awry, that Bob Dole was sinking, and that the best they could do was to save control of Congress. It can never be known whether Congress was saved for the Republicans because of this shift, or whether Clinton was beatable in any event, but it is certainly the case that Dole was deprived of ammunition that might have proven quite useful. Thus, by the end of the 104th Congress, Republicans had completely abandoned the strategy used by almost every preparatory congress to contribute to a presidential victory. Consequently, the 104th Congress contributed little to issue development in the 1996 election. Clinton was able to become the president of welfare reform and limited government and was allowed to dodge numerous potential wedge issues.

This is not, of course, to say that the 104th Congress was insignificant. At the very least, it stopped Clinton's attempted reprise of the Great Society, and while it is too early to render a definitive judgment, the 104th Congress may yet prove to have been enormously important. Its significance will not lie in how it drove partisan change at the presidential level but in how it redefined the playing field of American politics. Bill Clinton survived, but he did so only by moving to the right. Furthermore, unlike 1946, 1994 survived, too, and may have inaugurated a period of enduring Republican control of Congress (or at least consistent competitiveness). If that is true, 1994 will be significant, indeed, as even incremental changes in policy accumulate. Nevertheless, in the end, the dealigned electorate remained dealigned; a small but possibly decisive segment decided it liked divided government and voted accordingly. Republicans, according to opinion polls, were on the right side of most issues,[45] accounting for their ability to take congressional control in 1994 and maintain it in 1996. But they made blunders, and there was no single unavoidable issue like currency or depression to drive a wedge between the parties and produce a permanent realignment. And events beyond the control of either party hurt the Republican drive. The Oklahoma City bombing by antigovernment radicals did more to revive Clinton and blunt the Republican appeal than any single action by Clinton himself, a result that is surely laced with irony.

Conclusion

The midterm elections of 1946 and 1994 were not what Republicans hoped and Democrats feared—the onset of a period of unified Republican control of government. In the end, 1946 was nothing more than a normal midterm. The conditions were not right for anything more, Republicans made mistakes, and Truman proved more politically adept than virtually anyone had expected. Many of the strategies used by preparatory congresses were ignored by Republicans, while others were turned on them by the more aggressive Democrats. Yet 1946, in retrospect, was a crucial year; in the view of Michael Barone, its aftermath was "a hinge in American history" from turmoil to confidence.[46] The 80th Congress, far from being a "Do-Nothing" Congress, shifted national policy in a variety of ways. Above all, it forced the president to end World War II on the home front, brought to a definitive close the era of New Deal activism, laid the foundation for two decades of bipartisan foreign policy, and guaranteed the continuation of conservative coalition dominance that began in 1938. While reversing the partisan fortunes of 1946, the election of 1948 failed to reverse the deeper impact of 1946. Republicans after 1994 were also disappointed at the presidential level. In many respects, Clinton learned from Truman in a way that the 104th Congress did not learn from the 80th. But the Republican congressional majorities survived Clinton's reelection, and both before and after 1996, those majorities also drove national policy in a new direction, forced the president to the center, and changed the landscape of American politics.

What lessons can be learned about midterm elections from studying 1946 and 1994? First, a significant change in the composition and control of Congress is important to checking the president and may, on average, indicate an opportunity for a preparatory congress, but it is not, in itself, enough to produce one. While superior party cohesion can be an important factor—in most preparatory congresses, the president's opposition has enjoyed superior cohesion—it is also clearly not sufficient. The in-party splits that Republicans exploited after 1894 and Democrats exploited after 1930 also existed in the 80th Congress but preceded a completely different outcome in the next presidential election. Party leadership *is* important; it was significant that, after both 1946 and 1994, the leadership of both parties was fairly evenly matched.

Furthermore, the capacity of midterm congresses to influence change at the presidential level is limited by the boundaries of other, potentially more crucial, political realities. Conciliation and high levels of legislative productivity were not successful strategies for congressional opponents of the president, who wanted to contribute to future party victories. Six of the eight preparatory congresses and both of the normal congresses preceding a party shift in the White House saw declining productivity, while six of the remaining eleven normal midterms (including 1946) saw increasing productivity. Yet obstruction and confrontation were useful to the congressional opposition only if instigated by Congress and carried out in an otherwise favorable political environment. As the 80th Congress demonstrated, the confrontation and obstruction that bore fruit for most of the preparatory congresses can be turned into an effective weapon against Congress itself if the president and his party are astute enough to take control of the confrontation agenda. The contrast between the defensive Hoover, who refused to call the 72nd Congress into special session to deal with the Depression, and Truman, who called the 80th Congress into special session twice and relished those opportunities to take the offensive, is instructive. The president's ability to take control of the confrontation agenda depends on a variety of factors, including the president's temperament, his political skills and instincts, cooperation from his party in Congress, mistakes made by the opposition (in the 104th Congress, perhaps over-aggressiveness), and the objective political circumstances of the time, including underlying attitudes and partisan strength in the electorate.

Thus, the political nature of the times was crucial. After 1946, despite postwar adjustments, the New Deal alignment was still essentially solid, and no powerful cross-cutting issue arose to shake it more than temporarily. Harry Truman and the Democrats possessed a larger base than the Republicans and were able to mobilize that base through crafty confrontation. After 1994, Republicans had to contend with the underlying operational liberalism of a philosophically conservative electorate as well as a tendency by a crucial portion of the electorate to distrust unified government.

Most midterms may be normal, but the 80th and 104th Congresses show that normal midterms—even those, like 1946, widely derided as irrelevant—can make a difference, serving as a powerful check on the president and his party and helping to establish a new direction for national policy. Beyond the (often crucial) national circumstances that establish the parameters for human choice and action, nothing is inevitable. If these cases are any indication, the difference between preparatory midterms and normal midterms lies in the combination of those circumstances with the relative astuteness of each side. Virtually every midterm opens up dangers for the president and opportunities for his opponents. Sometimes presidents falter, sometimes they survive, and sometimes they survive only at the expense of their program. But they can take nothing for granted.

Conclusion

Do American midterm elections matter? Does it matter that the president's party in midterm elections almost invariably loses congressional seats, state legislative seats, and governorships, and not infrequently loses control of one or both congressional chambers? This was the question presented at the beginning of our discussion. Much scholarly energy has been directed at the important question of why the midterm curse is such a consistent feature of American politics, but little has addressed the arguably more crucial question of what difference it makes. This effort began with two propositions. First, midterm elections do matter—often more than is generally acknowledged and sometimes enormously. Second, they usually matter by representing an additional check on the president and his party. It is now clear that a substantial body of evidence supports both of those propositions.

The check presented by midterm elections is to some extent both constitutional and extraconstitutional in nature. The midterm election is itself mandated by the Constitution, and numerous constitutional checks are reinforced by it, ranging from separation of powers to bicameralism to federalism to the very principle of constitutionalism. Yet it is the extraconstitutional factor of institutionalized two-party competition which is central to the check imposed by midterms. Indeed, the hypothesis of midterm elections as a check depends vitally on an assumption that party is important and that shifts against the president's party can and do harm him politically. Above all, the party system ensures that there is a permanent opposition to the president, an organized force pledged to using the tools offered by the Constitution to check the president which is positioned to benefit from the political momentum and leadership transfusion offered by midterms. In turn, the midterm pattern itself has played a crucial role in guaranteeing a vigorous two-party system.

And just as the pattern of partisan oscillation is central to the check of the midterm election, the voting behavior of the public is at the heart of the pattern of partisan oscillation. Although that voting behavior remains mysterious to observers who cannot agree on whether the coattails, surge-and-decline, referendum, or presidential-penalty model best explains it, it is not a constitutional factor. The practice of presidents to claim that their power is derived from an electoral mandate is not part of the Constitution; indeed, it may be contrary to the original nonplebiscitary and antidemagogic spirit of the Constitution. Yet that practice leaves presidents open to attack when midterm elections seem to nullify or undermine their original mandate. And the effects of midterm elections at the state level are directly proportional to the number of states that choose to elect their officers in midterm years. That choice is left entirely up to the states, themselves; the Constitution stipulates only that each state be guaranteed a "republican form of government." Thus, extraconstitutional factors give power to the midterm check, even as some of those same factors are bolstered by it.

At the very least, the president's task is made more difficult even by normal midterm elections. He loses tangibly, in seats (an average of thirty-three House and two Senate seats) and in intraparty composition. The president's strongest intraparty allies tend to be hurt most, while his partisan opponents have an opportunity to begin constructing a new coalition—a fact that helps explain why midterm elections can have such an important impact even when the seat shift between parties is modest or when party control of Congress is not exchanged. He also loses intangibly through lost political leverage and momentum. Momentum is a rather ephemeral factor, and it clearly does not assure that those benefiting from it will actually prevail in the next elections. But the psychological boost usually experienced by the opposition party in midterm elections helps to ensure the continuing vigor and competitiveness of that party. Both regular midterm elections and special elections usually produce these results, although regular midterm elections are more likely than special elections to produce significant changes in actual seats. The president's opposition is revitalized to some extent and is often able to claim a counter mandate that nullifies the president's electoral mandate from two years before. These claims are usually supported by journalistic analysis.

The increasingly plebiscitary nature of the presidency—the degree to which presidents claim power based on public opinion and their own electoral victory—makes such a counter mandate particularly threatening to them. That both presidents and their opposition understand this phenomenon is made evident by the way presidents so consistently try to explain midterm election setbacks in terms that preserve their original mandate, while the opposition party in Congress just as consistently makes the opposite argument. The plausibility of these explanations is constrained by objective factors, most notably the actual extent of seat change and whether party control of Congress shifted, but every midterm has the potential of calling into question the very foundation of the president's plebiscitary power. Even relatively small losses by the president's party, which are rarely avoided in the pattern of midterm elections, can complicate his life and give succor to his opponents in myriad ways.

Even midterm elections that are often dismissed as irrelevant can carry great import below the surface. The preeminent example is 1946, the year Republicans seized control of Congress for the first time since the Great Depression. Despite widespread speculation at the time that the 1946 midterm elections heralded the end of Democratic dominance—or, at the very least, the end of Harry Truman—Truman was reelected in 1948 and Democrats simultaneously recaptured both houses of Congress. As a result, scholars have tended to downplay the elections of 1946, largely subscribing to Truman's depiction of the "Do-Nothing" 80th Congress. In reality, however, the 80th Congress was far from being a do-nothing body. As the Congress responsible for passing the Marshall Plan and military aid to Greece and Turkey, it played a crucial role in establishing the parameters of a bipartisan foreign policy of containment. And in keeping with the capacity of midterm elections to serve as an added check on the president, the 80th Congress forced Harry Truman and national policy in a very different direction than they might otherwise have taken. If Truman controlled the issue agenda in 1948, it was only partly because he was more astute and aggressive than the Republicans. It was largely because he had already co-opted or otherwise defused the powerful issues that led to Republican successes in 1946. Despite victory in 1948, Truman was unable to significantly expand the New Deal.

Finally, even the average midterm election has evolved into an important check on the president and his party at the state level. Because the midterm presidential penalty is also typically present in gubernatorial and legislative elections, and because three-fourths of states now elect their governors in midterm years, state government is also greatly affected by midterm trends. In some respects, these effects are immediate. The president's opposition, for example, gains an immediate boost in morale from successes at the state level just as it does from those at the national level—a boost that can conceivably translate into better fundraising and more vigorous campaigning.

In many respects, however, the most important effects of midterm elections at the state level are long term in nature. The electoral tide against the president's party helps bring in new opposition leadership, which can later (sometimes much later) run for higher offices from the U.S. House to the presidency. The opposition gains governorships, which are important to the long-term construction of viable state parties. It also gains strength for redistricting battles, which are likely to have a marginal but nevertheless potentially decisive impact on the partisan composition of Congress. By some estimates, the narrow Republican margin of control from 1994 through the remainder of the decade was owed to a favorable redistricting that followed a better-than-usual showing by the president's party in the 1990 midterm elections. Finally, influence on state government is important because states are an important part of the federal system, capable of obstructing national policy and offering alternative policies. When midterm gubernatorial elections go against the president's party, his opposition has an enhanced capacity to put forward a competing policy agenda at the subnational level, an agenda that might ultimately (as in the case of welfare reform in the 1990s) reach up to the national level to displace the preferences of the president. In each of these cases, the effects will be intertwined with numerous other factors and may not be fully evident for years. The anti-administration pattern of state midterm elections thus serves less as an immediate check than as a long-term mechanism ensuring balance between the parties and between their policy agendas.

It is this basic fact about midterm elections—that even average midterm years damage presidents—which has led some analysts to argue that the counter tendency of those elections represents another check on the president. Yet midterm elections clearly hold the potential for fulfilling a more creative role. Preparatory midterms—midterms that end up contributing to a change in White House control—provide the president's opposition with a platform for new issues or new issue presentation, a means of regaining confidence after a string of electoral setbacks, and a means of developing emerging political talent. Especially when the opposition party takes or strengthens its control of Congress, it can stymie the president, refusing to pass legislation he wants. It can also present an alternative program, forcing unpopular vetoes and seriously disrupting the president's control over the political agenda. The strengthened opposition in Congress can maneuver to exacerbate splits in the president's party, splits that are often quite damaging. Altogether, the opposition has an opportunity to demonstrate superior leadership and, what is perhaps more important, to deny the president the ability to showcase his own leadership. In almost every one of the preparatory congresses elected in midterm years, legislative productivity fell substantially. While there are only two examples since 1894, this potential effect of midterm elections seems to be operative in the largest changes of all—periods of long-term partisan realignment. Both the 54th Congress, elected in 1894, and the 72nd Congress, elected in 1930, followed this general pattern, depriving the president of legislation, sharpening partisan differences on crucial issues like currency and social welfare, and demonstrating more competent leadership than that offered by the president and his party. Midterm congresses preceding other less dramatic but important periods of change proceeded in much the same way.

In the calibrating midterm elections of 1938, 1982, and 1986, essentially popular presidents (Franklin Roosevelt and Ronald Reagan) were slowed in their efforts to bring about fundamental changes. In many respects, those midterm elections represented a consolidation of the president's position: in 1938 Republicans generally acknowledged the legitimacy of the New Deal and claimed to be seeking to make it more efficient, while Democrats in midterm elections in the 1980s largely conceded the conservative direction of policy while protesting the speed or precise manner of change. At the same time, the election results ensured that the president's program would be stalled and softened.

Proof of the importance of the midterm check can be seen by way of the two great exceptions in this study—the elections of 1934 and 1962, when the president's party gained seats or broke even. The two exceptions were central to the expansion of the federal government in the twentieth century. Liberal Democratic gains in the 1934 midterms both permitted and required Franklin Roosevelt to proceed with the so-called Second New Deal of the Social Security Act, the Wagner Act, the Fair Labor Standards Act, and others. In 1962, Democratic Senate gains and a mere four-seat loss in the House gave needed momentum to John F. Kennedy's New Frontier and later assured the votes for many of the Great Society programs of Lyndon Johnson. In both cases, changes in party composition went well beyond the aggregate seat gains; in either case, even average midterm losses suffered by the president's party might have derailed passage of these programs. The advantages traditionally gained by the president's opposition in midterm elections accrued to the president, himself, from compositional changes to the perception of mandate and momentum to issue development. Again, in 1998, the midterm pattern was broken, very possibly saving Bill Clinton's presidency. These elections truly were the exceptions that prove the rule.

David Mayhew began the project of categorizing midterm elections when he argued for the existence of a small number of innovative midterms (1810, 1866, 1910, and 1938) that had profound influence on future events. The categorization of midterm elections as normal, preparatory, calibrating, or exceptional focuses, as does Mayhew's, on the question of what difference midterms actually make. And, as Mayhew argues, changes in party composition are crucial and overall partisan seat shifts are often not the most important factor. The preparatory election of 1978 saw a very modest Republican seat gain, while 1946 and 1994—normal midterms in the long run—saw massive gains by the president's opponents. Yet it would be too easy to dismiss partisan seat changes as unimportant. The four categories of midterms, while exhibiting substantial internal variations, nevertheless show a fairly clear pattern on average. The president's party has performed progressively better in moving from preparatory to calibrating to normal elections (exceptions, by definition, being the best category for the president) (table 8.1). The concept of innovative midterms, as defined by Mayhew, can cross these categories and thus remains a useful nomenclature. For example, 1910 and 1938 fall in the categories of preparatory and calibrating elections, but both had profound long-term impact on politics and policy. And 1994 may come to fit Mayhew's conception of an innovative midterm—if Republican control is long lasting and brings substantial, if incremental, policy change—without being a preparatory election in the sense of preceding a shift of presidential control.

Taken together, midterm elections are not the poor stepchild of the

Table 8.1   Average Results by Midterm Category, 1894–1998
(Presidential Party Losses or Gains)

Midterm Category	Number	House	Senate	(%) Chamber(s) lost*
Preparatory	8	-47.5	-6.9	50
Calibrating	3	-34.0	-4.3	33
Normal	13	-33.0	-2.4	23
Exceptions	3	+3.3	+4.3	0

*Indicates in how many instances one or both legislative chambers moved from presidential partisan control to opposition partisan control. If one takes into account working control, rather than simply partisan control, the percentage of calibrating midterms in which the president lost control of one or both houses of Congress rises from 33 percent to 100 percent.

American electoral process. Not every midterm election is of great significance, but neither is every presidential election. After all, what was really settled by the presidential elections of 1840, 1888, or 1924? More than a few midterm elections have been easily as important as a presidential election, and indeed more than a few presidential elections have been driven in large measure by the midterm elections that preceded them. Midterm elections have launched realignments, begun and ended periods of great reform, stopped or (less frequently) propelled major presidential projects, and introduced scores of political figures who went on to play an important part in American political history. The three major bursts of federal activism in the twentieth century were both initiated and ended in midterm elections: 1910 through 1918, 1930 through 1938 (or perhaps 1946), and 1958 through 1966. The mid-century period of Eisenhower consensus really began in 1950 and ended in 1958; the deep salience of the tax issue at the national level stretched from 1978 to 1990, when George Bush's tax increase destroyed Republican hopes of Senate gains; the rightward movement of American electoral politics began in 1966 and was accelerated in 1978 and 1994. (Democrats hope, although it is too early to say, that this movement ended with the 1998 exception.) To a large extent, the story of American politics in the twentieth century is the story of midterm elections.

Midterm Elections as an Independent Variable

Midterm elections cannot be seen purely as dependent variables in American politics. Consideration of what follows midterm elections is as important as consideration of what precedes them. Yet, just as midterm elections are not merely products of the past, neither are they divorced from the past. They are both independent and dependent variables. Or perhaps a better way of putting it is that they are an integral part of the chain of political events. The question is then transformed: in what ways are midterm elections dependent variables, and in what ways do they assert an independent role?

Midterm elections can be seen as dependent variables in at least two ways. First, the results are highly dependent on the previous presidential election. At a minimum, the question of which party gains and which party loses is almost predetermined according to which party holds the White House. Furthermore, if there is truth to the coattails or surge-and-decline explanations for the midterm pattern, the *extent* of the out-party's gains is also heavily influenced by the size of the president's margin and coattails.

Hence, the argument is often made that midterm election results really just represent a return to equilibrium. Second, as part of a chain of events, rather than as free-standing events in themselves, the results and consequences of midterm elections are often difficult to disentangle from the surrounding context and subterranean trends in American politics. If a president is defeated for reelection after a major midterm election setback, it is not self-evident, without further investigation, whether the midterm contributed to the president's plight (as in the preparatory midterms) or whether the midterm simply reflected the same deeper political trend that later drove the president from office (as was the case in 1974). It is important not to overstate the capacity of midterm elections to influence future events as opposed to merely registering latent voter concerns. Administrations may naturally age, as well, suffering from gridlock that is a product of time, itself, rather than of unfortunate midterm election results.

Yet it is difficult to see how midterm elections can be declared to be simply a return to equilibrium, when the state of equilibrium is defined by the historical results of congressional elections held in both presidential and midterm years. In a sense, the answer is baked into that question. There appears to be a natural equilibrium in large part precisely because midterm elections have historically had the effect of restoring balance over time. Indeed, in some respects that is exactly the point: midterm elections consistently have the effect of restoring an equilibrium that would not necessarily have existed without them. And by restoring an equilibrium, they can profoundly affect the future.

This study has identified several specific ways in which midterm elections can serve an independent role—that is, produce or contribute to events that would not have happened without the midterm. Even if the party balance is simply restored to equilibrium, *it is restored*. And overall composition is at least as important as party numbers, meaning that the membership turnover produced by midterms can carry consequences far beyond partisan shifts. Just as midterm elections register and reveal existing voter preferences, they also change the strategic situation facing the president and both parties in Congress. Furthermore, it is no small thing to register otherwise inchoate voter preferences: the very act of registering those preferences in an election can have negative effects on the president's standing that would otherwise not occur. Most notably, shifting political momentum would not occur automatically without the stimulus of the midterm election, and the antiplebiscitary effect would not occur at all; the perceived mandate embedded in an election can be nullified only by another election.

Midterms and the new congresses they produce clearly can also influence the development of issues, providing both an avenue for testing during the midterm campaign and an avenue for action in Congress. Historical evidence strongly suggests that declines in legislative productivity, increases in vetoes, and falling presidential support scores are directly related to midterm elections. Midterm elections cannot create issues out of nothing, but midterm elections and post-midterm congresses can elevate certain issues and define them in ways that are different from what might have been. Likewise, the president's opposition would develop new leaders with or without midterms, but midterm elections combined with the midterm pattern provides them with disproportionate opportunities to do so.

If a party's candidates are aided by national party tides, and if the election of a president usually produces a tide for his party, it is worth remembering that, in the absence of midterm elections, the out-party could count on a national tide running in its direction roughly only once every eight or twelve years, since only rarely do parties surrender control of the White House after just one term. In extreme cases, the out-party might enjoy such a tide but once in two decades or more.[1] Midterm elections give the out-party a nearly automatic party tide once every four years for as long as it is the out-party. In any given twelve-year party hold on the White House, the typical out-party will enjoy a favorable party tide three times more often than it would if midterms did not exist.

Intraparty splits exist independently of electoral activity, but just as presidential elections often stimulate those splits, midterm elections can do so as well. Competition for nominations, as well as the pressures of seeking votes in an unfriendly electoral arena and later of governing with a reduced party cohort in Congress, can expose and even exacerbate party divisions. Simultaneously, the opposition has a ready-made opportunity in midterm elections to begin constructing an alternative electoral coalition on the basis of any serious split that might be evident in the in-party.

Altogether, effects produced independently by midterm elections are likely to be the result of an accumulation of individually marginal but intertwined factors—marginal not in the sense of unimportant but in the sense of not ordinal. In other words, midterms do not guarantee outright presidential failure; they make the president's success more difficult, and his opponents' success more likely, than would otherwise have been the case, all other things being equal. Ultimately, every midterm is an opportunity for the opposition. In the realm of probabilities, this study contains some predictive power. Large seat shifts are more likely than small seat shifts to precede a change of party in the White House; post-midterm con--

gresses that feature low productivity and high levels of confrontation are also more likely to precede such a change; and instances in which the president's party breaks the midterm pattern are likely to precede success for the president's agenda. (In Bill Clinton's case, the primary item on his agenda in November 1998 was probably to remain in office.) Yet, aside from these and other broad probabilities, there is no rigorous predictive authority here, because there is no guarantee that the political actors will take full advantage of their opportunity. If this were not true—if midterm elections only passively registered public opinion that was already set on an unchangeable course—then not only would Franklin Roosevelt have been elected president in 1932, but Thomas Dewey would have been elected in 1948 and Bob Dole in 1996.

Consequently, midterm elections, while potentially dramatic in their consequences, must be seen as highly contingent events. The ultimate outcome—both in terms of election results and in terms of longer-range consequences—depends on a wide variety of factors. Parameters are set by objective circumstances, including events, intraparty relations, deep trends in public opinion, partisan identification, and electoral behavior. The skill of the president is matched against the skill of his opponents. And the degree of change in the election results—how many seats won or lost, partisan or ideological control of chambers—can place limits around future interpretations and events. Preparatory elections and the resulting congresses can be declared preparatory elections only after the fact. They do not make change inevitable; indeed, at the time there is often confusion about the long-term significance of the midterm election. Rather, they create opportunities that are skillfully utilized by the president's opposition. The president's response is also crucial. Presidential rigidity has been an important contributing factor in realizing the potential of the preparatory elections. It was not just Republican mistakes that kept 1946 and 1994 from becoming preparatory elections; it was the ability of Harry Truman and Bill Clinton to adapt to new circumstances and to co-opt some of the opposition's most powerful themes.

In this sense, the theory of contingent realignment proposed by Chubb, Peterson, and Zingale can serve as a touchstone for the study of midterm elections generally.[2] In this view, realignments are more a process than an event—a process defined by contingency, in which one party is given an opportunity but in which there are no guarantees about how it will use that opportunity. Midterm elections may almost always serve as a check, but how and to what degree remains dependent on contingent factors.

Altogether, as a check, midterm elections are a complex mixture of the tangible and intangible, the interpartisan and intrapartisan, the constitutional and the extraconstitutional, the short-term and the long-term, the national and the subnational, the merely negative and the creative. Dependent for their power on party, midterm elections help to assure the continuing viability of two-party competition. Scholars will, and should, continue in their attempts to uncover the hidden mechanisms driving the midterm pattern. We cannot know with certainty that the pattern will extend indefinitely into the future just because it has characterized the past; 1998 proves this, although it was surrounded by circumstances unique enough that we should hesitate to consider it more than an aberration. But as long as the anti-administration essence of the midterm pattern continues, midterm elections will continue operating as a check, exerting a profound influence on the course of American politics. And even should the midterm curse, itself, become less consistent over time, every midterm election will hold the potential of filling that role.

APPENDIX A
Presidential and Opposition Bases Determined by Convention or Primary Votes by Region

Cleveland (1884 Democratic Convention
1st ballot)
Northeast 57.0%*
Midwest 56.0%*
South   39.3%#
West   31.0%#
Border   28.4%#

McKinley (1896 Republican Convention
1st ballot)
Border   98.7%*
Midwest   89.6%*
South   87.5%*
West   70.5%*
Northeast 30.2%#

T. Roosevelt (1912 Republican
Convention; counts votes for Roosevelt
and not voting)
Midwest   57.4%*
Northeast 51.6%*
Border   46.2%#
West   29.2%#
South   20.6%#

Taft (1912 Republican Convention)
South   74.6%*
West   65.0%*
Border   52.6%*
Northeast 47.4%#
Midwest   24.8%#

Wilson (1912 Democratic Convention,
45th and penultimate ballot)
Midwest   86.9%*
Northeast 52.6%*
South   52.2%*
West   48.8%#
Border   9.0%#

Harding (1920 Republican Convention,
10th ballot)
South   88.5%*
Border   85.9%*
Northeast 67.0%*
Midwest   51.7%*
West   29.4%#

Coolidge: No competitive convention.
Inherited Harding's base and opposition.

Hoover (1928 Republican Convention)
West   96.6%*
Northeast 94.3%*
Border   87.4%*
South   86.1%*
Midwest   41.8%#

F. Roosevelt (1940 Democratic
Convention)
Midwest   96.9%*
West   89.4%*
Northeast 84.8%*
Border   82.3%*
South   75.7%#

Truman (1948 Democratic Convention)
Border   100%*
Midwest   99.7%*
West   99.7%*
Northeast 95.2%*
South   12.3%#

Eisenhower (1952 Republican
Convention, pre-shift)
Northeast 83.0%*
Border   54.3%*
South   48.8%#
West   34.6%#
Midwest   26.3%#

Kennedy (1960 Democratic Convention)
Northeast 78.1%*
Midwest 77.4%*
West 56.8%*
Border 29.3%#
South 2.5%#

Johnson: No competitive convention.
Inherited Kennedy's base and opposition.

Nixon (1968 Republican Convention,
pre-shift)
Border 75.7%*
South 72.9%*
Midwest 51.5%*
West 47.7%#
Northeast 28.8%#

Ford (1976 Republican Convention)
Northeast 87.0%*
Midwest 70.9%*
Border 62.0%*
South 25.5%#
West 18.2%#

Carter (1976 Democratic primary
results)
South 54.4%*
Border 52.1%*
Midwest 48.7%#
Northeast 33.2%#
West 21.2%#

Reagan (1976 Republican Convention)
West 81.8%*
South 74.5%*
Border 38.0%#
Midwest 29.0%#
Northeast 12.8%#

Bush (average 1980 and 1988 mean
Republican primary results)
Northeast 47.8%*
West 44.7%*
Midwest 44.6%*
South 38.5%#
Border 37.9%#

Clinton (1992 Democratic primary
results)
South 63.3%*
Midwest 50.3%*
West 46.3%#
Northeast 43.0%#
Border 42.4%#

*=President's intraparty regional base
#=President's intraparty opposition base
Source: Guide to U.S. Elections, 2d ed. (Washington, D.C.: Congressional Quarterly, 1985); *Congressional Quarterly Weekly Report,* July 9, 1988, 1896; *Congressional Quarterly Weekly Report,* Special Democratic Convention Issue, July 4, 1992, 69.

Cutoff level dividing president's base from opposition base is 50 percent in all cases except for Hoover and Franklin Roosevelt, where cutoff was established at 80 percent, and George Bush, where cutoff was established at 40 percent. Unfortunately, primary results (which were used for Carter, Bush, and Clinton) do not take into account support received in caucus states. Nevertheless, they are a more valid measure of intraparty support than are convention delegates in these three cases, since the convention outcomes were not in doubt and most, if not all, opposing candidates had withdrawn.

It should be pointed out that Republican congressional strength in the South was minimal until the 1960s, ranging from three to eleven. Consequently, the South cannot be considered a meaningful political base for any Republican president or his intraparty opponents until Richard Nixon. Nevertheless, on several occasions Republican representation in the South turned over by half a dozen seats in one election, so it was important to include the South in overall national base calculations.

APPENDIX B
Presidential Explanations for Midterm Losses by Year

Year	President	Losses	Explanations
1946	Truman	55*/12*	Economy[1]
1950	Truman	29/6	History Local conditions[2]
1954	Eisenhower	18*/1*	History Local conditions No repudiation of admin[3]
1958	Eisenhower	48/13	Not a deliberate act by voters Not a repudiation of admin. (pointed to 1956)[4] GOP started campaign too late[5]
1962	Kennedy	4/+3	History[6]
1966	Johnson	47/4	History Local conditions (GOP governor coattails & vacancies) National conditions (backlash)[7]
1970	Nixon	12/+2	History Local conditions Victory (in Senate) Not a referendum on Nixon[8]
1974	Ford	48/5	Economy Watergate Mandate on inflation[9] Not a referendum on Ford[10]
1978	Carter	15/3	History Not a referendum[11] Losses held down because of public support for spending cuts[12]

Year	President	Losses	Explanations
1982	Reagan	26/+1	History Economy Victory (in Senate)[13]
1986	Reagan	5/8*	Poor GOP turnout Not a repudiation (pointed to 1984) Victory (in governships)[14]
1990	Bush	8/1	History[15]
1994	Clinton	52*/8*	National desire for change Presidential responsibility Failure to convey message Voters did not understand benefits 　(dumb voters) Balance: voters like divided 　government Not a repudiation[16] Dem. Congress did not end gridlock[17] Mandate for smaller, less intrusive 　government[18] * Loss of party control

1. John D. Morris, "Truman Rejects Resignation Idea, Plans 'National Welfare' Policy," *New York Times,* November 8, 1946, 19.

2. "News Conference, November 16, 1950," *Public Papers of the President, Harry S. Truman,* 1950, 713–14.

3. "News Conference, November 3, 1954," *Public Papers of the President, Dwight Eisenhower,* 1954, 1009–19.

4. "News Conference, November 5, 1958," *Public Papers of the President, Dwight Eisenhower,* 1958, 827–38.

5. "Nixon Says Loss Was 'Inevitable,'" *New York Times,* November 5, 1958, 8.

6. "News Conference, November 20, 1962," *Public Papers of the President, John F. Kennedy,* 1962, 834–43.

7. "The President's News Conference at the LBJ Ranch, November 10, 1966," *Public Papers of the President, Lyndon B. Johnson,* 1966 Vol. II, 1357–62.

8. "Remarks to Reporters on the Results of the 1970 Elections, November 4, 1970," *Public Papers of the President, Richard Nixon,* 1068–70; Richard W. Semple Jr., "Nixon is Said to Be 'Pleased' with Election Result," *New York Times,* November 4, 1970, 21; "Washington tensions increase as both parties claim election gains," *National Journal,* November 17, 1970, 2426.

9. "Statement on the Results of the 1974 Election, November 5, 1974," *Public Papers of the President, Gerald R. Ford,* 1974, 579; "Question and Answer Session at Society of Professional Journalists Meeting, November 14," *Public Papers of the President, Gerald R. Ford,* 1974, 596–613.

10. Carol Kilpatrick, "Mansfield Pledges to Work with Ford," *Washington Post,* November 7, 1974, A2.

11. "News Conference, November 9, 1978," *Public Papers of the President, Jimmy Carter,* 1978, vol. 2, 1986.

12. Edward Walsh, "Carter Performance on Campaign Trail: 28 Tries and 12 Hits," *Washington Post,* November 9, 1978, A9.

13. "Remarks at Question and Answer Session with Reporters on the Congressional Elections, November 3, 1982," *Public Papers of the President, Ronald Reagan,* 1982, vol. 2, 1420–23.

14. "Remarks at a White House Briefing for Senior Staff on the Congressional and Gubernatorial Election Results, November 5, 1986," *Public Papers of the President, Ronald Reagan,* 1986, vol. 2, 1517–19.

15. "Remarks Announcing the Resignation of William J. Bennett as Director of National Drug Control Policy and a Question and Answer Session with Reporters, November 8, 1990," *Public Papers of the President George Bush,* 1990, vol. 2, 1571.

16. Weekly Compilation of Presidential Documents 30, November-December 1994, "News Conference, November 9, 1994," 2339-48.

17. Edward Walsh, "Democrats Wonder Whether Sea Change Is Plea for Centrism," *Washington Post,* November 10, 1994, A27.

18. Ruth Marcus, "Clinton Reiterates Vow to Pursue New Democrat Agenda," *Washington Post,* November 11, 1994, A14.

APPENDIX C
Opposition Party Congressional Explanations for Midterm Gains by Year

Year	Cong. Party	Seats Gained	Explanations
1946	Republican	55*/12*	Ideological/ policy mandate[1]
1950	Republican	29/6	Ideological/ policy mandate Scandal/integrity[2]
1954	Democratic	18*/1*	Ike's popularity held down gains[3]
1958	Democratic	48/13	Balance: Not a mandate for disunity[4]
1962	Republicans	4/-3	[No explanation at congressional level]
1966	Republican	47/4	Anti-administration Balance: two party competition[5]
1970	Democratic	12/-2	Party mandate Anti-administration Balance: centrism No clear message Low GOP exposure held down gains[6]
1974	Democratic	48/5	Anti-administration Economy Scandal (Watergate) Ideological mandate Balance—centrism[7]
1978	Republican	15/3	Ideological mandate[8]
1982	Democratic	26/-1	Anti-administration Economy Balance: centrism[9]
1986	Democratic	5/8*	Anti-administration Policy mandate Economy Balance[10]

Year	Cong. Party	Seats Gained	Explanations
1990	Democratic	8/1	Party mandate Ideological mandate Economy Low GOP exposure held down gains[11]
1994	Republican	52*/8*	Ideological mandate Party mandate Anti-administration[12]

* Gain of party control

1. "Ives Sees Mandate to Restore Freedom," New York Times, November 6, 1946, 2; "Hoover Sees U.S. Moving To the Goal of Free Men," New York Times, November 6, 1946, 2; "Vandenberg Sees Victory for United Foreign Policy," New York Times, November 7, 1946, 4; "Taft Looks to Progress," New York Times, November 7, 1946, 5; "Martin Says Party Is Ready For Job," New York Times, November 7, 1946, 11.

2. Walter Waggoner, "Acheson Declares He Will Not Resign or Change Policies," New York Times, November 9, 1950, 1; "Backers See Taft 1952 Party Choice," New York Times, November 9, 1950, 1, 24; Clayton Knowles, "Democratic Chiefs Asked to Explain Losses in Election," New York Times, November 10, 1950, 1.

3. "Elections: The Whats of the 'Squeak,'" Newsweek, November 15, 1954, 31–37.

4. W. H. Lawrence, "Rayburn Bars a Tax Cut," New York Times, November 8, 1958, 1, 13.

5. John W. Finney, "G.O.P. Chiefs Call Results 'Victory,'" New York Times, November 9, 1966, 33; "The New Congress," Newsweek, November 21, 1966, 38.

6. Warren Weaver Jr., "Gains Made by Muskie, Humphrey and Kennedy," New York Times, November 5, 1970, 26; John W. Finney, "Senators Expect Relations with Nixon to be the Same," New York Times, November 5, 1970, 27; Rep. Sikes, Congressional Record—House, November 16, 1970, 37431; Sen. Mansfield, Congressional Record—Senate, November 17, 1970, 37548–49; Rep. Price, Congressional Record—House, November 17, 1970, 37748–49.

7. David S. Broder, "Nationwide Sweep Nets 6 Governors, Over 30 in House," Washington Post, November 6, 1974, A1, A10; Lou Cannon, "GOP Left with White House," Washington Post, November 6, 1974, A1, A10; Spencer Rich, "Senate Takes a Tiny Step to the Left," Washington Post, November 7, 1974, A7; Lou Cannon and Jules Witcover, "A New Role in Leadership is Foreseen," Washington Post, November 7, 1974, A1; Rep. Evins, Congressional Record—House, November 18, 1974, 36297–98.

8. "The New Tilt," Newsweek, November 20, 1978, 46–47.

9. Lou Cannon and Walter Pincus, "President's Hill Coalition is Jeopardized," Washington Post, November 3, 1982, A1; Dan Balz and Margot Hornblower, "Democrats Gain 26 Seats in House," Washington Post, November 4, 1982, A21; Helen Dewar, "President Will Face a Bolder Congress," Washington Post, November 4, 1982, A1, A25; Sen. Byrd, Congressional Record—Senate, November 29, 1982, 27662; Rep. Alexander, Congressional Record—House, November 29, 1982, 27764; Rep. Hamilton, Congressional Record—House, November 29, 1982, 27903; Rep. Hamilton, Congressional Record—November 30, 1982, 28133.

10. Helen Dewar and Spencer Rich, "GOP's Class of '80 Runs into Trouble 2nd Time Around," Washington Post, November 5, 1986, A31; Paul Taylor, "Senate to Have 55 Democrats," Washington Post, November 6, 1986, A1, A53; David S. Broder, "Both Parties Put on Notice: Voters Are Ready for Change," Washington Post, November 6, 1986, A1, A56.

11. Paul Taylor and Maralee Schwartz, "Helms, Most Other Hill Incumbents Prevail," *Washington Post,* November 7, 1990, A1, A26; John E. Yang and Helen Dewar, "Democrat Gains in Congress Spell Trouble for Bush," *Washington Post,* November 8, 1990, A43; Paul Taylor, "Restive Voters Pick Change at State Level, Stability on Hill," *Washington Post,* November 8, 1990, A1, A42.

12. Dan Balz, "Party Controls Both Houses for First Time Since '50s," *Washington Post,* November 9, 1994, A1; Dale Russakoff, "Gingrich Vows Cooperation," *Washington Post,* November 9, 1994, A21; Dan Balz, "Clinton, GOP Leaders Offer Cooperation," *Washington Post,* November 10, 1994, A1; Rep. Doolittle, *Congressional Record*—House, November 29, 1994, E2301–4.

APPENDIX D
President's Party Congressional Explanations for Losses by Year

Year	Party	Seats Lost	Explanations
1946	Democratic	55*/12*	Anti-administration Desire for change[1]
1950	Democratic	29/6	Anti-administration Scandal National conditions Centrism Senate GOP coattails[2]
1954	Republican	18*/1*	No repudiation of admin. Pres. did not campaign enough National conditions[3]
1958	Republican	48/13	[No explanation at congressional level]
1962	Democratic	4/+3	[No explanation at congressional level]
1966	Democratic	47/4	Anti-administration Centrism (LBJ moved too fast)[4]
1970	Republican	12/+2	Centrism (Nixon polarized)[5]
1974	Republican	48/5	Anti-administration Watergate National conditions Desire for change Pres. not responsible[6]
1978	Democratic	15/3	[No explanation at congressional level]
1982	Republican	26/+1	Anti-administration Desire for change National conditions No repudiation of pres.[7]
1986	Republican	5/8*	History Poor campaign[8]

Year	Party	Seats Lost	Explanations
1990	Republican	8/1	History Poor campaign Desire for change[9]
1994	Democratic	52*/8*	Anti-administration Centrism[10]

* Loss of party control

1. John D. Morris, "Change Accepted by Party Leaders," *New York Times,* November 7, 1946, 7; Arthur Krock, "Landslide Result," *New York Times,* November 7, 1946, 1.

2. "Anderson Blames the Brennan Plan," *New York Times,* November 9, 1950, 39; Clayton Knowles, "Democratic Chiefs Asked to Explain Losses in Election," *New York Times,* November 10, 1950, 1; "Truman on the Strait and Narrow," *Newsweek,* November 20, 1950, 24; Sen. Holland, Congressional Record, November 29, 1950, 15960–61.

3. William S. White, "Democrats Offer Harmony in Rule of 84th House," *New York Times,* November 5, 1954, 1; "Elections: The Whats of the 'Squeak,'" *Newsweek,* November 15, 1954, 31–37.

4. "The New Congress," *Newsweek,* November 21, 1966, 38.

5. Sen. Hatfield, *Congressional Record,* November 17, 1970, 37589–94.

6. Lou Cannon, "GOP Left with White House," *Washington Post,* November 6, 1974, A1, A10; Lou Cannon and Jules Witcover, "A New Role In Leadership is Foreseen," *Washington Post,* November 7, 1974, A1, A10; Rep. Talcott, *Congressional Record*—House, November 20, 1974, 36798.

7. Lou Cannon and Walter Pincus, "President's Hill Coalition is Jeopardized," *Washington Post,* November 3, 1982; Dan Balz and Margot Hornblower, "Democrats Gain 26 Seats in House," *Washington Post,* November 4, 1982, A21; Helen Dewar, "President Will Face a Bolder Congress," *Washington Post,* November 4, 1982, A1, A25; Rep. Goodling, *Congressional Record*—House, November 29, 1982, 27765.

8. Edward Walsh and Ward Sinclair, "Democrats Expand Majority as Few Incumbents Lose," *Washington Post,* November 5, 1986, A31, A37; Paul Taylor, "Senate to Have 55 Democrats," *Washington Post,* November 6, 1986, A1, A53.

9. David S. Broder, "Mixed Results Signal Voters' Impatience," *Washington Post,* November 7, 1990, A1, A26.

10. David S. Broder, "Sharp Turn to the Right Reflects Doubts About Clinton, Democrats," *Washington Post,* November 9, 1994, A1; David S. Broder, "Vote May Signal GOP Return as Dominant Party," *Washington Post,* November 10, 1994, A1; Edward Walsh, "Democrats Wonder Whether Sea Change Is Plea for Centrism," *Washington Post,* November 10, 1994, A27, A29; Rep. Harman, *Congressional Record*—House, November 29, 1994, H11439.

APPENDIX E
Media Assessment of Midterm Elections, 1894–1994

Year	New York Times Commentary
1994	National election results were "a powerful body blow to Bill Clinton and a repudiation of his party's conduct in Congress."[1]
1990	"What did yesterday's election prove? Not much."[2]
1986	Elections should "powerfully revitalize" liberals; however, "voters sent messages to both sides . . . compromise and conciliation must be the first priority for both houses, both parties, and both branches."[3]
1982	"President Reagan asked the electorate for a mandate to 'stay the course.' What he got was a message to go with the flow . . . 'Reaganomics' doesn't wash with the folks back home . . . the flow is to the center."[4]
1978	"as miscellaneous as any election in recent memory. The clearest theme is that there is no theme." However, tax revolt is shown to be an "enduring force."[5]
1974	Democrats made "handsome gains" due to the national issues of economy, Watergate, and the Ford pardon.[6]
1970	Nixon's "social issue" strategy failed.[7]
1966	"the Republican party has achieved a decisive victory . . . [which] can only be interpreted as a serious setback for [LBJ]. the nation has, in effect, flashed a 'Caution—Go Slow' signal to the Johnson Administration."[8]
1962	"The voters have given no dramatic new mandate to Congress," though pattern of results "does provide a degree of comfort for the Kennedy Administration" and "represents some indication of confidence" in JFK.[9]
1958	". . . there has been a leftward swing." Democrats capitalized on economic and foreign policy issues, and "possibly above all—on the Administration leadership issue."[10]
1954	"The results bespeak no great triumph for either party."[11]
1950	National trend is "indisputably Republican . . . the Democratic 'Fair Deal' has met with a resounding check . . . No good reason remains . . . for the President to insist upon his oft-repeated claim that he has a 'mandate from the people' for such measures."[12]

Year	New York Times Commentary

1946   Results "leave no doubt that there has been a swing of sentiment on a nationwide scale against the Democratic Administration."[13]

1942   "A decisive Republican victory . . . an important reverse for the administration."[14]

1938   "That the results of the elections constitute a sharp reversal for the Roosevelt Administration is undeniable." Results showed "a movement of the American people toward the middle of the road."[15]

1934   ". . .an overwhelming popular endorsement . . . an individual triumph for the President."[16]

1930   ". . .the heavy blows dealt Republicans by the voters will everywhere be taken as a repudiation of President Hoover's leadership" though issues of depression and prohibition brought backlash against whole party; Republicans were struck down "by a revolution which is peaceful but none the less decisive and politically devastating."[17]

1926   "Judged by the outcome of the Senatorial elections, the Republican Party and the Coolidge Administration appear to have received a severe rebuke from the country."[18]

1922   "[R]esentment against the course of the Republican Party in Congress, and against the accumulated mistakes of the Administration, burst into flame."[19]

1918   Elections left "the balance of political power very much where it was before . . . the people, though very much besought by opposition leaders, have not been moved to express their disapproval of his Administration."[20]

1914   "[T]he verdict is not favorable to [Wilson] or to his party . . . The Republican Party has renewed its strength."[21]

1910   Voters punished Republicans "for betrayals of their interests and disobedience to their will . . . What a wonderful and quick regeneration has been wrought in the Democratic Party in this year."[22]

1906   Results were "not likely to disturb" Republicans too much.[23]

1902   "There is a strong current of opinion against the Republican policy . . . The Democratic Party comes out of the campaign in a much better shape than it has been in a decade."[24]

1898   Results were "a distinct and severe blow to the administration . . . a vote of censure."[25]

1894   Democrats were punished "because the policy of the party has not been carried out." Democrats allowed popular sentiment to be "baffled and betrayed, and it is rebuked in the only way open to the voters, by the accession of the rival party."[26]

1. "Republican Gains and Obligations," New York Times, November 9, 1994, A26.
2. "Day of Decision: What Decision?," New York Times, November 7, 1990, A30.
3. "Reagan's Winter," New York Times, November 6, 1986, A34.
4. "The Center Rediscovered," New York Times, November 4, 1982, A26.
5. "One the One Hand...," New York Times, November 9, 1978, A26.
6. "Up to the Democrats," New York Times, November 7, 1974, A44.

7. "The Electoral Struggle," *New York Times,* November 4, 1970, A46; "...Mixed Election Results...," *New York Times,* November 5, 1970, A46.

8. "The Republican Tide," *New York Times,* November 9, 1966, 38.

9. "The 88th Congress," *New York Times,* November 8, 1962, 38.

10. "The National Picture," *New York Times,* November 6, 1958, 36.

11. "The Congressional Election," *New York Times,* November 4, 1954, A30.

12. "The Voice of the Voters," *New York Times,* November 9, 1950, 32.

13. "The House Goes Republican," *New York Times,* November 6, 1946, A22.

14. Arthur Krock, "A National Trend," *New York Times,* November 4, 1942, A1.

15. "The Elections," *New York Times,* November 10, 1938, 26.

16. "Mr. Roosevelt's New Responsibility," *New York Times,* November 8, 1934, 22.

17. "The Republican Debacle," *New York Times,* November 5, 1930, 22.

18. Richard V. Oulahan, *New York Times,* November 4, 1926, A1; see also "Butler Beaten," *New York Times,* November 3, 1926, A22.

19. "The Great Reaction," *New York Times,* November 8, 1922, A14.

20 . "A Close Congressional Election," *New York Times,* November 6, 1918, 16.

21. "The Verdict of the Nation," *New York Times,* November 4, 1914, A6; "The People's Way," *New York Times,* November 5, 1914, A10.

22. "The Political Revolution," *New York Times,* November 9, 1910, 8.

23. "The House of Representatives," *New York Times,* November 7, 1906, A8.

24. "The Republican Check," *New York Times,* November 5, 1902, A8.

25. "The Country to Mr. M'Kinley," *New York Times,* November 9, 1898, A6; "Business and the Elections," *New York Times,* November 10, 1898, A6.

26. "Congress," *New York Times,* November 7, 1894, 4.

APPENDIX F

Special Elections for House and Senate, 1944–1994: Number of Special Elections and Net Partisan Shift for or against the President's Party

	House		Senate	
	Elections	*Net Shift*	*Elections*	*Net Shift*
1945–46	8	-1	8	-3
1947–48	4	0	3	0
1949–50	10	0	6	-2
1951–52	10	-2	4	-2
1953–54	8	-2	9	0
1955–56	3	0	3	+2
1957–58	10	0	4	-1
1959–60	8	+1	3	-1
1961–62	12	0	6	0
1963–64	12	-2	2	0
1965–66	10	+1	3	-1
1967–68	6	-1	0	0
1969–70	14	-2	2	0
1971–72	10	0	2	0
1973–74	10	-4	0	0
1975–76	7	0	1	-1
1977–78	6	-4	2	-1
1979–80	7	-1	0	0
1981–82	3	0	0	0
1983–84	9	+1	1	+1
1985–86	5	0	1	-1
1987–88	7	+1	0	0
1989–90	11	-1	1	0
1991–92	6	-1	2	-1
1993–94	7	-2	2	-1
Total	201	-20	65	-12
Average	8.0	-.8	2.4	-.5

Source: Norman J. Ornstein, Thomas E. Mann, and Michael J. Malbin, *Vital Statistics on Congress 1995–96* (Washington, D.C.: *Congressional Quarterly,* 1996), 53–54. Adjustments were made to remove special elections held simultaneously with general elections, such as the California special Senate election held in November 1992.

NOTES

Introduction

1. Many Latin American constitutions also utilize a presidential system with midterm congressional elections, but the regularity of both presidential and midterm elections in Latin America has been frequently interrupted by political disorder and military government.

2. Nelson Polsby, "The Institutionalization of the U. S. House of Representatives," *American Political Science Review* 62 (March 1968): 144–168.

3. There are two possible ways of conceiving presidential coattails: a simple measurement of how many seats (if any) the presidential winner's party gains in Congress, and a more sophisticated (though also much more difficult to calculate) measure of how his party would have done had he not been at the top of the ticket. Much scholarly evidence has pointed to the declining coattails of victorious presidential candidates during most of the twentieth century by both measurements. See John. A. Ferejohn and Randall L. Calvert, "Presidential Coattails in Historical Perspective," *American Journal of Political Science* 28 (February 1984): 127–46.

4. See Barbara Hinckley, "Interpreting House Midterm Elections: Toward Measurement of the In-Party's 'Expected' Loss of Seats," *American Political Science Review* 61 (October 1967): 694–700.

5. See Bruce I. Oppenheimer, James A. Stimson, and Richard W. Waterman, "Interpreting U.S. Congressional Elections: The Exposure Thesis," *Legislative Studies Quarterly* 11 (May 1986): 227–47.

6. Angus Campbell, "Surge and Decline: A Study of Electoral Change," *Public Opinion Quarterly* 24 (1960): 387–419.

7. See Robert Ansenau and Raymond Wolfinger, "Voting Behavior in Congressional Elections" (paper presented at annual meeting of the American Political Science Association, New Orleans, La., September 1973).

8. Richard Born, "Surge and Decline, Negative Voting, and the Midterm Loss Phenomenon: A Simultaneous Choice Analysis," *American Journal of Political Science* 34 (August 1990): 615–45; James E. Campbell, *The Presidential Pulse of Congressional Elections* (Lexington: University Press of Kentucky, 1993).

9. Anthony Downs, *An Economic Theory of Democracy* (New York: Harper & Row, 1957).

10. Gerald H. Kramer, "Short-Term Fluctuation in U.S. Voting Behavior," *American Political Science Review* 65 (March 1971): 131–43.

11. Howard S. Bloom and H. Douglas Price, "Voter Response to Short-Run Economic Conditions: The Asymmetric Effect of Prosperity and Recession," *American Political Science Review* 69 (December 1975): 1240–55.

12. See Henry W. Chappell Jr. and William R. Keech, "A New View of Political Accountability for Economic Performance," *American Political Science Review* 79 (March 1985): 10–27.

13. James E. Piereson, "Presidential Popularity and Midterm Voting at Different Electoral Levels," *American Journal of Political Science* 19 (November 1975): 683–702.

14. Edward R. Tufte, *Political Control of the Economy* (Princeton: Princeton University Press, 1978).

15. For example, Michael B. MacKuen, Robert S. Erikson, and James A. Stimson argue that partisan identification and presidential approval are both dependent on the variable of economic perceptions. "Macropartisanship," *American Political Science Review* 83 (December 1989): 1125–42.

16. See Edward W. Chester, "Is the 'All Politics is Local' Myth True? The 1982 House Races as a Case Study," *Journal of Social, Political, and Economic Studies* 14 (Spring 1989): 99–116. According to Chester, only 38 percent of House candidates mentioned constituency service in their 1982 campaign literature and only 19 percent mentioned "pork"; in contrast, virtually all candidates mentioned national issues.

17. Donald E. Stokes and Warren E. Miller, "Party Government and the Salience of Congress," *Public Opinion Quarterly* 26 (Winter 1962): 531–46.

18. See George J. Stigler, "General Economic Conditions and National Elections," *American Economics Review* 63 (May 1973): 160–67; Francisco Arcelus and Allan H. Meltzer, "The Effect of Aggregate Economic Variables on Congressional Elections," *American Political Science Review* 69 (December 1975): 1232–39; Morris P. Fiorina, "Economic Retrospective Voting in American National Elections: A Micro-Analysis," *American Journal of Political Science* 22 (May 1978): 426–43; John R. Owens and Edward C. Olson, "Economic Fluctuations and Congressional Elections," *American Journal of Political Science* 24, (August 1980): 469–93; Lyn Ragsdale, "The Fiction of Congressional Elections as Presidential Events," *American Politics Quarterly* 8 (October 1980): 375–98.

19. See Alan I. Abramowitz, Albert D. Cover, and Helmut Norpoth, "The President's Party in Midterm Elections: Going from Bad to Worse," *American Journal of Political Science* 30 (August 1986): 562–76; Albert D. Cover, "Presidential Evaluations and Voting for Congress," *American Journal of Political Science* 30 (November 1986): 786–801; Albert D. Cover, "Party Competence Evaluations and Voting for Congress," *Western Political Quarterly* 39 (June 1986): 304–12.

20. Gary C. Jacobson and Samuel Kernell, *Strategy and Choice in Congressional Elections* (New Haven: Yale University Press, 1981); Gary C. Jacobson, *The Politics of Congressional Elections,* 3rd ed. (New York: HarperCollins, 1992); Gary C. Jacobson, *The Electoral Origins of Divided Government: Competition in U.S. House Elections, 1946–1988* (Boulder: Westview Press, 1990).

21. See Robert S. Erikson, "The Puzzle of Midterm Loss," *Journal of Politics* 50 (November 1988): 1011–29; Alberto Alesina and Howard Rosenthal, "Partisan Cycles in Congressional Elections and the Macroeconomy," *American Political Science Review* 83 (June 1989): 373–98.

22. Samuel Kernell, "Presidential Popularity and Negative Voting: An Alternative

Explanation to the Midterm Decline of the President's Party," *American Political Science Review* 71 (March 1977): 44–66.

23. See Priscilla L. Southwell, "The Mobilization Hypothesis and Voter Turnout in Congressional Elections, 1974–1982," *Western Political Quarterly* 41(June 1988): 273–87.

24. Robert S. Erikson and Gerald C. Wright, "Voters, Candidates, and Issues in Congressional Elections," in *Congress Reconsidered*, 6th ed., eds. Lawrence C. Dodd and Bruce I. Oppenheimer (Washington, D.C.: Congressional Quarterly Press, 1997), 135.

25. Morris P. Fiorina, *Divided Government*, 2d ed. (Boston: Allyn & Bacon, 1996).

26. See John R. Petrocik and Joseph Doherty, "The Road to Divided Government," in *Divided Government: Change, Uncertainty, and the Constitutional Order*, ed. Peter F. Galderisi (Lanham, Md.: Rowman & Littlefield, 1996), 85–107.

27. See James E. Campbell, "Presidential Coattails and Midterm Losses in State Legislatures," *American Political Science Review* 80 (March 1986): 45–63; Dennis M. Simon, Charles W. Ostrom Jr., and Robin F. Marra, "The President, Referendum Voting, and Subnational Elections in the United States," *American Political Science Review* 85 (December 1991): 1177–92.

Studies of British by-elections, Canadian by-elections, and German Land elections—all roughly analogous to U.S. midterm elections—have uncovered evidence of referendum voting and surge-and-decline effects. See Christopher J. Anderson and Daniel S. Ward, "Barometer Elections in Comparative Perspective," *Electoral Studies* 14 (1995), 1–14; Christopher J. Anderson, Appleton, and Daniel S. Ward, *The Causes and Consequences of Barometer Elections* (paper prepared for the annual meeting of the Midwest Political Science Association, April 1996)

28. David R. Mayhew, "Innovative Midterm Elections," in *Midterm: The Elections of 1994 in Context*, ed. Philip A. Klinkner (Boulder: Westview Press, 1996), 157–70.

29. Alberto Alesina and Howard Rosenthal, *Partisan Politics, Divided Government, and the Economy* (Cambridge: Cambridge University Press, 1995), 83.

1. Midterm Elections and Checks and Balances in the American System

Epigraphs: Richard E. Neustadt, *Presidential Power and the Modern Presidents* (New York: The Free Press, 1990), 77; Barbara Hinckley, "Interpreting House Midterm Elections: Toward Measurement of the In-Party's 'Expected Loss of Seats,'" *American Political Science Review* 61 (September 1967): 700.

1. James Madison, *Federalist* 47, in *The Federalist Papers*, ed. Clinton Rossiter (New York: New American Library, 1960), 301.

2. David Mayhew, *Divided We Govern* (New Haven: Yale University Press, 1991), 118. In total, Mayhew calculates that 152 important laws were passed in the first half of presidential terms, 115 in the second half—a decline of 24.3 percent.

3. Jong R. Lee, "Presidential Vetoes from Washington to Nixon," *Journal of Politics* 37 (May 1975): 522–46.

4. Lee, 540–41.

5. Gary W. Copeland, "When Congress and the President Collide: Why Presidents Veto Legislation," *Journal of Politics* 45 (August 1983): 696–710.

6. Of twenty-six presidential administrations in this period, only twelve experienced an increase in vetoes after the midterm; thirteen saw a decline (though five were declines of only one), and one was unchanged. There were increased override attempts

and/or successes after midterms in eighteen administrations, with only three declining and five unchanged.

7. See James P. Pfiffner, *The Modern Presidency* (New York: St. Martin's Press, 1994), 146.

8. Gary King and Lyn Ragsdale, *The Elusive Executive* (Washington, D.C.: Congressional Quarterly, 1988), 73–74.

9. Jon R. Bond and Richard Fleisher, *The President in the Legislative Arena* (Chicago: University of Chicago Press, 1990), 78–79.

10. For discussion of the advantages and disadvantages of presidential support scores, see Bond and Fleisher, 54–71.

11. Alberto Alesina and Howard Rosenthal, *Partisan Politics, Divided Government, and the Economy* (Cambridge: Cambridge University Press, 1995).

12. Seat changes from 1894–1994 are found in Norman J. Ornstein, Thomas E. Mann, and Michael J. Malbin, *Vital Statistics on Congress 1995–1996* (Washington, D.C.: Congressional Quarterly Press, 1996), 53. Ornstein, Mann, and Malbin count 1902 results as a nine-seat Republican gain, but it is counted as a sixteen-seat loss here. As the authors noted, the size of Congress was expanded after 1900, and while Republicans gained nine seats, Democrats gained twenty-five, leaving a net Republican loss of sixteen.

13. Exactly one-third (33 or 34) are normally up for election in any midterm election in accordance with the staggered terms, but the figure often goes higher due to special Senate elections to fill vacancies due to early resignations or deaths in the Senate.

14. Alan I. Abramowitz and Jeffrey A. Segal, "Determinants of the Outcomes of Senate Elections," *Journal of Politics* 48 (May, 1986): 433–39.

15. See Alan I. Abramowitz, Albert D. Cover, and Helmut Norpoth, "The President's Party in Midterm Elections: Going from Bad to Worse," *American Journal of Political Science* 30 (August 1986): 562–76.

16. Ornstein, Mann, and Malbin, 200. John W. Kingdon points out that a high degree of party regularity exists despite relatively weak party leadership, and traces party regularity to constituency characteristics as well as the common experience of waging campaigns against the other party. See John W. Kingdon, *Congressmen's Voting Decisions,* 3d ed. (Ann Arbor: University of Michigan Press, 1989), 120–22.

17. See Robert S. Erikson and Gerald C. Wright, "Voters, Candidates, and Issues in Congressional Elections," in *Congress Reconsidered,* 6th ed., eds. Lawrence C. Dodd and Bruce I. Oppenheimer (Washington, D.C.: Congressional Quarterly Press, 1997), 132–61.

18. See Philip A. Klinkner, *The Losing Parties: Out-Party National Committees* (New Haven: Yale University Press, 1994).

19. Alberto Alesina and Howard Rosenthal, *Partisan Politics, Divided Government, and the Economy* (Cambridge: Cambridge University Press, 1995).

20. David R. Mayhew, "Innovative Midterm Elections," 165–68.

21. David W. Brady, *Critical Elections and Congressional Policy Making* (Stanford: Stanford University Press, 1988).

22. Convention cases were selected to best illustrate regional/factional differences and presidents' true bases of support, so undisputed renominations of incumbent presidents were not used. The conventions used were 1884 Democratic (Cleveland),

1896 Republican (McKinley), 1912 Republican (Theodore Roosevelt and Taft), 1912 Democratic (Wilson), 1920 Republican (Harding), 1928 Republican (Hoover), 1940 Democratic (Franklin Roosevelt), 1948 Democratic (Truman), 1952 Republican (Eisenhower), 1960 Democratic (Kennedy), 1968 Republican (Nixon), and 1976 Republican (Ford and Reagan). Primary results by region were used from 1976 Democratic primaries (Carter) and 1992 Democratic primaries (Clinton), while 1980 and 1988 mean Republican primary results were averaged for Bush. In the case of Franklin Roosevelt, the 1932 convention was discarded in favor of 1940 because in 1932 his main opponent (Al Smith) was also from New York and drove southern support toward FDR to an unnatural degree due to Smith's Catholicism. Lyndon Johnson's circumstances and policy choices make a continuation of Kennedy's 1960 base more appropriate for him in 1966 than using Johnson's own 1960 convention performance. Like Johnson, Coolidge was assigned the previous president's base and opposition areas. For the data used to assign the president's base and oppositional regions, see Appendix A.

23. The regional analysis, of course, will often indirectly capture an ideological dimension as well. These fourteen cases were those in which contemporary accounts or subsequent historical analysis specifically emphasized an ideological shift. Sometimes this shift was consistent with the regional shift, while on other occasions region obscured the deeper philosophical shift. For example, in 1982, although the regional breakdown did not indicate a shift against Ronald Reagan, 25 percent of House Republican freshmen (the so-called "Reagan robots") lost, a loss rate twice that of the party as a whole.

24. Ornstein, Mann, and Malbin, *Vital Statistics on Congress 1995–96*, 203.

25. Bond and Fleisher, 87.

26. Bond and Fleisher, 92. Before midterms, presidents from 1953–1984 held an average effective base of 133.4 votes in the House, which fell to 114.3 votes after midterms.

27. James P. Pfiffner, *The Modern Presidency* (New York: St. Martin's Press, 1994), 146.

28. Bond and Fleisher, 120. For a similar view, see also George C. Edwards III, *At The Margins* (New Haven: Yale University Press, 1989), in which he argues that partisan and ideological composition of Congress is much more important to presidential success than is presidential skill.

29. Matthew Soberg Shugart, "The Electoral Cycle and Institutional Sources of Divided Government," *American Political Science Review* 89 (June 1995): 328.

30. Shugart, 331. The countries Shugart examined were Argentina, Brazil, Chile, Colombia, Costa Rica, Ecuador, El Salvador, France, the Philippines, Portugal, the United States, and Venezuela. While American midterms produce divided government 50 percent of the time, the international total is approximately 37 percent.

31. Pearl Olive Ponsford, *Evil Results of Mid-Term Congressional Elections and a Suggested Remedy* (Los Angeles: University of Southern California Press, 1937).

32. Lloyd Cutler, "To Form a Government," in *Separation of Powers: Does It Still Work?*, eds. Robert A. Goldwin and Art Kaufman (Washington, D.C.: American Enterprise Institute, 1986).

33. See David R. Mayhew, *Divided We Govern;* Morris Fiorina, *Divided Government,* 2d ed. (Boston: Allyn & Bacon, 1996); E. Scott Adler and Charles M. Cameron, "The

Macro-Politics of Congress: The Enactment of Significant Legislation 1947–1992," cited in Fiorina, *Divided Government*, 163–67.

34. See Sean Kelley, "Divided We Govern: A Reassessment," *Polity* 25 (1993): 475–84.

35. Bond and Fleisher, 74–75; Leroy N. Riselbach, "It's the Constitution, Stupid!," in *Divided Government: Change, Uncertainty, and the Constitutional Order*, ed. Peter F. Galderisi (Lanham, Md.: Rowman & Littlefield, 1996), 115.

36. Roberta Q. Herzberg, "Unity versus Division: The Effect of Divided Government on Policy Development," in *Divided Government: Change, Uncertainty, and the Constitutional Order*, ed. Peter F. Galderisi (Lanham, Md.: Rowman & Littlefield, 1996), 174.

37. V. O. Key, *Politics, Parties, & Pressure Groups*, 5th ed. (New York: Thomas Y. Crowell Company, 1964), 545.

38. Midterm elections have produced a shift from a unified Congress to a split Congress in 1842, 1846, 1854, 1858, 1874, 1882, 1890, 1910, and 1930; the reverse occurred in 1794, 1878, and 1986.

39. See Fiorina, *Divided Government*, 169–70.

40. See Jeffrey Tulis, *The Rhetorical Presidency* (Princeton: Princeton University Press, 1987); Samuel Kernell, *Going Public*, 2d ed. (Washington, D.C.: Congressional Quarterly Press, 1993).

41. Richard Neustadt, *Presidential Power*, 78.

42. Mary E. Stuckey, *The President as Interpreter-in-Chief* (Chatham, N.J.: Chatham House Publishers, 1991).

43. Kernell, 234.

44. See James Ceaser, *Presidential Selection: Theory and Development* (Princeton: Princeton University Press, 1978); Tulis, *The Rhetorical Presidency*.

45. Neustadt, *Presidential Power*.

46. See Charles O. Jones, *The Presidency in a Separated System* (Washington, D.C.: Brookings Institution, 1994); Robert A. Dahl, "Myth of the Presidential Mandate," *Political Science Quarterly* 105, no. 3 (1990): 355–72; Stanley Kelley Jr., *Interpreting Elections* (Princeton: Princeton University Press, 1983).

47. Presidential explanations of midterm election losses are taken primarily from *Public Papers of the President* from Harry S. Truman to George Bush and *Weekly Compilation of Presidential Documents* (30) for Bill Clinton. These comments were generally delivered in news conferences or written statements offered shortly after the elections. For purposes of this analysis, "presidential" explanations also include statements by vice presidents, chairmen of the president's national party committee, and White House spokesmen, who are assumed to be speaking for the administration; these comments are found in the same news sources reviewed for congressional explanations below.

48. "News Conference, November 5, 1958," *Public Papers of the President*, Dwight Eisenhower (Washington, D.C.: Government Printing Office, 1959), 828.

49. "News Conference, November 9, 1994," *Weekly Compilation of Presidential Documents* 30 (November–December 1994): 2339–48.

50. "Statement on the Results of the 1974 Election, November 1974," *Public Papers of the President*, Gerald Ford (1974), 579. Ruth Marcus, "Clinton Reiterates Vow to Pursue New Democrat Agenda," *Washington Post*, November 11, 1994, A14.

51. Edward Walsh, "Democrats Wonder Whether Sea Change Is Plea for Centrism," *Washington Post*, November 10, 1994, A27.

In partisan terms, there was no difference between Democratic and Republican presidents in use of the historical explanation, local conditions explanation, policy mandate explanation, and dumb voter explanation. Republicans were more likely than Democrats to claim victory on the basis of non-House elections (undoubtedly because their poor record in the House through most of this period left them little choice), to blame campaign shortcomings, and to explicitly deny that the elections were a referendum. Democrats were slightly more likely than Republicans to point to national conditions, to accept personal responsibility, to claim voters wanted divided government, and to blame their own Congress, although the partisan discrepancy in the last three cases were all traceable to Bill Clinton.

52. Studying congressional interpretations of midterm election results is a much more difficult task than examining congressional responses. The president is one figure whose statements are systematically recorded and easily available. Examination of congressional reaction is much more dependent on media outlets and, hence, on the author's selection of outlets and on journalistic selection of sources and quotes. Thus, conclusions regarding Congress cannot be made as securely as conclusions regarding the president.

Congressional explanations are taken primarily from the *New York Times* (1946–1970) and *Washington Post* (1974–1994), supplemented by *Newsweek* magazine, *Congressional Quarterly Weekly Report*, and *The National Journal*. To provide a documentary source equivalent to the *Public Papers of the President*, the *Congressional Record* was also consulted, though only in years when a lame-duck Congress met shortly after the election. For purposes of this paper, comments issuing from the parties' congressional campaign committees are considered congressional comments. Journalistic sources were examined through the Friday after the election (if daily) or in the first issue after the election (if weekly); *Congressional Record* entries were examined for the first three days of the lame-duck session.

The key measurement used is whether or not a given explanation was offered following each election; how frequently these explanations were offered within elections is a separate question and is not treated. Because a large part of the analysis consists of a comparison of presidential with congressional explanations, and because there are 535 members of Congress and only one president, measuring actual frequencies would have skewed the results and seriously complicated the analysis.

53. In addition, there was occasionally a second variety of interpretation offered: explanation for why the opposition party did not gain as many seats as expected. Presidential popularity and low exposure on the part of the president's party in Congress were each offered. On one occasion, the opposition offered no explanation at all in the sources surveyed in a year when the president's losses were far below average (1962). In that year, outside of Congress, Richard Nixon blamed his California gubernatorial loss on the Cuban crisis, an interpretation shared on the national level by political correspondents. See Gladwin Hill, "Nixon Denounces Press as Biased," *New York Times*, November 8, 1962, 1, 18; "The 'In' Party's Dramatic Triumph," *Newsweek*, November 19, 1962, 31.

Overall, from 1946 through 1994 Republicans were slightly more likely to claim an ideological/policy mandate, while Democrats have been more likely to claim that voters wished to restore balance to government and much more likely to claim that economic concerns were central. Democrats were more likely than Republicans to claim an anti-administration mandate, were slightly more likely to claim a party mandate, and were the only party to claim that the elections were a standoff. Each party pointed to scandal once.

54. See "Anderson Blames the Brennan Plan," *New York Times,* November 9, 1950, 39; Sen. Holland, *Congressional Record*—Senate, November 29, 1950, 15960–15961; David Broder, "Vote May Signal GOP Return as Dominant Party," *Washington Post,* November 10, 1994, A1.

On one occasion, the president (Eisenhower) was implicitly blamed not for dragging down the party but for not campaigning hard enough to take advantage of his popularity. William S. White, "Democrats Offer Harmony in Rule of 84th House," *New York Times,* November 5, 1954, 1.

55. *New York Times,* November 9, 1966, 1.

56. *New York Times,* November 9, 1966, 38.

57. *Newsweek,* November 21, 1966, 31.

58. *Time,* November 18, 1966, front cover.

59. Gary C. Jacobson, *The Politics of Congressional Elections,* 3d ed. (New York: HarperCollins, 1992), 182.

60. Jacobson, *The Politics of Congressional Elections,* 49.

61. Donley T. Studlar and Lee Sigelman, "Special Elections: A Comparative Perspective," *British Journal of Political Science* 17 (April 1987): 255.

62. Christopher J. Anderson, Andrew M. Appleton, and Daniel S. Ward, "The Causes and Consequences of Barometer Elections," paper presented at the 1996 annual meeting of the Midwest Political Science Association, 17. See also Lee Sigelman, "Special Elections to the U.S. House: Some Descriptive Generalizations," *Legislative Studies Quarterly* 6 (November 1981): 577–88.

63. Sigelman, 577–88. In presidential years from 1954 through 1978, two-thirds of party turnover in special elections benefited the president's party; in midterm years, more than 80 percent of party turnover hurt the president's party.

64. Anderson, Appleton, and Ward, 18.

65. Anderson, Appleton, and Ward, 20.

66. Anderson, Appleton, and Ward, 11–12.

67. Anderson, Appleton, and Ward, 12.

68. *Causes and Consequences,* 8.

69. See Peter Roff, "Housekeeping," *National Review,* August 17, 1998, 24–25.

70. "Terminated in Texas," *Newsweek,* June 14, 1993, 37.

71. *Congressional Quarterly Weekly Report,* May 8, 1993, 1173.

72. *Congress and the Nation 1989–1992,* vol. 8 (Washington, D.C.: Congressional Quarterly Press, 1993), 8.

73. Sigelman, 578.

74. "Elections: The Run-Off," *Newsweek,* May 29, 1961, 26–27.

75. Mitchell won the special election by 24 votes out of about 33,000 cast, and lost the general election by 130 out of the same vote total.

76. For an interesting discussion of special elections in the South in the 1980s and early 1990s, see James M. Glaser, *Race, Campaign Politics, and Realignment in the South* (New Haven: Yale University Press, 1996).

77. King and Ragsdale, 73–74.

78. William A. Glaser, "Hindsight and Significance," in *Public Opinion and Congressional Elections*, eds. William N. McPhee and William A. Glaser (New York: Free Press, 1962).

79. David W. Brady, *Critical Elections and Congressional Policy-Making* (Stanford: Stanford University Press, 1988); Barbara Sinclair, *Congressional Realignment: 1925–1978* (Austin: University of Texas Press, 1982).

80. John D. Morris, "Change Accepted by Party Leaders," *New York Times*, November 7, 1946, 7.

81. "What the GOP Is Doing," *Newsweek*, November 17, 1958, 21.

82. See Josiah Lee Auspitz, "GOP Electoral Strategy Full of Holes," *Washington Post*, November 8, 1970, A12.

83. David S. Broder and Ann Devroy, "A Sobering Experience," *Washington Post*, November 8, 1990, A41, 43.

84. Edward Walsh, "Democrats Wonder if Sea Change is a Plea for Centrism," *Washington Post*, November 10, 1994, A27.

85. The six significant intraparty challenges in this period were counted as 1912 (Taft vs. Roosevelt and LaFollette), 1948 (Truman vs. Thurmond and Wallace), 1968 (Johnson vs. McCarthy), 1976 (Ford vs. Reagan), 1980 (Carter vs. Kennedy), and 1992 (Bush vs. Buchanan). The case of 1948 was included even though the challenge came in the form of third parties because both third parties were essentially discontented factions of the Democratic Party.

2. State Midterm Elections

1. See V. O. Key Jr. and Corinne Silverman, "Party and Separation of Powers: A Panorama of Practice in the States," in *American State Politics: Readings for Comparative Analysis*, ed. Frank Munger (New York: Thomas Y. Crowell, 1966), 452–55.

2. V. O. Key Jr., *American State Politics: An Introduction* (New York: Alfred A. Knopf, 1966), 30.

3. See Austin Ranney, "Parties in State Politics," in *Politics in the American States: A Comparative Perspective*, 2d ed., eds. Herbert Jacob and Kenneth N. Vines (Boston: Little, Brown, and Company, 1971), 100. Oklahoma elects the largest number of statewide officials—fourteen.

4. See Dennis M. Simon, "Presidents, Governors, and Electoral Accountability," *Journal of Politics* 51 (May 1989): 286–303.

5. Key, *American State Politics*, 26–29.

6. James E. Campbell, "Presidential Coattails and Midterm Losses in State Legislative Elections," *American Political Science Review* 80 (March 1986): 45–63.

7. John E. Chubb, "Institutions, the Economy, and the Dynamics of State Elections," *American Political Science Review* 82 (March 1988): 133–54 .

8. James E. Peireson, "Presidential Popularity and Midterm Voting at Different Electoral Levels," *American Journal of Political Science* 19 (November 1975): 683–94; Dennis M. Simon, Charles W. Ostrom Jr., and Robin F. Marra, "The President, Referendum Voting, and Subnational Elections in the United States," *American Political Science Review* 85 (December 1991): 1177–92.

9. James E. Peireson, "Determinants of Candidate Success in Gubernatorial Elections, 1910–1970," unpublished paper, 1974. Cited by Malcolm E. Jewell and David M.

Olson, *American State Parties and Elections* (Honewood, Ill.: Dorsey Press, 1978), 243.

10. See Gregory A. Caldiera and Samuel C. Patterson, "Bringing Home the Votes: Electoral Outcomes in State Legislative Races," *Political Behavior* 4 (1982): 33–67.

11. See Ranney, "Parties in State Politics," 105.

12. Chubb, 149.

13. "Good" years were years when the president's approval was in excess of 45 percent and had fallen less than 15 percent since the previous election; "mediocre" years were years when presidential approval was either less than 45 percent or had fallen at least 15 percent; and "bad" years were years when approval was both less than 45 percent and had fallen at least 15 percent.

14. Dennis M. Simon, "Presidents, Governors, and Electoral Accountability," *Journal of Politics* 51 (May 1989): 286–303.

15. John F. Bibby, "Patterns in Midterm Gubernatorial and State Legislative Elections," *Public Opinion* (February/March 1983): 42.

16. Bibby, 45.

17. Chubb, 150.

18. Key, *American State Politics*, 33.

19. Bibby, 46.

20. Sarah McCally Morehouse, *State Politics, Parties and Policy* (New York: Holt, Rinehart & Winston, 1980), 203. For a general treatment of governor as party leader, see chapter 11.

21. See, for example, Jewell and Olson, 65–71.

22. See Jewell and Olson; Morehouse; Coleman B. Ransone Jr., *The American Governorship* (Westport, Conn.: Greenwood Press, 1982), 127.

23. See, for example, Lynn Muchmore and Thad L. Beyle, "The Governor as Party Leader," *State Government* 53 (Spring 1980): 121–24.

24. Bibby, 46.

25. Key, *American State Politics*, 79.

26. This figure includes Theodore Roosevelt and Calvin Coolidge, who were governors immediately before attaining their party's vice-presidential nomination. They then succeeded to the Oval Office when the president died. Charles Evans Hughes was the sole member of this group to hold an intermediate office between governorship and nomination to a presidential ticket; he served as Chief Justice of the U.S. Supreme Court.

27. See Larry J. Sabato, *Good-bye to Goodtime Charlie: The American Governorship Transformed,* 2d ed. (Washington, D.C.: Congressional Quarterly Press, 1983), chapter 6, 183–202.

28. Joseph A. Schlesinger, "The Politics of the Executive," in *Politics in the American States: A Comparative Analysis,* 2d ed., eds. Herbert Jacob and Kenneth N. Vines (Boston: Little, Brown and Company, 1971), 213.

29. Gary C. Jacobson, *The Politics of Congressional Elections,* 3d ed. (New York: HarperCollins, 1992), 47; see generally 47–49. Also Jacobson, *The Electoral Origins of Divided Government* (Boulder, Colo.: Westview Press, 1990), chapter 4, 45–74.

30. Bibby, 46.

31. See Sabato, *Good-bye to Goodtime Charlie,* 33–45. See also Joseph A. Schlesinger, *Ambition and Politics: Political Careers in the United States* (Chicago: Rand McNally, 1966), chapter 6, 89–118.

32. Sabato, *Good-bye to Goodtime Charlie,* 46–47; Schlesinger, 213.

33. Robert S. Erikson, "Malapportionment, Gerrymandering, and Party Fortunes in Congressional Elections," *American Political Science Review* 66 (December 1972): 1243. On 1970, see also Amihai Glazer, Bernard Grofman, and Marc Robbins, "Partisan and Incumbency Effects of 1970s Congressional Redistricting," *American Journal of Political Science,* 31 (August 1987): 680–707.

34. "The New Tilt," *Newsweek,* November 20, 1978, 46.

35. Alan I. Abramowitz, "Partisan Redistricting and the 1982 Congressional Elections," *Journal of Politics* 45 (August, 1983): 767–70. See also Alan Ehrenhalt, "Reapportionment and Redistricting" in *The American Elections of 1982,* eds. Thomas Mann and Norman Ornstein (Washington, D.C.: American Enterprise Institute, 1983), 44–71. As perhaps the most extreme single-state example, Democrats in California likely redistricted themselves into possession of five seats after 1980. See Bruce Cain, "Assessing the Partisan Effects of Redistricting," *American Political Science Review* 79 (June 1985): 320–33.

36. See Morris Fiorina, *Divided Government,* 2d ed. (Boston: Allyn & Bacon, 1996), 16; Thomas E. Mann, "Is the House Unresponsive to Change?," in *Elections American Style, ed. A.* James Reichley (Washington, D.C.: Brookings Institution, 1987), 269–75; Gary C. Jacobson, *The Politics of Congressional Elections,* 3d ed. (New York: HarperCollins, 1992), 10–15; Andrew W. Robertson, "American Redistricting in the 1980s: The Effect on Midterm Elections," *Electoral Studies* 2 (1983): 113–29. For general skepticism on the partisan effects of redistricting, see Richard Born, "Partisan Intentions and Election Day Realities in the Congressional Redistricting Process," *American Political Science Review* 79 (1985): 317

37. Bruce E. Cain and Janet C. Campagna, "Predicting Partisan Redistricting Disputes," *Legislative Studies Quarterly* 12 (May 1987): 265–74.

38. Susan A. Banducci and Jeffrey A. Karp, "Electoral Consequences of Scandal and Reapportionment in the 1992 House Elections," *American Politics Quarterly* 22 (January 1994): 3–26.

39. David Lublin, cited in Fiorina, *Divided Government,* 137. See also Gary C. Jacobson, "Divided Government and the 1994 Elections," in *Divided Government: Change, Uncertainty, and the Constitutional Order,* ed. Peter F. Galderisi (Lanham, Md.: Rowman & Littlefield, 1996), 76–77; Gary C. Jacobson, "The 1994 House Elections in Perspective," in *Midterm: The Elections of 1994 in Context,* ed. Philip A. Klinkner (Boulder: Westview Press, 1996), 18–19.

40. Charles S. Bullock, "Affirmative Action Districts: In Whose Faces Will They Blow Up?," *Campaigns and Elections* , April 1995, 22; see also Kevin A. Hill, "Does the Creation of Majority Black Districts Aid Republicans? An Analysis of the 1992 Congressional Elections in Eight Southern States," *Journal of Politics* 57 (May 1995): 384–401.

41. Richard C. Born, "Partisan Intentions and Election Day Realities in the Congressional Redistricting Process," *American Political Science Review* 79 (1985): 304–19.

42. Abramowitz, "Partisan Redistricting," 770.

43. Republicans actually held six more state senators (out of almost 2,000) and twenty-six more state representatives (out of almost 4,500) after the 1990 elections than they had after the 1988 elections.

44. Gov. Martinez of Florida faced a tough reelection campaign against popular former Sen. Lawton Chiles under any circumstances, but Ann Richards of Texas defeated Republican Chilton Williams by a narrow margin after trailing for most of the campaign.

45. Alexander Hamilton, *Federalist* 17, in *The Federalist Papers,* ed. Clinton Rossiter (New York: New American Library, 1960), 118–122.

46. See Parris N. Glendening, "The Public's Perception of State Government and Governors," *State Government* 53 (Summer 1980): 115–20.

47. See particularly Alexander Hamilton, *Federalist* 17, and James Madison, *Federalist* 45–46.

48. See Larry J. Sabato, *The Party's Just Begun* (Glenview, Ill.: Scott, Foresman, & Co., 1988), 63–65.

49. Federalism scholar Martha Derthick calls the state half of this dialogue "talking back." Martha Derthick, "The Enduring Features of American Federalism," *Brookings Review* 7 (summer 1989): 34–38.

50. See Terry Sanford, *Storm Over the States* (New York: McGraw-Hill, 1967), 53–68; Ira Scharansky, *The Maligned States,* 2d ed. (New York: McGraw-Hill, 1978); David Osborne, *Laboratories of Democracy* (Boston: Harvard Business School Press, 1990); Ann O'M. Bowman and Richard C. Kearney, *The Resurgence of the States* (Englewood Cliffs N.J.: Prentice-Hall, 1986), 187–248.

51. Sanford, *Storm Over the States,* 4.

52. Of course, these movements also ultimately shifted their attention to the national level, either because too many states remained unresponsive or because the states were simply inadequate to deal with certain national concerns.

53. For example, Governors Tommy Thompson of Wisconsin and John Engler of Michigan requested waivers allowing greater experimentation with welfare. The Clinton administration granted the waivers (political considerations were highly relevant in 1996) but was clearly uncomfortable with the direction of state policy. Those states gave the administration the choice of leaving itself open to charges of hypocrisy by rejecting the waivers or legitimizing policy innovation that expanded the parameters of the debate perhaps beyond where the administration preferred.

54. See Jack Tweedie, "Changing the Face of Welfare," *State Legislatures* 21 (December 1995): 15–17. Interestingly, Democratic and Republican governors were equally likely to pursue welfare reform after 1994, although there can be little doubt that the Republican tide of 1994 was the driving factor across party lines.

55. Campbell, "Presidential Coattails," 61.

56. For a broad discussion of the revitalization of the gubernatorial office, see Sabato, *Good-bye to Goodtime Charlie.*

57. Bowman and Kearney, 29–31.

58. Sabato, *Goodbye to Good–time Charlie,* 164.

3. Midterm Elections as the Vanguard of Change: Part 1, Realignment and the Elections of 1894 and 1930

Epigraph: David W. Brady, "Critical Elections and Clusters of Policy Changes," *British Journal of Political Science* 8 (January 1978): 81.

1. Angus Campbell, in his three-fold classification of elections, identified both 1896 and 1932 (as well as 1860) as realignments. Gerald Pomper, who employed a four-fold

classification scheme, categorized 1932 as a realigning election and 1896 as a "converting" election in which the old majority party remained the majority but the bases of both parties were significantly reconstituted. Campbell, "A Classification of the Presidential Elections," in *The American Voter*, ed. Angus Campbell, Philip E. Converse, Warren E. Miller, and Donald E. Stokes (New York: John Wiley & Sons, 1960); Gerald Pomper, "Classification of Presidential Elections," *Journal of Politics* 29 (August 1967): 535-66.

2. V. O. Key, "A Theory of Critical Elections," *Journal of Politics* 17 (February 1955): 3–18.

3. Campbell, "A Classification of the Presidential Elections"; Charles Sellers, "The Equilibrium Cycle in Two–Party Politics," *Public Opinion Quarterly* 29 (Spring 1965): 16–38; Pomper, "Classification of Presidential Elections"; Walter Dean Burnham, *Critical Elections and the Mainsprings of American Elections* (New York: W.W. Norton, 1970); Paul Allen Beck, "The Electoral Cycle and Patterns of American Politics," *British Journal of Political Science* 9 (April 1979): 129–56; Kristi Anderson, *The Creation of a Democratic Majority, 1928–1936* (Chicago: University of Chicago Press, 1979); Robert S. Erikson and Kent L. Tedin, "The 1928–1936 Partisan Realignment: The Case for the Conversion Hypothesis," *American Political Science Review* 75 (December 1981): 951–62; James L. Sundquist, *Dynamics of the Party System*, rev. ed. (Washington, D.C.: The Brookings Institution, 1983); Byron E. Shafer ed., *The End of Realignment: Interpreting American Electoral Eras* (Madison: University of Wisconsin Press, 1991).

4. Paul Lechner, "Partisan Realignments and Congressional Behavior," *American Politics Quarterly* 4 (April 1976): 223–33; Stuart Elaine MacDonald and George Rabinowitz, "The Dynamics of Structural Realignment," *American Political Science Review* 81 (September 1987): 775–86.

5. MacDonald and Rabinowitz, 778.

6. Jerome M. Clubb, William H. Flanigan, and Nancy H. Zingale, *Partisan Realignment: Voters, Parties, and Government in American History* (Beverly Hills: Sage, 1980), 160.

7. Sundquist, 301.

8. J. Richard Piper, "Party Realignment and Congressional Change," *American Politics Quarterly* 11 (October 1983): 487.

9 . Walter Dean Burnham, Jerome M. Clubb, and William A. Flanigan, "Partisan Realignment:A Systemic Perspective," in *The History of American Political Behavior*, eds. Joel H. Silbey, Allan G. Bogne, and William H. Flanigan (Princeton: Princeton University Press, 1978), 71–72.

10. For example, see David W. Brady, *Critical Elections and Congressional Policy Making* (Stanford: Stanford University Press, 1988); Barbara Sinclair, *Congressional Realignment: 1925–1978* (Austin: University of Texas Press, 1982); Clubb, Flanigan, and Zingale, *Partisan Realignment*.

11. MacDonald and Rabinowitz, 780–783.

12. Pearl Olive Ponsford, *Evil Results of Mid-Term Congressional Elections and a Suggested Remedy* (Los Angeles: University of Southern California Press, 1937), 39.

13. "Congress," *New York Times*, November 7, 1894, 4.

14. Burnham, Clubb, and Flanigan, 66.

15. Brady, 58; also see J. Rogers Hollingsworth, *The Whirligig of Politics: The Democracy of Cleveland and Bryan* (Chicago: University of Chicago Press, 1963), 28;

George H. Mayer, *The Republican Party 1854–1964* (New York: Oxford Press, 1964), 243.

16. Paul Kleppner, *Continuity and Change in Electoral Politics, 1893–1928* (Westport: Greenwood Press, 1987), 28; Richard W. Waterman, "Institutional Realignment: The Composition of the U.S. Congress," *Western Political Quarterly* 43 (March 1990): 81–92.

17. Burnham, Clubb, and Flanigan, 69.

18. Brady, 66–67.

19. Brady, 52–53.

20. Ronald M. Peters Jr., *The American Speakership* (Baltimore: Johns Hopkins University Press, 1990), 73; also William A. Robinson, *Thomas B. Reed: Parliamentarian* (New York: Dodd, Mead, and Company, 1930), 324. For a sample of contemporary commentary on the 54th Congress, see "Record of the First Session of Congress," *The Literary Digest,* June 20, 1896, 225–27. One analyst observed that "Congress . . . pays little heed either to [Cleveland's] appeals for necessary legislation or to his warnings against wasteful expenditures." George Walton Green, "Mr. Cleveland's Second Administration," *Forum,* July 1896, 556.

21. Mayer, 243.

22. Clarence A. Stern, *Protectionist Republicanism* (Ann Arbor: Edwards Brothers, 1971), 53; see also Mayer, 243–44.

23. George B. Galloway, *History of the House of Representatives,* 2d ed. (New York: Thomas Y. Crowell Company, 1976), 375.

24. Ponsford, 43.

25. There is a variety of ways of measuring vetoes. The first and most obvious is the raw number of vetoes. However, when drawing comparisons across years, this measure does not always paint an accurate picture because of fluctuations in legislative productivity. Hence, some sort of percentage or proportion makes sense. In this study, I will use the proportion or ratio of vetoes to public bills passed. This measure has its own shortcomings, primarily that some vetoes were cast against private rather than public bills. However, this proportion makes the most sense if one is attempting to construct an index that measures both legislative policy-making productivity and the president's willingness to confront Congress.

26. Ponsford, 43; Carlton Jackson, *Presidential Vetoes 1792–1945* (Athens: University of Georgia Press, 1967), 162–64.

27. Arthur Wallace Dunn, *From Harrison to Harding,* vol. 1 (Port Washington, N.Y.: Kennikat Press, 1971), 165.

28. Stern, *Protectionist Republicanism,* 53.

29. Stern, 54; Brady, 77.

30. Kirk H. Porter and Donald Bruce Johnson, *National Party Platforms: 1840–1960* (Urbana: University of Illinois Press, 1961), 93, 107.

31. Mayer, 243.

32. Stern, *Protectionist Republicanism,* 54.

33. See Ponsford, 42–43; Mayer, 243–44; Francis Curtis, *The Republican Party,* vol. 2 (New York: The Knickerbocker Press, 1904), 312–16; Rexford G. Tugwell, *Grover Cleveland* (New York: Macmillan Co., 1968), 269.

34. "The Presidency and Mr. Reed," *The Atlantic Monthly,* February 1896, 255.

35. Robinson, 331.

36. Brady, 76.

37. Margaret Leech, *In the Days of McKinley* (New York: Harper & Brothers, 1959), 78–83.

38. Dunn, 165.

39. H. C. Lodge, "Our Duty to Cuba," *Forum,* May 1896, 286.

40. From the *Baltimore Herald,* an independent newspaper, cited in "Record of the First Session of Congress," *The Literary Digest,* June 20, 1896, 227.

41. Kirk H. Porter and Donald Bruce Johnson, *National Party Platforms: 1840–1960* (Urbana: University of Illinois Press, 1961), 108.

42. Porter and Johnson, 99–100.

43. Porter and Johnson, 93–95, 99, 109.

44. Samuel Kernell and Michael McDonald, "Political Strategy and the Transformation of the Post Office from Patronage to Service," paper presented at the annual meeting of the Western Political Science Association, San Francisco, Calif., March 1996.

45. Hollingsworth, 28–31; R. Hal Williams, *Years of Decision: American Politics in the 1890s* (New York: John Wiley and Sons, 1978), 93–95.

46. Kleppner, 25.

47. Robinson, *Thomas B. Reed: Parliamentarian,* 255, 324.

48. Michael E. Welch, *The Presidencies of Grover Cleveland* (Lawrence: University of Kansas, 1988), 205.

49. Welch, 206–7; Hollingsworth, 17.

50. Hollingsworth, 34–35.

51. See Jerome H. Clubb and Santa A. Traugott, "Partisan Cleavage and Cohesion in the House of Representatives," *Journal of Interdisciplinary History* 8 (winter 1977): 375–401.

52. Welch, 202.

53. Hollinsworth, 43.

54. Stern, 54.

55. Brady, 103.

56. See Edgar Eugene Robinson, *The Roosevelt Leadership, 1933–1945* (Philadelphia: J. D. Lippincott Company, 1955), 48.

57. Jordan A. Schwarz, *The Interregnum of Despair: Hoover, Congress, and the Depression* (Urbana: University of Chicago Press, 1970), 21.

58. Waterman, "Institutional Realignment," 81–92.

59. Arthur M. Schlesinger Jr., *The Crisis of the Old Order, 1919–1933* (Boston: Houghton Mifflin Company, 1957), 224.

60. Richard V. Oulahan, "Democratic Landslide Sweeps Country," *New York Times,* November 5, 1930, 1.

61. "The Republican Debacle," *New York Times,* November 5, 1930, 22.

62. "The Next Congress," *New York Times,* November 5, 1930, 22.

63. Hoover detected a mandate in 1929 to protect the integrity of the Constitution, vigorously enforce the laws, maintain economy in public expenses, regulate business to prevent domination of communities, avoid entanglement in controversies in foreign countries, reorganize the federal government, expand public works, promote welfare activities affecting education and the home, and ameliorate agricultural problems. *Public Papers of the President of the United States: Herbert Hoover* (Washington, D.C.: Government Printing Office, 1974), 10.

64. Ponsford, 54.

65. Schwartz, 62–64.

66. Galloway, 375.

67. Ponsford, 57; Schwarz, 114–39, 146; Herbert Hoover and Calvin Coolidge, *Campaign Speeches of 1932* (Garden City: Doubleday, Doran & Company, Inc., 1933), 11; William Starr Myers and Walter H. Newton, *The Hoover Administration: A Documented Narrative* (New York: Charles Scribner's Sons, 1936), 181, 200.

68. Total vetoes actually fell from 19 to 18, but legislative productivity had fallen almost in half.

69. Barbara Deckard Sinclair, "Party Realignment and the Transformation of the Political Agenda: The House of Representatives 1925–1938," *American Political Science Review* 71 (September 1977): 948.

70. Peters, 112.

71. F. R. Kent, "Why Congress Acts That Way," *American Magazine*, October 1932, 18.

72. Ponsford, 54.

73. See Sinclair, *Congressional Realignment*, 34; David R. Mayhew, "Innovative Midterms," in *Midterm: The 1994 Elections in Context,* ed. Philip A. Klinkner (Boulder: Westview Press, 1996), 162.

74. Brady, 108; Sinclair, "Party Realignment and the Transformation of the Political Agenda," 944. Brady holds that the social welfare dimension first appeared in the 72nd Congress, while Sinclair maintains that it first appeared in the 71st Congress but exploded in the 72nd.

75. Martin L. Fausold, *The Presidency of Herbert C. Hoover* (Lawrence: University of Kansas Press, 1985), 149.

76. Myers and Newton, 188.

77. For example, see Victor von Szeliski, "The Distribution of Income," *The Commonweal*, July 6, 1932, 262–64; George E. Sokolosky, "Will Revolution Come?," *The Atlantic Monthly*, August 1932, 189–90.

78. Myers and Newton, 200.

79. Schwarz, 105.

80. Schwarz, 126–27.

81. Milton Derber, "The New Deal and Labor," in *The New Deal: The National Level,* eds. John Braeman, Robert H. Bremner, and David Brody (Columbus: Ohio State University Press, 1975), 118.

82. See Charles Willis Thompson, "Today and Next November," *The Commonweal*, June 1, 1932, 119–20; Charles Willis Thompson, "The Cold Grey Morning After," *The Commonweal*, July 20, 1932, 302–3; Clinton W. Gilbert, "The People Against Pork," *The Atlantic Monthly*, August 1932, 129–39.

83. Thompson, "Today and Next November," 120.

84. Porter and Johnson, 350, 340.

85. Hoover, 6.

86. Hoover, 15–21.

87. Porter and Johnson, 331–33.

88. Franklin D. Roosevelt, *The Public Papers and Addresses of Franklin D. Roosevelt,* vol. 1 (New York: Russell and Russell, 1938), 837, 851–59.

89. Basil Rauch, *The History of the New Deal 1933–1938* (New York: Creative Age Press, Inc., 1944), 27.

90. Schlesinger, 227–28. See also Ponsford, 56.

91. Schwarz, 54–59.

92. Schwarz, 51–53.

93. For a discussion of Republican congressional divisions, see Schwartz, 45–46, 59; Robinson, *The Roosevelt Leadership*, 37, 59–61.

94. Schwarz, 20. Capper had been appointed to fill the vacancy left by Hoover's vice president, former Senator Charles Curtis, and was running in a special election in 1930 to finish the remainder of Curtis's term.

95. Schwarz, 20–21.

96. Sinclair, "Party Realignment," 944.

97. Schwarz, 114.

98. Clubb, Flanigan, and Zingale, *Partisan Realignment*, 239–44.

99. Mayhew, 165–68.

100. Schwarz, 19.

101. See "A Record of the First Session of Congress," *The Literary Digest*, June 20, 1896, 225–27; Thompson, "Today and Next November," 120; Gilbert, "The People Against Pork," 134.

102. MacDonald and Rabinowitz, 779.

4. Midterm Elections as the Vanguard of Change: Part 2. More Preparatory Midterms

1. Three incidents particularly contributed to Taft's difficulties. First, after promising downward tariff revision, Taft accepted the Payne-Aldrich tariff of 1909, written by Republican conservatives who desired and delivered no such thing. Second, he took sides against Roosevelt's friend Gifford Pinchot in an intraadministration dispute between Pinchot and Interior Secretary Richard Ballinger. Finally, while privately hoping for the resignation of House Speaker Joseph Cannon, Taft appeared publicly to have taken Cannon's side against House insurgents. In the famed March 1910 revolt, Cannon was stripped of many of his powers by a coalition of Democrats and insurgent Republicans.

2. George F. Mowry, *The Era of Theodore Roosevelt: 1900–1912* (New York: Harper & Brothers, 1958), 261.

3. Mowry, 266–68.

4. See Henry F. Pringle, *The Life and Times of William Howard Taft*, vol. 2 (New York: Farrar and Rinehart, Inc., 1939), 570–72.

5. Mowry, 272.

6. David R. Mayhew, "Innovative Midterms" in *Midterm: The Elections of 1994 in Context*, ed. Philip A. Klinkner (Boulder: Westview Press, 1996).

7. James Holt, *Congressional Insurgents and the Party System 1909–1936* (Cambridge: Harvard University Press, 1967), 41.

8. George H. Mayer, *The Republican Party: 1854–1964* (New York: Oxford Press, 1964), 315.

9. John Milton Cooper Jr., *Pivotal Decades: The United States 1900–1920* (New York: W.W. Norton, 1990), 162.

10. Kenneth W. Hechler, *Insurgency: Personalities and Politics of the Taft Era* (New York: Columbia UNiversity Press, 1940), 187.

11. Hechler, 187.

12. Holt, 40–41; see also Mayer, 318.

13. See Mowry, 291; Holt, 46–47.

14. Lewis L. Gould, *Reform and Regulation: American Politics, 1900–1916* (New York: John Wiley & Sons, 1978), 105.

15. "The Political Revolution," *New York Times*, November 9, 1910, 8.

16. Mowry, 273; see also Gould, 135.

17. Cooper, 163.

18. Gould, 133.

19. Pearl Olive Ponsford, *Evil Results of Mid–term Elections and a Suggested Remedy* (Los Angeles: University of Southern California Press, 1937), 46.

20. Mayer, 319.

21. Mayer, 319.

22. Mayhew, 160.

23. Telford Taylor, *Grand Inquest: The Story of Congressional Investigations* (New York: Ballantine, 1961), 81–84.

24. Kirk H. Porter and Donald Bruce Johnson, *National Party Platforms: 1840–1960* (Urbana: University of Illinois Press, 1961), 168–75, 183–88.

25. Mayer, 333–34.

26. Mayer, 351–52; see also Seward W. Livermore, *Politics is Adjourned: Woodrow Wilson and the War Congress 1916–1918* (Middletown: Wesleyan University Press, 1966), 88–98.

27. Cooper, 312.

28. Livermore, 135.

29. On Wilson's appeal, see Mayer, 353; Ponsford, 48–49; Livermore, 220–23; Arthur Walworth, *America's Moment: 1918* (New York: W.W. Norton, 1977), 110–13; Herbert Hoover, *The Ordeal of Woodrow Wilson* (New York: McGraw-Hill, 1958), 14–17.

30. Livermore, 223.

31. Livermore, 210.

32. Livermore, 211–12.

33. Livermore, 215.

34. Ironically, these words were uttered by Sen. John W. Weeks of Massachusetts, one of the few incumbent Republicans to lose in 1918.

35. Mayer, 353.

36. Paul Kleppner, *Continuity and Change in Electoral Politics, 1893–1928* (Westport: Greenwood Press, 1987), 125.

37. For a detailed analysis, see Livermore, 220–46.

38. Cooper, 312.

39. Hoover, 77.

40. Ponsford, 52.

41. Charles Jones, *The Minority Party in Congress* (Boston: Little, Brown, and Company, 1970), 86.

42. John D. Hicks, *Republican Ascendancy 1921–1933* (New York: Harper Torchbooks, 1960), 24.

43. Burl Noggle, *Into the Twenties* (Urbana: University of Illinois Press, 1974), 48; also Ponsford, 50–52.

44. Livermore, 246.

45. Mayer, 359.

46. Mayer, 359, 366.

47. William A. Glaser, "Hindsight and Significance," in *Public Opinion and Congressional Elections*, eds. William N. McPhee and William A. Glaser (New York: Free Press, 1962), 274.

48. William S. White, "Coalition Is Likely," *New York Times*, November 9, 1950, A1.

49. "The Election," *Time*, November 13, 1950, 19–20.

50. See Arthur Krock, "A 'Landslide' Which Went That-a-Way," *New York Times*, November 9, 1950, A32; "The Voice of the Voters," *New York Times*, November 9, 1950, A32.

51. "The Voice of the Voters."

52. "News Conference, November 16, 1950," *Public Papers of the President*, Harry S. Truman 1950, 713–14; Walter Waggoner, "Acheson Declares He Will Not Resign or Change Policies," *New York Times*, November 9, 1950, 1; "Backers See Taft 1952 Party Choice," *New York Times*, November 9, 1950, 1, 24; Clayton Knowles, "Democratic Chiefs Asked to Explain Losses in Election," *New York Times*, November 10, 1950,1.

53. Arthur Krock, "Voting Record Set," *New York Times*, November 8, 1950, A1.

54. Harold F. Gosnell, *Truman's Crises* (Westport: Greenwood Press, 1980), 484. Indeed, McFarland lost to Barry Goldwater in 1952.

55. Glaser, 277. See also Gosnell, 453–59.

56. *Congress and the Nation 1945–1964* (Washington, D.C.: Congressional Quarterly Service, 1965), 11.

57. Glaser, 275.

58. Glaser, 275.

59. Glaser, 277–81.

60. *Congress & the Nation 1945–1964*, 11.

61. Gosnell, 484.

62. Mayer, 480.

63. See David R. Mayhew, *Divided We Govern* (New Haven: Yale University Press, 1991), 13–25.

64. Elmo R. Richardson, *The Presidency of Dwight D. Eisenhower* (Lawrence: The Regents Press of Kansas, 1979), 141.

65. Dwight D. Eisenhower, *Waging Peace: 1956–1961* (Garden City: Doubleday & Company, Inc., 1965), 377.

66. Eisenhower, 381.

67. Richardson, 134.

68. Robert L. Branyan and Lawrence A. Larsen, *The Eisenhower Administration 1953–1961: A Documentary History*, vol. 2 (New York: Random House, 1971), 943–45.

69. Branyan and Larsen, 792.

70. "News Conference, November 5, 1958," *Public Papers of the President*, Dwight Eisenhower 1958 (Washington, D.C.: Government Printing Office, 1959), 827–38.

71. W. H. Lawrence, "Rayburn Bars a Tax Cut," *New York Times*, November 8, 1958, 1, 13.

72. "The National Picture," *New York Times*, November 6, 1958, 36.

73. *Congress and the Nation 1945–1964* (Washington: Congressional Quarterly Service, 1965), 31.

74. Henry Z. Scheele, "Executive–Legislative Relations: Eisenhower and Halleck," in *Reexamining the Eisenhower Presidency*, ed. Shirley Anne Warshaw (Westport: Greenwood Press, 1993), 143.

75. Eisenhower, *Waging Peace*, 393–95.

76. Jones, *The Minority Party in Congress*, 87.

77. James L. Sundquist, *Politics and Policy: The Eisenhower, Kennedy, and Johnson Years* (Washington, D.C.: The Brookings Institution, 1968), 450–51.

78. Branyan and Larsen, 793.

79. Gary King and Lyn Ragsdale, *The Elusive Executive* (Washington, D.C.: Congressional quarterly, 1988), table 2.13.

80. Eisenhower, *Waging Peace*, 699–701.

81. For an analysis of public opinion on federal activism in this time period, see Sundquist, *Politics and Policy*, 440–70.

82. *Congress and the Nation*, 32.

83. See Sundquist, *Politics and Policy*, 456–57.

84. Sundquist, *Politics and Policy*, 441.

85. Rhodes Cook, "No Longer Certain They Like Ike, Voters Punish His Allies in Congress," *Congressional Quarterly Weekly Report*, April 15, 1995, 1061.

86. Edward G. Carmines and James A. Stimson, *Issue Evolution: Race and the Transformation of American Politics* (Princeton: Princeton University Press, 1989), 70.

87. Cook, "No Longer Certain," 1061.

88. See Michael Barone, *Our Country: The Shaping of America from Roosevelt to Reagan* (New York: Free Press, 1990), 303–6.

89. Norman J. Ornstein, Thomas E. Mann, and Michael J. Malbin, *Vital Statistics on Congress 1995–1996* (Washington, D.C.: CQ Press, 1996), 203.

90. See Matt Pinkus, "Democratic Study Group," in *The Encyclopedia of the United States Congress,* vol. 2, eds. Donald C. Bacon, Roger H. Davidson, and Morton Keller eds. (New York: Simon & Schuster, 1995), 633–34; Sundquist, 529.

91. Carmines and Stimson, 63, 70–71.

92. See Emmet John Hughes, *The Ordeal of Power* (New York: Atheneum, 1963), 271; Jones, 110; Eisenhower, *Waging Peace*, 382–84.

93. Quoted in Scheele, 143.

94. Sundquist, 496–97.

95. Herbert S. Parmet, *The Democrats: The Years After FDR* (New York: Macmillan, 1976), 231.

96. "1966 Elections—A Major Republican Comeback," *Congressional Quarterly Weekly Report*, November 11, 1966, 2773.

97. "1966 Elections—A Major Republican Comeback," 2787.

98. See "Elections," *Time*, November 18, 1966, 24; *The 1966 Elections* (Washing-ton, D.C.: Republican National Committee, 1967).

99. "GOP '66: Back on the Map," *Newsweek*, November 21, 1966, 31.

100. "The New Congress," *Newsweek*, November 21, 1966, 38.

101. "The Republican Tide," *New York Times*, November 9, 1966, 38.

102. "GOP '66," 31.

103. "The New Congress," 38–43.

104. "GOP '66," 31.

105. Thomas Byrne Edsall and Mary D. Edsall, *Chain Reaction: The Impact of Race, Rights, and Taxes on American Politics* (New York: W.W. Norton, 1991), 60.

106. "The New Congress," 38.

107. "GOP '66," 34.

108. See "The New Congress," 43; also "1966 Elections—A Major Republican Comeback," 2773.

109. Ornstein, Mann, and Malbin, 203.

110. Barone, *Our Country*, 414.

111. *Congress and the Nation 1965–1968*, vol. 2 (Washington, D.C.: Congressional Quarterly Service, 1969), 8–13.

112. See "Text of Addresses by Rep. Ford and Sen. Dirksen," *Congressional Quarterly Weekly Report*, January 27, 1967, 130–34.

113. See Kenneth Crawford, "Republican Plan," *Newsweek*, November 28, 1966, 35; *Congress and the Nation 1965–1968*, 13.

114. "Elections," 23, 28.

115. Stephen Hess and David S. Broder, *The Republican Establishment: The Present and Future of the G.O.P.* (New York: Harper & Row, 1967), 9, 11.

116. Hess and Broder, 1.

117. See *The 1966 Elections*.

118. "Elections," 29.

119. See Gregory S. Thielemann, "The Rise and Stall of Southern Republicanism in Congress," *Social Science Quarterly* 73, no. 1 (March 1992): 123–35.

120. See "Elections," 23, 27.

121. Edsall and Edsall, 61.

122. "1966 Elections—A Major Republican Comeback," 2774.

123. See "GOP '66," 31; "Elections," 28. Nixon had predicted, amid much skepticism, a Republican gain of 40 in the House, 3 in the Senate, 6 governorships, and about 700 state legislative seats.

124. Richard M. Nixon, *The Memoirs of Richard Nixon* (New York: Grossett and Dunlap, 1978), 275.

125. Nixon, 277.

126. Barone, 416.

127. Theodore H. White, *The Making of the President 1968* (New York: Pocket Books, 1969), 42.

128. "On the One Hand . . . ," *New York Times*, November 9, 1978, A26.

129. Austin Ranney, "The Carter Administration," in *The American Elections of 1980*, ed. Austin Ranney (Washington, D.C.: American Enterprise Institute, 1981), 28.

130. See "The New Tilt," *Newsweek*, November 20, 1978, 44–47.

131. Several analyses concurred that Republicans had lost 5–15 seats due to redistricting, but that number was, of course, far from the number needed to gain a House majority. See Alan Ehrenhalt, "Reapportionment and Redistricting," in *The American Elections of 1982*, eds. Thomas E. Mann and Norman J. Ornstein (Washington, D.C.: American Enterprise Institute, 1983); Alan I. Abramowitz, "Partisan Redistricting and the 1982 Congressional Elections," *Journal of Politics* 45, no. 3 (August 1983): 767–71; Barone, 625.

132. See "The New Tilt," 46–47.

133. "On the One Hand," A26.

134. See Paul Craig Roberts, *The Supply-Side Revolution* (Cambridge: Harvard University Press, 1984), especially chapter 3.

135. "The New Tilt," 44.

136. "The New Tilt," 44.

137. Philip Williams and Graham Wilson, "The American Mid-Term Elections," *Political Studies* 27 (December 1979): 608.

138. "The Penny-Wise 96th," *Newsweek*, November 20, 1978, 55.

139. *Congress & the Nation Vol. V, 1977–1980* (Washington, D.C.: Congressional Quarterly, 1981), 16–17.

140. *Congress and the Nation 1977–80*, 16.

141. *Congress & the Nation Vol. V, 1977–1980*, 11–14.

142. *Congress & the Nation 1977–80*, 16.

143. "Leaning Right," *Newsweek*, November 20, 1978, 55.

144. "The Penny–Wise 96th," 55–56. See also Hedrick Smith, "Social Reforms and Arms Accord Likely to Face Snag on Capitol Hill," *New York Times*, November 8, 1978, A1, A22; Robert G. Kaiser, "In the Upper Chamber, Things Seem to Be Going— Right," *Washington Post*, November 9, 1978, A15.

145. See "New Right: 'Many Times More Effective' Now," *Electing Congress* (Washington, D.C.: Congressional Quarterly, 1978), 21–25.

146. Richard Cohen, "The 96th Congress—Who'll Be Calling the Shots?" *National Journal*, November 11, 1978, 1805.

147. Jimmy Carter, *Keeping Faith* (New York: Bantam Books, 1982), 539.

148. David S. Broder, "The Changing Order," *Washington Post*, November 9, 1978, A1.

149. Wilson Carey McWilliams, *The Politics of Disappointment: American Elections 1976–1994* (Chatham, N.J.: Chatham House, 1995), 45.

150. Barone, *Our Country*, 577.

151. George F. Will, "Clinton Feels His Own Pain," *Newsweek*, November 24, 1997, 84.

152. Martin Tolchin, "Carter Plans Rise in Defense Budget and Lower Deficits," *New York Times*, November 10, 1978, A1.

153. "The New Tilt," 44.

154. "The New Tilt," 45.

155. Eric M. Uslaner, M. Margaret Conway, Gary C. Jacobson, and Samuel Kernell, "Interpreting the 1974 Congressional Election," *American Political Science Review* 80 (June 1986): 591–95. Uslaner and Conway maintain that the election represented a rather direct referendum, while Jacobson and Kernell say Watergate and the economy affected the outcome indirectly through the altered calculations of strategic politicians. Jack M. McLeod, Jane D. Brown, and Lee B. Barker ("Watergate and the 1974 Congressional Elections," *Public Opinion Quarterly* 41 [Summer 1977]: 179–95) maintain that the effects of Watergate were less extensive and more complex than generally understood at the time.

156. Mayhew, 162.

157. Mayhew's calculations, based on a combination of contemporary journalistic and subsequent scholarly appraisals of legislation, determined that the four change congresses passed a total of 37 major laws, compared with 57 passed by the four preceding congresses. That decline was approximately twice as steep as the average decline for the other seven post-midterm congresses.

158. See *Congress and the Nation 1965–68*, 8–13.

5. The Calibrating Elections: Midterm Thermidor

1. James MacGregor Burns, *Roosevelt: The Lion and the Fox* (New York: Harcourt, Brace and Company, 1956), 348.

2. James T. Patterson, *Congressional Conservatism and the New Deal* (Lexington: University of Kentucky Press, 1967), 249.

3. Patterson, 189.

4. On the "purge," see Patterson, 250–87; Burns, *Roosevelt*, 358–64; William E. Leuchtenburg, *Franklin D. Roosevelt and the New Deal* (New York: Harper & Row, 1963), 267–69; James A. Farley, *Jim Farley's Story: The Roosevelt Years* (New York: Whittlesly House, 1948; reprint, Westport, Conn.: Greenwood Press, 1984), 146.

5. George H. Mayer, *The Republican Party 1854–1964* (New York: Oxford University Press, 1964), 449.

6. See Sean J. Savage, *Roosevelt: The Party Leader 1932–1945* (Lexington: University of Kentucky Press, 1991), 155–58.

7. Patterson, 285, 287.

8. Savage, 159.

9. Farley, 148.

10. Raymond Moley, *After Seven Years* (New York: Harper & Brothers, 1939), 364.

11. James MacGregor Burns, *The Crosswinds of Freedom* (New York: Alfred A. Knopf, 1989), 114.

12. Leuchtenburg, 271.

13. Patterson, 290; Burns, *Roosevelt*, 365.

14. Patterson, 290.

15. Patterson, 289.

16. "Beat Even Santa Claus, Comments Vandenberg," *New York Times*, November 10, 1938, 16.

17. Arthur Krock, "Taxpayers Revolt," *New York Times*, November 10, 1938, 15.

18. Arthur Krock, "Win Back 10 States," *New York Times*, November 9, 1938, A1.

19. See David L. Porter, *Congress and the Waning of the New Deal* (Port Washington, N.Y.: Kennikat Press, 1980).

20. Patterson, 332.

21. Burns, *Roosevelt*, 370.

22. See Basil Rauch, *The History of the New Deal* (New York: Creative Age Press, 1944), 325–26.

23. George Wolfskill and John A. Hudson, *All But the People: Franklin D. Roosevelt and His Critics 1933–39* (London: Macmillan, 1969), 291. For similar appraisals, see Barbara Sinclair, *Congressional Realignment: 1925–1978* (Austin: University of Texas, 1982), 33; Leuchtenburg, 272–74.

24. See David R. Mayhew, "Innovative Midterm Elections," in *Midterm: The Elections of 1994 in Context,* ed. Philip A. Klinkner (Boulder: Westview Press, 1996), 160–61.

25. Leuchtenburg, 274.

26. Mayhew, 160–61.

27. "The Elections," *New York Times*, November 10, 1938, 26.

28. Albert R. Hunt, "National Politics and the 1982 Campaign," in *The American Elections of 1982,* eds. Thomas E. Mann and Norman J. Ornstein (Washington, D.C.: AEI, 1983), 2.

29. Dilys M. Hill and Phil Williams, "The Reagan Legacy," in *The Reagan Presidency,* eds. Dilys M. Hill, Raymond A. Moore, and Phil Williams (New York: St. Martin's Press, 1990), 234.

30. Hill and Williams, "The Reagan Legacy," 234.

31. See Charles M. Tidmarch, Lisa J. Hyman, and Jill E. Sorkin, "Press Issue Agendas in the 1982 Congressional and Gubernatorial Election Campaigns," *Journal of Politics* 46, no. 4 (November 1984): 1226–42. This survey of 12 metropolitan newspapers confirmed that, at least in congressional races, the agenda of the 1982 elections was dominated by "the political economy of the Reagan presidency."

32. *Elections '82* (Washington, D.C.: Congressional Quarterly, Inc., 1982), 1. See also Hunt, 26.

33. Hunt, 38.

34. Hunt, 18.

35. Thomas E. Mann and Norman J. Ornstein, "Sending a Message: Voters and Congress in 1982," in *The American Elections of 1982,* eds. Thomas E. Mann and Norman J. Ornstein (Washington, D.C.: AEI, 1983), 147.

36. Priscilla Southwell, "The Mobilization Hypothesis and Voter Turnout in Congressional Elections, 1974–1982," *Western Political Quarterly* 41 (June 1988): 273–87.

37. Dan Balz and Margot Hornblower, "Democrats Solidifying House Gains," *Washington Post,* November 3, 1982, A25.

38. *Elections '82,* 1–2.

39. *Elections '82,* 5.

40. Mann and Ornstein, 139–40.

41. See Alan Ehrenhalt, "Reapportionment and Redistricting," in *The American Elections of 1982,* eds. Thomas E. Mann and Norman J. Ornstein (Washington, D.C.: AEI, 1983), 44–71; Alan I. Abramowitz, "Partisan Redistricting and the 1982 Congressional Elections," *Journal of Politics* 45, no. 3 (August 1983): 767–71. Ehrenhalt estimated the Democratic gain from redistricting at 5–10 seats, while Abramowitz pointed out that Democrats significantly improved their "swing ratio" only in the 17 states where they had total control over the redistricting process. Michael Barone offered a somewhat more impressionistic estimate of 15 seats; *Our Country: The Shaping of America from Roosevelt to Reagan* (New York: Free Press, 1990), 625.

42. Mann and Ornstein, 143.

43. See John C. McAdams and John R. Johannes, "The Voter in the 1982 House Elections," *American Journal of Political Science* 28, no. 4 (November 1984): 778–81; Alan I. Abramowitz, "National Issues, Strategic Politicians, and Voting Behavior in the 1980 and 1982 Congressional Elections," *American Journal of Political Science* 28, no. 4 (November 1984): 710–21; Adam Clymer, "Democrats Victors in Key Races in a Wave of Reagan Discontent," *New York Times,* November 3, 1982, A1.

44. Gary C. Jacobson, *The Politics of Congressional Elections,* 3rd ed. (New York: HarperCollins, 1992), 172–182.

45. Jacobson, 174–75; Mann and Ornstein, 142.

46. Mann and Ornstein, 137.

47. David S. Broder, "Elections Boost Democratic Strength," *Washington Post,* November 3, 1982, A1.

48. *Time,* November 15, 1982, front cover; "The Center Rediscovered," *New York Times,* November 4, 1982, A26.

49. Lou Cannon and Walter Pincus, "President's Hill Coalition is Jeopardized," *Washington Post*, November 3, 1982, A1; Dan Balz and Margot Hornblower, "Democrats Gain 26 Seats in House," *Washington Post*, November 4, 1982, A21; Helen Dewar, "President Will Face a Bolder Congress," *Washington Post*, November 4, 1982, A1, A25; Sen. Byrd, *Congressional Record*—Senate, November 29, 1982, 27662; Rep. Alexander, *Congressional Record*—House, November 29, 1982, 27764; Rep. Hamilton, *Congressional Record*—House, November 29, 1982, 27903; Rep. Hamilton, *Congressional Record*—November 30, 1982, 28133.

50. Mann and Ornstein, 134. See also Steven V. Roberts, "Republicans Meet Setbacks in House," *New York Times*, November 3, 1982, A1; Cannon and Pincus, "President's Hill Coalition is Jeopardized," A1; Helen Dewar, "President Will Face A Bolder Congress," *Washington Post*, November 4, 1982, A1.

51. Hedrick Smith, "New House Seems Less In-Tune With Reagan," *New York Times*, November 4, 1982, A1; Jones, 42.

52. Charles O. Jones, "Ronald Reagan and the U.S. Congress: Visible-Hand Politics," in *The Reagan Legacy: Promise and Performance*, ed. Charles O. Jones (Chatham, N.J.: Chatham House, 1988), 42. See also Mann and Ornstein, 148–50.

53. Hunt, 40.

54. Mann and Ornstein, 134–35.

55. The proportion of Democrats identified as being part of the party's base grew from 79 percent to 91 percent in the House and from 72 percent to 80 percent in the Senate. Jon R. Bond and Richard Fleisher, *The President in the Legislative Arena* (Chicago: University of Chicago Press, 1990), 87.

56. See Mann and Ornstein, 150–51.

57. Jones, 44.

58. See Dick Kirschten, "Building Bridges," *National Journal*, November 8, 1986, 2701–2.

59. Sen. Pete Domenici (N.M.) and Republican pollster Richard Wirthlin, for example, both argued that it had been a mistake not to nationalize the election as much as possible. See Paul Taylor, "Senate to Have 55 Democrats," *Washington Post*, November 6, 1986, A1, A53.

60. Ronald Brownstein, "The End of the Road," *National Journal*, November 8, 1986, 2671.

61. For more discussion of the extreme localism of the 1986 elections, see William Schneider, "Return to Normalcy," *National Journal*, November 8, 1986, 2708–10; Pippa Norris, "1986 U.S. Elections: National Elections or Pluralistic Diversity?," *Political Quarterly* 58, no. 2 (April/June 1987): 194–201; Paul R. Abramson, John H. Aldrich, and David W. Rohde, *Change and Continuity in the 1984 Elections*, rev. ed. (Washington, D.C.: Congressional Quarterly Press, 1987), 316, 319–25.

62. David Brady and Morris Fiorina, "The Ruptured Legacy: Presidential-Congressional Relations in Historical Perspective," in *Looking Back on the Reagan Presidency*, ed. Larry Berman (Baltimore: Johns Hopkins University Press, 1990), 283.

63. See Schneider, "Return to Normalcy."

64. Richard E. Cohen, "Back in the Saddle," *National Journal*, November 8, 1986, 2677.

65. Norris, 199.

66. "Democrats on the Spot," *Newsweek*, November 17, 1986, 28.

67. Brownstein, "End of the Road," 2671.

68. Brownstein, "End of the Road," 2671.

69. Kirschten, "Building Bridges," 2701.

70. Helen Dewar and Spencer Rich, "GOP's Class of '80 Runs Into Trouble 2nd Time Around," *Washington Post*, November 5, 1986, A31; Paul Taylor, "Senate to Have 55 Democrats," *Washington Post*, November 6, 1986, A1, A53; David S. Broder, "Both Parties Put on Notice: Voters Are Ready for Change," *Washington Post*, November 6, 1986, A1, A56.

71. Steven Reilly, "Managing Party Support: Reagan as Party Leader," in *The Reagan Years: The Record in Presidential Leadership,* ed. Joseph Hogan (New York: Manchester University Press, 1990), 131.

72. Brady and Fiorina, 274.

73. See Nigel Bowles, "Reagan and Congress," in *The Reagan Years: The Record in Presidential Leadership,* ed. Joseph Hogan (New York: Manchester University Press, 1990), 115.

74. Reilly, 129.

75. "Democrats on the Spot," 28.

76. See, for example, Hill and Williams, 235.

77. Edward Walsh, "In the End, Bork Himself Was His Own Worst Enemy," *Washington Post*, October 24, 1987, A16.

78. Norman J. Ornstein, Thomas E. Mann, and Michael J. Malbin, *Vital Statistics on Congress 1993–1994* (Washington, D.C.; Congressional Quarterly Press, 1994), 212–13. Only the Veterans Affairs Committee saw a greater decline of 18 percentage points. Abramson, Aldrich, and Rohde pointed to the Judiciary Committee as the "clearest example" of "significant ideological change" among Senate committees (331).

79. Those nine were Adams (Wash.), Conrad (N.D.), Daschle (S.D.), Fowler (Ga.), Graham (Fla.), Mikulski (Md.), Reid (Nev.), Sanford (N.C.), and Shelby (Ala.). Fifty Senate votes would have been enough because Vice President George Bush would have cast the tie-breaking vote in favor.

80. Walsh, A16.

6. The Dogs That Did Not Bark: Exceptions That Shaped History

1. Republicans in 1902 gained nine seats, but Democrats gained 25, an outcome made possible by an expansion in the size of the House. Consequently, Republicans suffered a net loss of 16.

2. Edgar Eugene Robinson, *The Roosevelt Leadership 1933–1945* (New York: De Capo Press, 1972), 147.

3. Arthur M. Schlesinger Jr., *The Coming of the New Deal* (Boston: Houghton Mifflin Company, 1959), 471–507.

4. William E. Leuchtenberg, *Franklin D. Roosevelt and the New Deal 1932–1940* (New York: Harper & Row, 1963), 93.

5. Robinson, 147.

6. Charles A. Moser, *Watershed and Ratifying Elections: A Historical View of the 1934 and 1954 Midterm Congressional Elections* (Washington, D.C.: The Free Congress Research & Educational Foundation, 1982), 7.

7. Leuchtenberg, 94. See also Robert S. McElvaine, *The Great Depression: America 1929–1941* (New York: Times Books, 1984), 253–54.

8. James MacGregor Burns, *The Crosswinds of Freedom* (New York: Alfred A. Knopf, 1989), 66.

9. See Arthur M. Schlesinger Jr., *The Politics of Upheaval* (Boston: Houghton Mifflin Co., 1960), 1–11; Paul K. Conkin, *FDR and the Origins of the Welfare State* (New York: Thomas Y. Crowell Company, 1967), 50; Burns, 70–71.

10. Schlesinger, *The Coming of the New Deal*, 505.

11. Luechtenberg, 116.

12. Roger Biles, *A New Deal for the American People* (Dekalb: Northern Illinois University Press, 1991), 118.

13. "Mr. Roosevelt's New Responsibility," New York Times, November 8, 1934, 22.

14. See Biles, 118; Moser, 8.

15. Anthony J. Badger, *The New Deal: The Depression Years, 1933–1940* (New York: The Noonday Press, 1989), 251.

16. Walter Dean Burnham, "Critical Realignment: Dead or Alive?," in *The End of Realignment? Interpreting American Electoral Eras*, ed. Byron E. Shafer (Madison: University of Wisconsin Press, 1991), 101–139.

17. "Mr. Roosevelt's New Responsibility," 22.

18. Arthur Krock, "Tide Sweeps Nation," *New York Times*, November 7, 1934, 1; Arthur Krock, "Republican Remolding Looms in Election Rout," *New York Times*, November 11, 1934, 1E.

19. Leuchtenberg, 117.

20. See James T. Patterson, *Congressional Conservatism and the New Deal* (Louisville: University of Kentucky Press, 1967), 250–55.

21. Conkin, 53.

22. McElvaine, 229.

23. Ronald A. Mulder, *The Insurgent Progressives in the United States Senate and the New Deal, 1933–1939* (New York: Garland Publishing, Inc., 1979), 86. See also McElvaine, 229.

24. Biles, 131.

25. Biles, 128.

26. Biles, 131.

27. See Burns, 76; Delbert Clark, "Roosevelt Recharts His Course," in *The New Deal*, ed. Carl N. Degler (Chicago: Quadrangle Books, 1970), 87.

28. Basil Rauch, *The History of the New Deal 1933–1938* (New York: Creative Age Press, Inc., 1944), 159.

29. See Wilbur J. Cohen and Thomas H. Eliot, "The Advent of Social Security," in *The Making of the New Deal: The Insiders Speak*, ed. Katie Louchheim (Cambridge: Harvard University Press, 1983), 153, 165.

30. Otis L. Graham Jr. and Elizabeth Koed, "New Deal," in *The Encyclopedia of the United States Congress*, eds. Donald C. Bacon, Roger H. Davidson, and Morton Keller (New York: Simon & Schuster, 1995), 1458.

31. Richard C. Burnweit, "Snell, Bertrand H.," in *The Encyclopedia of the United States Congress*, eds. Donald C. Bacon, Roger H. Davidson, and Morton Keller (New York: Simon & Schuster, 1995), 1838; see also Charles O. Jones, *The Minority Party in Congress* (Boston: Little, Brown and Company, 1970), 34.

32. George B. Galloway, *History of the House of Representatives*, 2d ed. (New York: Thomas Y. Crowell Company, 1976), 375.

33. Kirk H. Porter and Donald Bruce Johnson, *National Party Platforms 1840–1960* (Urbana: University of Illinois Press, 1961), 360–63.

34. Schlesinger, *The Politics of Upheaval*, 422.

35. Schlesinger, *The Politics of Upheaval*, 424.

36. Milton Derber, "The New Deal and Labor," in *The New Deal: The National Level*, eds. John Braeman, Robert H. Bremner, and David Brody (Columbus: Ohio State University Press, 1975), 129.

37. Schlesinger, *The Politics of Upheaval*, 424.

38. W. Phillips Shively, "A Reinterpretation of the New Deal Realignment," *Public Opinion Quarterly* 35 (Winter 1971–72): 621–24. Shively compared *Literary Digest* polls with actual results from 1924–36. The *Literary Digest*, of course, had a strong middle-class and professional bias, but Shively found that its poll results did not differ markedly from the actual voting outcomes until 1936, indicating that class differences in party coalitions did not emerge until then.

39. Helen Fuller, "Kennedy's First Congress," *The New Republic*, October 27, 1962, 12.

40. Arthur M. Schlesinger Jr., *A Thousand Days* (Boston: Houghton Mifflin, 1965), 256–57.

41. Schlesinger, *A Thousand Days*, 757; Carroll Kilpatrick, "The Kennedy Style and Congress," in *John F. Kennedy and the New Frontier*, ed. Aida DiPace Donald (New York: Hill and Wang, 1966), 52; Hugh Sidey, *John F. Kennedy, President*, new ed. (New York: Atheneum, 1964), 353.

42. Theodore C. Sorenson, *Kennedy* (New York: Harper & Row, 1965), 688.

43. Sidey, 354.

44. See Tom Wicker, "Voting in Nation Narrow in Scope," *New York Times*, November 6, 1962, A1.

45. Wicker, "Voting in Nation," A1.

46. See "Whose Victory Was It?," *The New Republic*, November 17, 1962, 4.

47. Tom Wicker, "President Elated," *New York Times*, November 8, 1962, A1.

48. Wicker, "President Elated," A1.

49. Schlesinger, *A Thousand Days*, 833.

50. Kilpatrick, 60; "The 88th Congress," *New York Times*, November 8, 1962, A38; "Viva La Difference," *The New Republic*, November 12, 1962, 2; "The 'In' Party's Dramatic Triumph," *Newsweek*, November 19, 1962, 31.

51. Cabell Phillips, "Kennedy and Democratic Aides Heartened by Victory at Polls," *New York Times*, November 8, 1962, A22.

52. Phillips, A22.

53. Sidey, *John F. Kennedy*, 362; "The 'In' Party's Dramatic Triumph," 31; "Viva La Difference," 2.

54. "Whose Victory Was It?," 4–5.

55. See George H. Mayer, *The Republican Party 1854–1964* (New York: Oxford University Press, 1964), 518.

56. Wicker, "President Elated," A1.

57. James L. Sundquist, *Politics and Policy: The Eisenhower, Kennedy, and Johnson Years* (Washington, D.C.: The Brookings Institution, 1968), 481.

58. James Pfiffner, *The Modern Presidency* (New York: St. Martin's Press, 1994), 146. Jon R. Bond and Richard Fleisher also calculate that Kennedy's support score in the

House increased after 1962 on important conflictual votes *(The President in the Legislative Arena* [Chicago: University of Chicago Press, 1990], 78).

59. Bond and Fleisher, 94.

60. Sundquist, 483.

61. Sundquist, 482.

62. Sundquist, 482.

63. For example, see Rebecca Carr, "GOP Eager to Finish Hearings," *Atlanta Constitution*, November 5, 1998, 1.

64. R. W. Apple Jr., "New Outlook on 2000 Race," *New York Times*, November 5, 1998, A1.

65. "Mr. Speaker," *U.S. News & World Report*, December 14, 1998, 9.

66. Jeanne Cummings, "Democrats Ready Quick Legislative Initiatives as GOP Aims to Recover From Election Results," *Wall Street Journal*, November 18, 1998, A24; see also Helen Dewar, "Democrats to Revive Health Measure," *Washington Post*, November 6, 1998, A4.

7. Normal Midterms

1. See George H. Mayer, *The Republican Party 1854–1964* (New York: Oxford, 1964), 265; Lewis L. Gould, *The Presidency of William Mckinley* (Lawrence: Regents Press of Kansas, 1980), 137, 169.

2. The size of the House had been increased as part of the 1900 reapportionment, so even though Republicans added 9, Democrats added 25, cutting the prior Republican margin by 16.

3. Lewis L. Gould, *The Presidency of Theodore Roosevelt* (Lawrence: University of Kansas Press, 1991), 71–72.

4. David Sarasohn, *The Party of Reform* (Jackson: University Press of Mississippi, 1989), 26.

5. George H. Mayer, *The Republican Party 1854–1964* (New York: Oxford University Press, 1964), 297.

6. Sarasohn, 21–27; Samuel Hays, "The Social Analysis of American Political History," *Political Science Quarterly* 80 (September 1965): 368.

7. Mayer, *The Republican Party 1854–1964*, 339.

8. John D. Hicks, *Republican Ascendancy 1921–1933* (New York: Harper & Brothers, 1960), 88.

9. "McNary-Haugen Farm Relief Bill," in *The Encyclopedia of the United States Congress*, vol. 3, eds. Donald C. Bacon, Roger H. Davidson, and Morton Keller (New York: Simon & Schuster, 1995), 1339.

10. "World War Two," in *The Encyclopedia of the United States Congress*, vol. 4, eds. Donald C. Bacon, Roger H. Davidson, and Morton Keller (New York: Simon & Schuster, 1995), 2152–54.

11. Michael Barone, *Our Country: The Shaping of America from Roosevelt to Reagan* (New York: Free Press, 1990), 484.

12. Harold F. Gosnell, *Truman's Crises: A Political Biography of Harry S Truman* (Westport: Greenwood Press, 1980), 316–18; Robert J. Donovan, *Conflict and Crisis: The Presidency of Harry S Truman, 1945–1948* (New York: W.W. Norton Company, 1977), 237–38; Cabell Phillips, *The Truman Presidency* (New York: Macmillan, 1966), 160.

13. Susan M. Hartmann, *Truman and the 80th Congress* (Columbia: University of Missouri Press, 1971), 1.

14. Jerome M. Clubb and Santa A. Traugott, "Partisan Cohesion and Cleavage in the U.S. House of Representatives," *Journal of Interdisciplinary History* 8 (Winter 1977): 383; Hartmann, 156.

15. See Ronald M. Peters Jr., *The American Speakership* (Baltimore: Johns Hopkins University Press, 1990), 127.

16. On the "dump Truman" attempt by Franklin Roosevelt's sons James, Elliott, and Franklin Jr., Mayor William O'Dwyer of New York, Mayor Frank Hague of Jersey City, Cook County Democratic Chairman Jake Avery, and leaders of the CIO and Americans for Democratic Action, see James W. Davis, *The President as Party Leader* (New York: Praeger, 1992), 24–25. General Dwight D. Eisenhower and Justice William O. Douglas were both targets of liberal draft efforts.

17. Hartmann, 211–12.

18. Peters, 127.

19. Hartmann, 197.

20. Gosnell, 327.

21. Harry S. Truman, *Memoirs: Years of Trial and Hope,* vol. 2 (Garden City: Doubleday & Company, Inc., 1956), 208.

22. Phillips, 162.

23. See Hartmann, 129; Donovan, 407–8.

24. See Louis H. Bean, *The Midterm Battle* (New York: Business Press, Inc., 1950).

25. David R. Mayhew, "Innovative Midterm Elections," in *Midterm: The Elections of 1994 in Context* ed. Philip A. Klinkner (Boulder: Westview, 1996), 169–70.

26. Michael Barone, *Our Country: The Shaping of America from Roosevelt to Reagan* (New York: Free Press, 1990), 203.

27. See James Boylan, *The New Deal Coalition and the Election of 1946* (New York: Garland Publishing, Inc. 1981).

28. Barone, 188.

29. Thomas E. Mann, "Is the House of Representatives Unresponsive to Political Change?," in *Elections American Style,* ed. A. James Reichley (Washington, D.C.: The Brookings Institution, 1987), 277.

30. "Interview with Timothy Russert and Tom Brokaw on 'Meet the Press,'" *Public Papers of the President of the United States: William J. Clinton,* 1993, vol. 2 (Washington, D.C.: Government Printing Office, 1994), 1930.

31. Peter Roff, "The Tsunami Effect: Why This November's Elections Are More Important Than You Think," *Rising Tide* 5 (Fall 1997): 21.

32. For a discussion of Republican efforts to nationalize the 1994 elections, see Gary C. Jacobson, "The 1994 House Elections in Perspective," in *Midterm: The Elections of 1994 in Context,* ed. Philip A. Klinkner (Boulder: Westview Press, 1996), 1–20.

33. See Franco Mattei, "Eight More in '94: The Republican Takeover of the Senate," in *Midterm: The Elections of 1994 in Context,* ed. Philip A. Klinkner (Boulder: Westview Press, 1996), 25.

34. William Schneider, "Clinton: The Reason Why," *National Journal,* November 12, 1994, 2630–32.

35. "Republican Gains and Obligations," *New York Times,* November 9, 1994, A26.

36."News Conference, November 9, 1994," *Weekly Compilation of Presidential Documents* 30 (November–December 1994): 2339–48; Ruth Marcus, "Clinton Reiterates Vow to Pursue New Democrat Agenda," *Washington Post*, November 11, 1994, A14; Edward Walsh, "Democrats Wonder Whether Sea Change Is Plea for Centrism," *Washington Post*, November 10, 1994, A27.

37. Dan Balz, "Party Controls Both Houses for First Time Since '50s," *Washington Post*, November 9, 1994, A1; Dale Russakoff, "Gingrich Vows Cooperation," *Washington Post*, November 9, 1994, A21; Dan Balz, "Clinton, GOP Leaders Offer Cooperation," *Washington Post*, November 10, 1994, A1; Rep. Doolittle, *Congressional Record*—House, November 29, 1994, E2301–04.

38. David S. Broder, "Sharp Turn to the Right Reflects Doubts About Clinton, Democrats," *Washington Post*, November 9, 1994, A1; David S. Broder, "Vote May Signal GOP Return as Dominant Party," *Washington Post*, November 10, 1994, A1; Walsh, "Democrats Wonder Whether Sea Change Is Plea for Centrism," A27, A29; Rep. Harman, *Congressional Record*—House, November 29, 1994, H11439.

39. Presidential press conference of April 18, 1995.

40. Alison Mitchell, "Despite His Reversals, Clinton Stays Centered," *New York Times*, July 28, 1996, A10.

41. At the time, the verdict was not so clear. By the end of the second shutdown, Clinton's approval rating had hit a one-year low of 43 percent.

42. See Mary McGrory, "A Democrats' Democrat," *Washington Post*, April 30, 1996, C4.

43. Carroll J. Doherty, "Clinton's Big Comeback Shown in Vote Score," *Congressional Quarterly Weekly Report*, December 21, 1996, 3427.

44. Doherty, 3427.

45. Everett Carll Ladd, "Survey Says? Little New," *The Weekly Standard*, June 17, 1996, 15–16; Jacobson, "The 1994 House Elections in Perspective," 2–9.

46. Barone, *Our Country*, 197.

Conclusion

1. There are three cases in American history when one party went twenty years or more between presidential victories: 1856–1884 (Democrats), 1892–1912 (Democrats), 1928–1952 (Republicans). In a fourth case, a party won the presidency only once within in a twenty-eight-year span (between 1964 and 1992, Democrats won once—1976).

2. See Jerome M. Clubb, William H. Flanigan, and Nancy H. Zingale, *Partisan Realignment* (Boulder: Westview Press, 1990).

BIBLIOGRAPHY

Abramowitz, Alan I. "National Issues, Strategic Politicians, and Voting Behavior in the 1980 and 1982 Congressional Elections." *American Journal of Political Science* 28 (November 1984): 710–21.

———"Partisan Redistricting and the 1982 Congressional Elections." *Journal of Politics* 45 (August 1983): 767–770.

Abramowitz, Alan I., Cover, Albert C., and Norpoth, Helmut. "The President's Party in Midterm Elections: Going from Bad to Worse." *American Journal of Political Science* 30 (August 1986): 562–76.

Abramowitz, Alan I. and Segal, Jeffrey A. "Determinants of the Outcomes of Senate Elections." *Journal of Politics* 48 (May 1986): 433–39.

Abramson, Paul R., Aldrich, John H., and Rohde, David W. *Change and Continuity in the 1984 Elections.* Rev. ed. Washington, D.C.: Congressional Quarterly Press, 1987.

Adler, Scott, and Cameron, Charles M. "The Macro-Politics of Congress: The Enactment of Significant Legislation 1947–1992," cited in Morris P. Fiorina, *Divided Government, 2nd ed.* (Boston: Allyn and Bacon, 1996), 163–67.

Alesina, Alberto, and Rosenthal, Howard. "Partisan Cycles in Congressional Elections and the Macroeconomy." *American Political Science Review* 83 (June 1989): 373–98.

———*Partisan Politics, Divided Government, and the Economy.* Cambridge: Cambridge University Press, 1995.

"Anderson Blames the Brennan Plan." *New York Times,* November 9, 1950, 39.

Anderson, Christopher J., Appleton, Andrew M., and Ward, Daniel S. "The Causes and Consequences of Barometer Elections." Paper presented for delivery at the annual meeting of the Midwest Political Science Association, 1996.

Anderson, Christopher J., and Ward, Daniel S. "Barometer Elections in Comparative Perspective." *Electoral Studies* 14 (1995): 1–14.

Anderson, Kristi. *The Creation of a Democratic Majority, 1928–1936.* Chicago: University of Chicago Press, 1979.

Ansenua, Robert, and Wolfinger, Raymond. "Voting Behavior in Congressional Elections." Paper presented at the annual meeting of the American Political Science Association, New Orleans, La., September 1973.

Apple, R.W. Jr. "New Outlook on 2000 Race." *New York Times,* November 5, 1998, A1.

Arselus, Francisco, and Meltzer, Allan H. "The Effect of Aggregate Economic Variables on Congressional Elections." *American Political Science Review* 69 (December 1975): 1232–39.

Auspitz, Josiah Lee. "GOP Electoral Strategy Full of Holes." *Washington Post*, November 8, 1970.

"Backers See Taft 1952 Party Choice." *New York Times*, November 9, 1950, 1.

Badger, Anthony J. *The New Deal:The Depression Years, 1933–1940*. New York: The Noonday Press, 1989.

Balz, Dan. "Clinton, GOP Leaders Offer Cooperation." *Washington Post*, November 10, 1994, A1.

———"Party Controls Both House for First Time Since '50s." *Washington Post*, November 9, 1994, A1.

Balz, Dan, and Hornblower, Margaret. "Democrats Gain 26 Seats in House." *Washington Post*, November 4, 1982, A21.

———"Democrats Solidifying House Gains." *Washington Post*, November 3, 1982, A25.

Banducci, Susan A., and Karp, Jeffrey A. "Electoral Consequences of Scandal and Re-apportionment in the 1992 House Elections." *American Politics Quarterly* 22 (January 1994): 3–26.

Barone, Michael. *Our Country: The Shaping of America from Roosevelt to Reagan*. New York: Free Press, 1990.

Bean, Louis H. *The Midterm Battle*. New York: Business Press, Inc., 1950.

"'Beat Even Santa Claus,' Comments Vandenberg." *New York Times*, November 10, 1938, 16.

Beck, Paul Allen. "The Electoral Cycle and Patterns of American Politics." *British Journal of Political Science* 9 (April 1979): 129–56.

Bibby, John F. "Patterns in Midterm Gubernatorial and State Legislative Elections." *Public Opinion* (February/March 1983): 41–46.

Biles, Roger. *A New Deal for the American People*. Dekalb: Northern Illinois University Press, 1991.

Bloom, Howard S., and Price, H. Douglas. "Voter Response to Short-Run Economic Conditions: The Asymmetric Effect of Prosperity and Recession." *American Political Science Review* 69 (December 1975): 1240–55.

Bond, Jon R., and Fleisher, Richard. *The President in the Legislative Arena*. Chicago: University of Chicago Press, 1990.

Born, Richard. "Partisan Intentions and Election Day Realities in the Congressional Redis-tricting Process." *American Political Science Review* 79 (1985): 305–19.

———"Surge and Decline, Negative Voting, and the Midterm Loss Phenome-non: A Simultaneous Choice Analysis." *American Journal of Political Science* 34 (August 1990): 615–45.

Bowles, Nigel. "Reagan and Congress." In *The Reagan Years:The Record in Presidential Leadership*, ed. Joseph Hogan. New York: Manchester University Press, 1990.

Bowman, Ann O'M., and Kearney, Richard C. *The Resurgence of the States*. Englewood Cliffs, N.J.: Prentice-Hall, 1986.

Boylan, James. *The New Deal Coalition and the Election of 1946*. New York: Garland Publishing, Inc., 1981.

Brady, David W. *Critical Elections and Congressional Policy Making*. Stanford: Stanford University Press, 1988.

———"Critical Elections and Clusters of Policy Changes." *British Journal of Political Science* 8 (January 1978): 79–99.

Brady, David, and Fiorina, Morris P. "The Ruptured Legacy: Presidential-Congressional Relations in Historical Perspective." In *Looking Back on the Reagan Presidency*, edited by Larry Berman. Baltimore: Johns Hopkins University Press, 1990.

Branyan, Robert L., and Larsen, Lawrence A. *The Eisenhower Administration 1953–1961: A Documentary History.* Vol. 2. New York: Random House, 1971.

Broder, David S. "Both Parties Put on Notice: Voters Are Ready for Change." *Washington Post*, November 6, 1986, A1.

———"The Changing Order." *Washington Post*, November 8, 1978, A1.

———"Elections Boost Democratic Strength." *Washington Post*, November 3, 1982, A1.

———"Sharp Turn to the Right Reflects Doubts About Clinton, Democrats." *Washington Post*, November 9, 1994, A1.

———"Vote May Signal GOP Return as Dominant Party." *Washington Post*, November 10, 1994, A4.

Broder, David S., and Devroy, Ann. "A Sobering Experience." *Washington Post*, November 8, 1990.

Brownstein, Ronald. "The End of the Road." *National Journal*, November 8, 1986, 2671.

Bullock, Charles S. "Affirmative Action Districts: In Whose Faces Will They Blow Up?" *Campaigns and Elections*, April 1995, 22–23.

Burnham, Walter Dean. *Critical Elections and the Mainsprings of American Politics.* New York: W. W. Norton, 1970.

———"Critical Realignment: Dead or Alive?" In *The End of Realign-ment: Interpreting American Electoral Eras*, edited by Byron E. Shafer. Madison: University of Wisconsin Press, 1991.

Burnham, Walter Dean, Clubb, Jerome M., and Flanigan, William H. "Partisan Re-alignment: A Systemic Perspective." In *The History of American Political Behavior*, edited by Joel H. Silbey, Allan G. Bogne, and William H. Flanigan. Princeton: Princeton University Press, 1978.

Burns, James MacGregor. *The Crosswinds of Freedom.* New York: Alfred A. Knopf, 1989.

———*Roosevelt: The Lion and the Fox.* New York: Harcourt, Brace and Company, 1956.

Burnweit, Richard C. "Snell, Bertrand H." In *The Encyclopedia of the United States Congress*, edited by Donald C. Bacon, Roger H. Davidson, and Morton Keller. New York: Simon and Schuster, 1995.

Cain, Bruce E. "Assessing the Partisan Effects of Redistricting." *American Political Science Review* 79 (June 1985): 320–33.

Cain, Bruce E., and Campagna, Janet C. "Predicting Partisan Redistricting Disputes." *Legislative Studies Quarterly* 12 (May 1987): 265–74.

Caldiera, Gregory A., and Patterson, Samuel C. "Bringing Home the Votes: Electoral Outcomes in State Legislative Races." *Political Behavior* 4 (1982): 33–67.

Calvert, Randall L. "Presidential Coattails in Historical Perspective." *American Journal of Political Science* 28 (February 1984): 127–46.

Campbell, Angus. "A Classification of the Presidential Elections." In *The American Voter*, edited by Angus Campbell, Philip E. Converse, Warren E. Miller, and Donald E. Stokes. New York: John Wiley and Sons, 1960.

———"Surge and Decline: A Study of Electoral Change." *Public Opinion Quarterly* 24 (1960): 387–419.

Campbell, James E. "Presidential Coattails and Midterm Losses in State Legislative Elections." *American Political Science Review* 80 (March 1986): 45–63.

———*The Presidential Pulse of Congressional Elections*. Lexington: University Press of Kentucky, 1993.

Cannon, Lou, and Pincus, Walter. "President's Hill Coalition is Jeopardized." *Washington Post*, November 3, 1982, A1.

Carmines, Edward G., and Stimson, James A. *Issue Evolution: Race and the Transformation of American Politics*. Princeton: Princeton University Press, 1989.

Carr, Rebecca. "GOP Eager to Finish Hearings." *Atlanta Constitution*, November 5, 1998, 1.

Carter, Jimmy. *Keeping Faith*. New York: Bantam Books, 1982.

Ceaser, James. *Presidential Selection: Theory and Development*. Princeton: Princeton University Press, 1978.

———"The Center Rediscovered." *New York Times*, November 4, 1982, A26.

Chapman, Richard N. "World War Two." In *The Encyclopedia of the United States Congress*, vol. 4, edited by Donald C. Bacon, Roger H. Davidson, and Morton Keller. New York: Simon and Schuster, 1995, 2149–2155.

Chappell, Henry W. Jr., and Keech, William R. "A New View of Political Accountability for Economic Performance." *American Political Science Review* 79 (March 1985): 10–27.

Chester, Edward W. "Is the 'All Politics is Local' Myth True? The 1982 House Races as a Case Study." *Journal of Social, Political, and Economic Studies* 14 (Spring 1989): 99–116.

Chubb, John E. "Institutions, the Economy, and the Dynamics of State Elections." *American Political Science Review* 82 (March 1988): 133–54.

Clark, Delbert. "Roosevelt Recharts His Course." In *The New Deal*, edited by Carl N. Degler. Chicago: Quadrangle Books, 1970.

Clubb, Jerome M., Flanigan, William H., and Zingale, Nancy H. *Partisan Realignment: Voters, Parties, and Government in American History*. Beverly Hills: Sage, 1980.

Clubb, Jerome M., and Traugott, Santa A. "Partisan Cleavage and Cohesion in the House of Representatives." *Journal of Interdisciplinary History* 8 (Winter 1977): 375–401.

Clymer, Adam. "Democrats Victors in Key Races in a Wave of Reagan Discontent." *New York Times*, November 3, 1982, A1.

Cohen, Richard E. "Back in the Saddle." *National Journal*, November 8, 1986, 2677.

———"The 96th Congress—Who'll Be Calling the Shots?" *National Journal*, November 11, 1978, 1804–1811.

Cohen, Wilbur J. and Eliot, Thomas H. "The Advent of Social Security." In *The Making of the New Deal: The Insiders Speak*, edited by Katie Loucheim. Cambridge: Harvard University Press, 1983.

"Congress." *New York Times*, November 7, 1894, 4.

Congress and the Nation 1989–1992. Vol. 8. Washington, D.C.: Congressional Quarterly Press, 1993.

Congress and the Nation 1977–1980. Vol. 5. Washington, D.C.: Congressional Quarterly Press, 1981.

Congress and the Nation 1965–1968. Vol. 2. Washington, D.C.: Congressional Quarterly Service, 1969.

Congress and the Nation 1945–1964. Vol. 1. Washington, D.C.: Congressional Quarterly Service, 1965.

Congressional Quarterly Guide to Elections, 2d. ed. Washington, D.C.: Congressional Quarterly Press, 1985.

Congressional Quarterly Weekly Report, May 8, 1993, 1173.

Conkin, Paul K. *FDR and the Origins of the Welfare State*. New York: Thomas Y. Crowell Company, 1967.

Cook, Rhodes. "No Longer Sure they Like Ike, Voters Punish His Allies in Congress." *Congressional Quarterly Weekly Report*, April 15, 1995, 1061.

Cooper, John Milton, Jr. *Pivotal Decades: The United States 1900–1920*. New York: W. W. Norton, 1990.

Copeland, Gary W. "When Congress and the President Collide: Why Presidents Veto Legislation." *Journal of Politics* 45 (August 1983): 696–710.

Cover, Albert D. "Party Competence Evaluations and Voting for Congress." *Western Political Quarterly* 39 (June 1986): 304–12.

———"Presidential Evaluations and Voting for Congress." *American Journal of Political Science* 30 (November 1986): 786–801.

Crawford, Kenneth. "Republican Plan." *Newsweek*, November 28, 1966, 35.

Cummings, Jeanne. "Democrats Ready Quick Legislative Initiatives as GOP Aims to Recover From Election Results." *Wall Street Journal*, November 18, 1998, A24.

Curtis, Francis. *The Republican Party*. Vol. 2. New York: Knickerbocker Press, 1904.

Cutler, Lloyd. "To Form a Government." In *Separation of Powers: Does It Still Work?*, edited by Robert A. Goldman and Robert Kaufman. Washington, D.C.: AEI, 1986.

Dahl, Robert A. "Myth of the Presidential Mandate." *Political Science Quarterly* 105, no. 3 (Fall 1990): 355–72.

Davis, James W. *The President as Party Leader*. New York: Praeger, 1992.

"Democrats on the Spot." *Newsweek*, November 17, 1986, 28.

Derber, Milton. "The New Deal and Labor." In *The New Deal: The National Level*, edited by John Braemen, Robert H. Bremner, and David Brody. Columbus: Ohio State University Press, 1975.

Derthick, Martha. "The Enduring Features of American Federalism." *The Brookings Review* (Summer 1989): 34–38.

Dewar, Helen. "Democrats to Revive Health Measure." *Washington Post*, November 6, 1998, A4.

———"President Will Face a Bolder Congress." *Washington Post*, November 4, 1982, A1.

Dewar, Helen, and Rich, Spencer. "GOP's Class of '80 Runs into Trouble Second Time Around." *Washington Post*, November 5, 1986, A31.

Doherty, Carroll J. "Clinton's Big Comeback Shown in Vote Score." *Congressional Quarterly Weekly Report*, December 21, 1996, 3427.

Donovan, Robert J. *Conflict and Crisis: The Presidency of Harry S Truman, 1945–1948*. New York: W. W. Norton Company, 1977.

Downs, Anthony. *An Economic Theory of Democracy*. New York: Harper and Row, 1957.

Dunn, Arthur Wallace. *From Harrison to Harding*. Vol. 1. Port Washington, N.Y.: Kennikat Press, 1971.

Edsall, Thomas Byrne, and Edsall, Mary D. *Chain Reaction: The Impact of Race, Rights, and Taxes on American Politics*. New York: W. W. Norton, 1991.

Edwards, George C., III. *At the Margins*. New Haven: Yale University Press, 1989.

Ehrenhalt, Alan. "Reapportionment and Redistricting." In *The American Elections of 1982*, edited by Thomas Mann and Norman Ornstein. Washington, D.C.: AEI, 1983, 44–71.

"The 88th Congress." *New York Times*, November 8, 1962, A38.

Eisenhower, Dwight D. *Waging Peace: 1956–1961*. Garden City: Doubleday, 1965.

"The Election." *Time*, November 13, 1950, 19–20.

"Elections." *Time*, November 18, 1966, 23–28.

"The Elections." *New York Times*, November 10, 1938, 26.

Elections '82. Washington, D.C.: Congressional Quarterly Press, 1983.

"Elections: The Runoff." *Newsweek*, May 29, 1961, 26–27.

Erikson, Robert S. "Malapportionment, Gerrymandering, and Party Fortunes in Congressional Elections." *American Political Science Review* 66 (December 1972): 1234–1245.

———"The Puzzle of Midterm Loss." *Journal of Politics* 50 (November 1988): 1011–29.

Erikson, Robert S., and Tedin, Kent L. "The 1928–1936 Partisan Realignment: The Case for the Conversion Hypothesis." *American Political Science Review* 75 (December 1981): 951–62.

Erikson, Robert S., and Wright, Gerald C. "Voters, Candidates, and Issues in Congressional Elections." In *Congress Reconsidered*, 6th ed., edited by Lawrence C. Dodd and Bruce I. Oppenheimer. Washington, D.C.: Congressional Quarterly Press, 1997.

Farley, James A. *Jim Farley's Story: The Roosevelt Years*. (New York: Whittlesly House, 1948.) Reprint, Westport: Greenwood Press, 1984.

Fausold, Martin L. *The Presidency of Herbert C. Hoover*. Lawrence: University of Kansas Press, 1985.

Fiorina, Morris P. *Divided Government*. 2d ed. Boston: Allyn and Bacon, 1996.

———"Economic Retrospective Voting in American National Elections: A Micro-Analysis." *American Journal of Political Science* 22 (May 1978): 426–43.

Fuller, Helen. "Kennedy's First Congress." *The New Republic*, October 27, 1962, 12–14.

Galloway, George B. *History of the House of Representatives*. 2d ed. New York: Thomas Y. Crowell Company, 1976.

Gilbert, Clinton W. "The People Against Pork." *The Atlantic Monthly* (August 1932): 129–39.

Glaser, James M. *Race, Campaign Politics, and Realignment in the South*. New Haven: Yale University Press, 1996.

Glaser, William A. "Hindsight and Significance." In *Public Opinion and Congressional Elections*, edited by William N. McPhee and William A. Glaser. New York: Free Press, 1962.

Glazer, Amihai, Grofman, Bernard, and Robbins, Marc. "Partisan and Incumbency Effects of 1970s Congressional Redistricting." *American Journal of Political Science* 31 (August 1987), 680–707.

Glendening, Parris N. "The Public's Perception of State Government and Governors." *State Government* 53 (Summer 1980): 115–120.

"GOP '66: Back on the Map." *Newsweek*, November 21, 1966, 31–34.

Gosnell, Harold F. *Truman's Crises*. Westport: Greenwood Press, 1980.

Gould, Lewis L. *Reform and Regulation: American Politics 1900–1916.* New York: John Wiley and Sons, 1978.

Graham, Otis L., Jr., and Koed, Elizabeth. "New Deal." In *The Encyclopedia of the United States Congress*, edited by Donald C. Bacon, Roger H. Davidson, and Morton Keller. New York: Simon and Schuster, 1995.

Green, George Walton. "Mr. Cleveland's Second Administration." *Forum*, July 1896, 540–557.

Hamilton, Alexander. *Federalist* 17. In *The Federalist Papers*, edited by Clinton Rossiter. New York: New American Library, 1960, 118–22.

Hartmann, Susan M. *Truman and the 80th Congress.* Columbia: University of Missouri Press, 1971.

Hays, Samuel P. "The Social Analysis of American Political History." *Political Science Quarterly* 80 (September 1965): 373–94.

Hechler, Kenneth W. *Insurgency: Personalities and Politics of the Taft Era.* New York: Columbia University Press, 1940.

Hertzberg, Roberta Q. "Unity versus Division: The Effect of Divided Government on Policy Development." In *Divided Government: Change, Uncertainty, and the Constitutional Order*, edited by Peter F. Galderisi. Lanham, Md.: Rowman and Littlefield, 1996.

Hess, Stephen, and Broder, David S. *The Republican Establishment: The Present and Future of the G.O.P.* New York: Harper and Row, 1967.

Hicks, John D. *Republican Ascendancy 1921–1933.* New York: Harper Torchbooks, 1960.

Hill, Dilys M., and Williams, Phil. "The Reagan Legacy." In *The Reagan Presidency*, edited by Dilys M. Hill, Raymond A. Moore, and Phil Williams. New York: St. Martin's Press, 1990.

Hill, Gladwin. "Nixon Denounces Press as Biased." *New York Times*, November 8, 1962, 1.

Hill, Kevin A. "Does the Creation of Majority Black Districts Aid Republicans? An Analysis of the 1992 Congressional Elections in Eight Southern States." *Journal of Politics* 57 (May 1995): 384–401.

Hinckley, Barbara. "Interpreting House Midterm Elections: Toward Measurement of the In-Party's 'Expected' Loss of Seats." *American Political Science Review* 61 (October 1967): 694–700.

Hollingsworth, J. Rogers. *The Whirligig of Politics: The Democracy of Cleveland and Bryan.* Chicago: University of Chicago Press, 1963.

Holt, James. *Congressional Insurgents and the Party System 1909–1936.* Cambridge: Harvard University Press, 1967.

Hoover, Herbert. *The Ordeal of Woodrow Wilson.* New York: McGraw Hill, 1958.

Hoover, Herbert, and Coolidge, Calvin. *Campaign Speeches of 1932.* Garden City: Doubleday, Doran, and Company, Inc., 1933.

Hughes, Emmet John. *The Ordeal of Power.* New York: Atheneum, 1963.

Hunt, Albert R. "National Politics and the 1982 Campaign." In *The American Elections of 1982*, edited by Thomas E. Mann and Norman J. Ornstein. Washington, D.C.: AEI, 1983.

"The 'In' Party's Dramatic Triumph." *Newsweek*, November 19, 1962, 31–50.

"Interview with Timothy Russert and Tom Brokaw on 'Meet the Press.'" *Public Papers of the President of the United States: William J. Clinton 1993.* Vol. 2. Washington, D.C.: Government Printing Office, 1994.

Jackson, Carlton. *Presidential Vetoes 1792–1945*. Athens: University of Georgia Press, 1967.

Jacobson, Gary C. "Divided Government and the 1994 Elections." In *Divided Government: Change, Uncertainty, and the Constitutional Order*, edited by Peter F. Galderisi. Lanham, Md.: Rowman and Littlefield, 1996.

———*The Electoral Origins of Divided Government: Competition in U.S. House Elections, 1946–1988*. Boulder: Westview Press, 1990.

———"The 1994 House Elections in Perspective." In *Midterm: The Elections of 1994 in Context*, edited by Philip A. Klinkner. Boulder: Westview Press, 1996.

———*The Politics of Congressional Elections*. 3rd ed. New York: HarperCollins, 1992.

Jacobson, Gary C., and Kernell, Samuel. *Strategy and Choice in Congressional Elections*. Boston: Little, Brown, 1983.

Jones, Charles O. *The Minority Party in Congress*. Boston: Little, Brown, and Company, 1970.

Kaiser, Robert G. "In the Upper Chamber, Things Seem to Be Going—Right." *Washington Post*, November 9, 1978, A15.

———*The Presidency in a Separated System*. Washington, D.C.: Brookings Institution, 1994.

———"Ronald Reagan and the U.S. Congress: Visible-Hand Politics." In *The Reagan Legacy: Promise and Performance*, edited by Charles O. Jones. Chatham, N.J.: Chatham House Publishers, 1988.

Kelley, Sean. "Divided We Govern: A Reassessment." *Polity* 25 (1993): 475–84.

Kelly, Stanley Jr. *Interpreting Elections*. Princeton: Princeton University Press, 1983.

Kent, F. R. "Why Congress Acts That Way." *American Magazine*, October 1932, 18–19.

Kernell, Samuel. *Going Public*. 2d ed. Washington, D.C.: Congressional Quarterly Press, 1993.

———"Presidential Popularity and Negative Voting: An Alternative Explanation to the Midterm Decline of the President's Party." *American Political Science Review* 71 (March 1977): 44–66.

Kernell, Samuel, and McDonald, Michael. "Political Strategy and the Transformation of the Post Office from Patronage to Service." Paper presented at the annual meeting of the Western Political Science Association, San Francisco, Calif., March 1996.

Key, V. O. *American State Politics: An Introduction*. New York: Alfred A. Knopf, 1966.

———*Politics, Parties, and Pressure Groups*. 5th ed. New York: Thomas Y. Crowell Company, 1964.

———"A Theory of Critical Elections." *Journal of Politics* 17 (February 1955): 3–18.

Key, V. O., and Silverman, Corinne. "Party and Separation of Powers: A Panorama of Practice in the States." In *American State Politics: Readings for Comparative Analysis*, edited by Frank Munger. New York: Thomas Y. Crowell, 1966.

Kilpatrick, Carroll. "The Kennedy Style and Congress." In *John F. Kennedy and the New Frontier*, edited by Aida DiPace Donald. New York: Hill and Wang, 1966.

King, Gary, and Ragsdale, Lyn. *The Elusive Executive*. Washington, D.C.: Congressional Quarterly, 1988.

Kingdon, John W. *Congressmen's Voting Decisions*. 3rd ed. Ann Arbor: University of Michigan Press, 1989.

Kirschten, Dick. "Building Bridges." *National Journal*, November 8, 1986, 2701–2.

Kleppner, Paul. *Continuity and Change in Electoral Politics, 1893–1928.* Westport, Conn.: Greenwood Press, 1987.

Klinkner, Philip A. *The Losing Parties: Out-Party National Committees.* New Haven: Yale University Press, 1994.

Knowles, Clayton. "Democratic Chiefs Asked to Explain Losses in Election." *New York Times,* November 10, 1950, 1.

Kramer, Gerald H. "Short-Term Fluctuation in U.S. Voting Behavior." *American Political Science Review* 65 (March 1971): 131–43.

Krock, Arthur. "A 'Landslide' Which Went That-a-Way." *New York Times,* November 9, 1950, 32.

———"Republican Remolding Looms in Election Rout," *New York Times,* November 11, 1934, 1E.

———"Taxpayers Revolt." *New York Times,* November 10, 1938, 15.

———"Tide Sweeps Nation." *New York Times,* November 7, 1934, 1.

———"Voting Record Set." *New York Times,* November 8, 1950, 1.

———"Win Back 10 States." *New York Times,* November 9, 1938, 1.

Ladd, Everett Carll. "Survey Says? Little New." *Weekly Standard,* June 17, 1996, 15–16.

Lawrence, D. H. "Rayburn Bars a Tax Cut." *New York Times,* November 8, 1958, 1.

"Leaning Right." *Newsweek,* November 20, 1978, 55.

Lechner, Paul. "Partisan Realignments and Congressional Behavior." *American Politics Quarterly* 4 (April 1976): 223–33.

Lee, Jong R. "Presidential Vetoes from Washington to Nixon." *Journal of Politics* 37 (May 1975): 522–46.

Leech, Margaret. *In the Days of McKinley.* New York: Harper and Brothers, 1959.

Leuchtenburg, William E. *Franklin D. Roosevelt and the New Deal.* New York: Harper and Row, 1963.

Livermore, Seward W. *Politics is Adjourned: Woodrow Wilson and the War Congress 1916–1918.* Middletown: Wesleyan University Press, 1966.

Lodge, H. C. "Our Duty to Cuba." *Forum,* May 1896, 278–287.

MacKuen, Michael B., Erikson, Robert S., and Stimson, James A. "Macropartisanship." *American Political Science Review* 83 (December 1989): 1125–42.

Madison, James. *Federalist 47.* In *The Federalist Papers,* edited by Clinton Rossiter. New York: New American Library, 1960, 300–308.

Mann, Thomas E. "Is the House Unresponsive to Change?" In *Elections American Style,* edited by A. James Reichley. Washington, D.C.: Brookings Institution, 1987.

Mann, Thomas E., and Ornstein, Norman J. "Sending a Message: Voters and Congress in 1982." In *The American Elections of 1982,* edited by Thomas E. Mann and Norman J. Ornstein. Washington, D.C.: AEI, 1983.

Marcus, Ruth. "Clinton Reiterates Vow to Pursue New Democrat Agenda." *Washington Post,* November 11, 1994, A14.

Mattei, Franco. "Eight More in '94: The Republican Takeover of the Senate." In *Midterm: The Elections of 1994 in Context,* edited by Philip A. Klinkner. Boulder: Westview Press, 1996.

Mayer, George H. *The Republican Party 1854–1964.* New York: Oxford University Press, 1964.

Mayhew, David R. *Divided We Govern.* New Haven: Yale University Press, 1991.

———— "Innovative Midterm Elections." In *Midterm: The Elections of 1994 in Context*, edited by Philip A. Klinkner. Boulder: Westview Press, 1996.

McAdams, John C., and Johannes, John R. "The Voter in the 1982 House Elections." *American Journal of Political Science* 28 (November 1984): 778–81.

McCleod, Jack M., Brown, Jane D., and Barker, Lee B. "Watergate and the 1974 Congressional Elections." *Public Opinion Quarterly* 41 (Summer 1977): 179–95.

McDonald, Stuart Elaine, and Rabinowitz, George. "The Dynamics of Structural Realignment." *American Political Science Review* 81 (September 1987): 775–86.

McElvaine, Robert S. *The Great Depression: America 1929–1941*. New York: Times Books, 1984.

McGrory, Mary. "A Democrats' Democrat." *Washington Post*, April 30, 1996, C4.

McWilliams, Wilson Carey. *The Politics of Disappointment: American Elections 1976–1994*. Chatham, N.J.: Chatham House Publishers, 1995.

Mitchell, Alison. "Despite His Reversals, Clinton Stays Centered." *New York Times*, July 28, 1996, A10.

Moley, Raymond. *After Seven Years*. New York: Harper and Brothers, 1939.

Morehouse, Sarah McCally. *State Politics, Parties and Policy*. New York: Holt, Rinehart and Winston, 1980.

Morris, John D. "Change Accepted by Party Leaders." *New York Times*, November 7, 1946, 5.

Moser, Charles A. *Watershed and Ratifying Elections: A Historical View of the 1934 and 1954 Midterm Congressional Elections*. Washington, D.C.: The Free Congress Research and Educational Foundation, 1982.

Mowry, George E. *The Era of Theodore Roosevelt: 1900–1912*. New York: Harper and Brothers, 1958.

"Mr. Roosevelt's New Responsibility." *New York Times*, November 8, 1934, 22.

"Mr. Speaker." *U.S. News and World Report*, December 14, 1998, 9.

Muchmore, Lynn, and Beyle, Thad L. "The Governor as Party Leader." *State Government* 53 (Spring 1980): 121–24.

Mulder, Ronald A. *The Insurgent Progressives in the United States Senate and the New Deal, 1933–1939*. New York: Garland Publishing, Inc., 1979.

Myers, William Starr, and Newton, Walter H. *The Hoover Administration: A Documented Narrative*. New York: Charles Scribner's Sons, 1936.

"The National Picture." *New York Times*, November 6, 1958, 36.

Neustadt, Richard E. *Presidential Power and the Modern Presidents*. New York: Free Press, 1990.

"The New Congress." *Newsweek*, November 21, 1966, 38–43.

"New Right: 'Many Times More Effective' Now." *Electing Congress*. Washington, D.C.: Congressional Quarterly Press, 1978.

"The New Tilt." *Newsweek*, November 20, 1978, 44–47.

"News Conference, November 9, 1994." *Weekly Compilation of Presidential Documents* 30 (November–December 1994).

"News Conference, November 5, 1958." *Public Papers of the President: Dwight Eisenhower 1958*. Washington, D.C.: Government Printing Office, 1959.

"News Conference, November 16, 1950." *Public Papers of the President: Harry S. Truman 1950*. Washington, D.C.: Government Printing Office, 1965.

"The Next Congress." *New York Times*, November 5, 1930, 22.

"1966 Elections—A Major Republican Comeback." *Congressional Quarterly Weekly Report*, November 11, 1966, 2773.

The 1966 Elections. Washington, D.C.: Republican National Committee, 1967.

Nixon, Richard M. *The Memoirs of Richard Nixon*. New York: Grossett and Dunlap, 1978.

Noggle, Burl. *Into the Twenties*. Urbana: University of Illinois Press, 1974.

Norris, Pippa. "1986 U.S. Elections: National Elections or Pluralistic Diversity?" *Political Quarterly* 58 (April/June 1987): 194–201.

O'Brien, Patrick G. "McNary-Haugen Farm Relief Bill." In *The Encyclopedia of the United States Congress*, vol. 3., edited by Donald C. Bacon, Roger H. Davidson, and Morton Keller. New York: Simon and Schuster, 1995, 1339.

"On the One Hand . . . " *New York Times*, November 9, 1978, A26.

Oppenheimer, Bruce I., Stimson, James A., and Waterman, Richard W. "Interpreting U.S. Congressional Elections: The Exposure Thesis." *Legislative Studies Quarterly* 11 (May 1986): 227–47.

Ornstein, Norman J., Mann, Thomas E., and Malbin, Michael J. *Vital Statistics on Congress 1993–1994*. Washington, D.C.: Congressional Quarterly Press, 1994.

———*Vital Statistics on Congress 1995–1996*. Washington, D.C.: Congressional Quarterly Press, 1996.

Osborne, David. *Laboratories of Democracy*. Boston: Harvard Business School Press, 1990.

Oulahan, Richard V. "Democratic Landslide Sweeps Country." *New York Times*, November 5, 1930, 1.

Owens, John R., and Olson, Edward C. "Economic Fluctuations and Congressional Elections." *American Journal of Political Science* 24 (August 1980): 469–93.

Parmet, Herbert S. *The Democrats: The Years After FDR*. New York: Macmillan, 1976.

Patterson, James T. *Congressional Conservatism and the New Deal*. Lexington: University of Kentucky Press, 1967.

"The Penny-Wise 96th." *Newsweek*, November 20, 1978, 44–47.

Peters, Ronald M., Jr. *The American Speakership*. Baltimore: Johns Hopkins University Press, 1990.

Petrocik, John R., and Doherty, Joseph. "The Road to Divided Government." In *Divided Government: Change, Uncertainty, and the Constitutional Order*, edited by Peter F. Galderisi. Lanham, Md.: Rowman and Littlefield, 1996.

Pfiffner, James P. *The Modern Presidency*. New York: St. Martin's Press, 1994.

Phillips, Cabell. "Kennedy and Democratic Aides Heartened by Victory at Polls." *New York Times*, November 8, 1962, A22.

———*The Truman Presidency*. New York: Macmillan, 1966.

Piereson, James E. "Determinants of Legislative Success in Gubernatorial Elections, 1910–1970." Unpublished paper cited in *American State Parties and Elections*, by Malcolm E. Jewell and David M. Olson. Homewood, Ill.: Dorsey Press, 1978.

———"Presidential Popularity and Midterm Voting at Different Electoral Levels." *American Journal of Political Science* 19 (November 1975): 683–702.

Pinkus, Matt. "Democratic Study Group." In *The Encyclopedia of the United States Congress*, vol. 2, edited by Donald C. Bacon, Roger H. Davidson, and Morton Keller. New York: Simon and Schuster, 1995, 633–34.

Piper, J. Richard. "Party Realignment and Congressional Change." *American Politics Quarterly* 11 (October 1983): 459–490.

"The Political Revolution." *New York Times*, November 8, 1910, 8.

Polsby, Nelson. "The Institutionalization of the U.S. House of Representatives." *American Political Science Review* 62 (March 1968): 144–168.

Pomper, Gerald. "Classification of Presidential Elections." *Journal of Politics* 89 (August 1967): 535–66.

Ponsford, Olive Pearl. *Evil Results of Midterm Elections and a Suggested Remedy*. Los Angeles: University of Southern California Press, 1937.

Porter, David L. *Congress and the Waning of the New Deal*. Port Washington, N.Y.: Kennikat Press, 1980.

Porter, Kirk H., and Johnson, Donald Bruce. *National Party Platforms: 1840–1960*. Urbana: University of Illinois Press, 1961.

"The Presidency and Mr. Reed." *Atlantic Monthly*, February 1896, 250–56.

Pringle, Henry F. *The Life and Times of William Howard Taft*. Vol. 2. New York: Farrar and Rinehart, Inc., 1939.

Public Papers of the President of the United States: Herbert Hoover. Washington, D.C.: Government Printing Office, 1974.

Ragsdale, Lyn. "The Fiction of Congressional Elections as Presidential Events." *American Politics Quarterly* 8 (October 1980): 375–93.

Ranney, Austin. "The Carter Administration." In *The American Elections of 1980*, edited by Austin Ranney. Washington, D.C.: AEI, 1981.

————"Parties in State Politics." In *Politics in the American States: A Comparative Perspective*, 2d ed., edited by Herbert Jacob and Kenneth N. Vines. Boston: Little, Brown, and Company, 1971.

Ransone, Carl B., Jr. *The American Governorship*. Westport, Conn.: Greenwood Press, 1982.

Rauch, Basil. *The History of the New Deal 1933–1938*. New York: Creative Age Press, Inc., 1944.

"A Record of the First Session of Congress." *The Literary Digest*, June 20, 1896, 225–27.

Reilly, Steven. "Managing Party Support: Reagan as Party Leader." In *The Reagan Years: The Record in Presidential Leadership*, edited by Joseph Hagan. New York: Manchester University Press, 1990.

"The Republican Debacle." *New York Times*, November 5, 1930, 22.

"Republican Gains and Obligations." *New York Times*, November 9, 1994, A26.

"The Republican Tide." *New York Times*, November 9, 1966, 38.

Richardson, Elmo R. *The Presidency of Dwight D. Eisenhower*. Lawrence: The Regents Press of Kansas, 1979.

Riselbach, Leroy N. "It's the Constitution, Stupid!" In *Divided Government: Change, Uncertainty, and the Constitutional Order*, edited by Peter F. Galderisi. Lanham, Md.: Rowman and Littlefield, 1996.

Roberts, Paul Craig. *The Supply-Side Revolution*. Cambridge: Harvard University Press, 1984.

Roberts, Steven V. "Republicans Meet Setbacks in House." *New York Times*, November 3, 1982, A1.

Robertson, Andrew W. "American Redistricting in the 1980s: The Effect on Midterm Elections." *Electoral Studies* 2 (August 1983): 113–29.

Robinson, Edgar Eugene. *The Roosevelt Leadership, 1933–1945*. Philadelphia: J. D. Lippincott Company, 1955.

Robinson, William A. *Thomas B. Reed: Parliamentarian*. New York: Dodd, Mead, and Company, 1930.

Roff, Peter. "Housekeeping." *National Review*, August 17, 1998, 24–25.

———"The Tsunami Effect: Why This November's Elections Are More Important Than You Think." *Rising Tide* 5 (Fall 1997): 21–23.

Roosevelt, Franklin D. *The Public Papers and Addresses of Franklin D. Roosevelt*. Vol. 1. New York: Russell and Russell, 1938.

Russakoff, Dale. "Gingrich Vows Cooperation." *Washington Post*, November 9, 1994, A21.

Sabato, Larry J. *Goodbye to Good-time Charlie: The American Governorship Transformed*. 2d ed. Washington, D.C.: Congressional Quarterly Press, 1983.

———*The Party's Just Begun*. Glenview, Ill.: Scott, Foresman and Co., 1988.

Sanford, Terry. *Storm Over the States*. New York: McGraw-Hill, 1967.

Savage, Sean J. *Roosevelt: The Party Leader 1932–1945*. Lexington: University of Kentucky Press, 1991.

Scheele, Henry Z. "Executive-Legislative Relations: Eisenhower and Halleck." In *Reexamining the Eisenhower Presidency*, edited by Shirley Anne Warshaw. Westport, Conn.: Greenwood Press, 1993.

Schlesinger, Arthur M., Jr. *The Coming of the New Deal*. Boston: Houghton Mifflin, 1959

———*The Crisis of the Old Order, 1919–1933*. Boston: Houghton Mifflin, 1957.

———*The Politics of Upheaval*. Boston: Houghton Mifflin, 1960.

———*A Thousand Days*. Boston: Houghton Mifflin, 1965.

Schlesinger, Joseph A. *Ambition and Politics: Political Careers in the United States*. Chicago: Rand McNally, 1966.

———"The Politics of the Executive." In *Politics in the American States: A Comparative Analysis*, 2d ed., edited by Herbert Jacob and Kenneth N. Vines. Boston: Little, Brown, and Company, 1971.

Schneider, William. "Clinton: The Reason Why." *National Journal*, November 12, 1994, 2630–2632.

———"Return to Normalcy." *National Journal*, November 8, 1986, 2708–10.

Schwarz, Jordan A. *Interregnum of Despair: Hoover, Congress, and the Depression*. Urbana: University of Illinois Press, 1970.

Sellers, Charles. "The Equilibrium Cycle in Two-Party Politics." *Public Opinion Quarterly* 29 (Spring 1965): 16–38.

Shafer, Byron E., ed. *The End of Realignment: Interpreting American Electoral Eras*. Madison: University of Wisconsin Press, 1991.

Shively, W. Phillips. "A Reinterpretation of the New Deal Realignment." *Public Opinion Quarterly* 35 (Winter 1971–72): 621–24.

Shugart, Matthew Soberg. "The Electoral Cycle and Institutional Sources of Divided Government." *American Political Science Review* 89 (June 1995): 327–55.

Sidey, Hugh. *John F. Kennedy, President* New edition. New York: Atheneum, 1964.

Sigelman, Lee. "Special Elections to the U.S. House: Some Descriptive Generalizations." *Legislative Studies Quarterly* 6 (November 1981): 577–88.

Simon, Dennis M. "Presidents, Governors, and Electoral Accountability." *Journal of Politics* 51 (May 1989): 286–303.

Simon, Dennis M., Ostrom, Charles W., Jr., and Marra, Robin F. "The President, Referendum Voting, and Subnational Elections in the United States." *American Political Science Review* 85 (December 1991): 1177–92.

Sinclair, Barbara. *Congressional Realignment: 1925–1978.* Austin: University of Texas Press, 1982.

Sinclair, Barbara Deckard. "Party Realignment and the Transformation of the Political Agenda: The House of Representatives 1925–1938." *American Political Science Review* 71 (September 1977): 940–953.

Smith, Hedrick. "New House Seems Less In-Tune with Reagan." *New York Times,* November 4, 1982, A1.

———"Social Reforms and Arms Accord Likely to Face Snag on Capitol Hill." *New York Times,* November 8, 1978, A1.

Sokolosky, George E. "Will Revolution Come?" *Atlantic Monthly* (August 1932): 189–90.

Sorenson, Theodore C. *Kennedy.* New York: Harper and Row, 1965.

Southwell, Priscilla L. "The Mobilization Hypothesis and Voter Turnout in Congressional Elections, 1974–1982." *Western Political Quarterly* 41 (June 1988): 273–87.

"Statement on the Results of the 1974 Election, November 1974." *Public Papers of the President: Gerald R. Ford 1974.* Washington, D.C.: Government Printing Office, 1975.

Stern, Clarence A. *Protectionist Republicanism.* Ann Arbor: Edwards Brothers, 1971.

Stigler, George J. "General Economic Conditions and National Elections." *American Economics Review* 63 (May 1973): 160–67.

Stokes, Donald E., and Miller, Warren E. "Party Government and the Salience of Congress." *Public Opinion Quarterly* 26 (Winter 1962): 531–46.

Stuckey, Mary E. *The President as Interpreter-in-Chief.* Chatham, N.J.: Chatham House Publishers, 1991.

Studlar, Donley T., and Sigelman, Lee. "Special Elections: A Comparative Perspective." *British Journal of Political Science* 17 (April 1987): 247–256.

Sundquist, James L. *Dynamics of the Party System.* Rev. ed. Washington, D.C.: Brookings Institution, 1983.

———*Politics and Policy: The Eisenhower, Kennedy, and Johnson Years.* Washington, D.C.: Brookings Institution, 1968.

Taylor, Paul. "Senate to Have 55 Democrats." *Washington Post,* November 6, 1986, A1.

Taylor, Telford. *Grand Inquest: The Story of Congressional Investigations.* New York: Ballantine, 1961.

"Terminated in Texas." *Newsweek,* June 14, 1993, 37.

"Text of Addresses by Rep. Ford and Sen. Dirksen." *Congressional Quarterly Weekly Report,* January 27, 1967, 130–34.

Thielemann, Gregory S. "The Rise and Stall of Southern Republicanism in Congress." *Social Science Quarterly* 73 (March 1992): 123–35.

Thompson, Charles Willis. "The Cold Grey Morning After." *Commonweal,* July 20, 1932, 302–3.

———"Today and Next November." *Commonweal,* June 1, 1932, 119–20.

Tidmarch, Charles M., Hyman, Lisa J., and Sorkin, Jill E. "Press Issue Agendas in the 1982 Congressional and Gubernatorial Election Campaigns." *Journal of Politics* 46 (November 1984): 1226–42.

Tolchin, Martin. "Carter Plans Rise in Defense Budget and Lower Deficits."*New York Times,* November 10, 1978, A1.

Truman, Harry S. *Memoirs: Years of Trial and Hope.* Vol. 2. Garden City: Doubleday, 1956.

Tufte, Edward R. *Political Control of the Economy.* Princeton: Princeton University Press, 1978.

Tugwell, Rexford G. *Grover Cleveland.* New York: Macmillan, 1968.

Tulis, Jeffrey. *The Rhetorical Presidency.* Princeton: Princeton University Press, 1987.

Tweedie, Jack. "Changing the Face of Welfare." *State Legislatures* 21 (December 1995): 15–17.

Uslaner, Eric M., Conway, M. Margaret, Jacobson, Gary C., and Kernell, Samuel. "Interpreting the 1974 Congressional Election." *American Political Science Review* 80 (June 1986): 591 95.

"Viva La Difference." *New Republic,* November 12, 1962, 2.

"The Voice of the Voters." *New York Times,* November 9, 1950, A32.

von Szeliski, Victor. "The Distribution of Income." *Commonweal,* July 6, 1932, 262–64.

Waggoner, Walter. "Acheson Declares He Will Not Resign or Change Policies." *New York Times,* November 9, 1950, 1.

Walsh, Edward. "Democrats Wonder Whether Sea Change Is Plea for Centrism." *Washington Post,* November 10, 1994, A27.

——— "In the End, Bork Himself Was His Own Worst Enemy." *Washington Post,* October 24, 1987, A16.

Walworth, Arthur. *America's Moment: 1918.* New York: W. W. Norton, 1977.

Waterman, Richard W. "Institutional Realignment: The Composition of the U.S. Congress." *Western Political Quarterly* 43 (March 1990): 81–92.

Welch, Michael E. *The Presidencies of Grover Cleveland.* Lawrence: University of Kansas Press, 1988.

"What the GOP Is Doing." *Newsweek,* November 17, 1958, 29–36.

White, Theodore H. *The Making of the President: 1968.* New York: Pocket Books, 1969.

White, William S. "Coalition is Likely." *New York Times,* November 9, 1950, A1.

——— "Democrats Offer Harmony in Rule of 84th House." *New York Times,* November 5, 1954, 1.

"Whose Victory Was It?" *The New Republic,* November 17, 1962, 4.

Wicker, Tom. "President Elated." *New York Times,* November 8, 1962, A1.

——— "Voting in Nation Narrow in Scope." *New York Times,* November 6, 1962, A1.

Will, George F. "Clinton Feels His Own Pain." *Newsweek,* November 24, 1997, 84.

Williams, Philip, and Wilson, Graham. "The American Mid-Term Elections." *Political Studies* 27 (December 1979): 601–9.

Williams, R. Hal. *Years of Decision: American Politics in the 1890s.* New York: John Wiley and Sons, 1978.

Wolskill, George, and Hudson, John A. *All but the People: Franklin D. Roosevelt and His Critics, 1933–39.* London: Macmillan Press, 1969.

INDEX

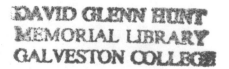